The Politics of Failed Policies

The Politics of Failed Policies

SARAH JAMES

OXFORD
UNIVERSITY PRESS

Oxford University Press is a department of the University of Oxford.
It furthers the University's objective of excellence in research, scholarship,
and education by publishing worldwide. Oxford is a registered trade mark of
Oxford University Press in the UK and in certain other countries.

Published in the United States of America by Oxford University Press
198 Madison Avenue, New York, NY 10016, United States of America.

© Oxford University Press 2025

All rights reserved. No part of this publication may be reproduced, stored in a retrieval system,
transmitted, used for text and data mining, or used for training artificial intelligence, in any form or
by any means, without the prior permission in writing of Oxford University Press, or as expressly
permitted by law, by license or under terms agreed with the appropriate reprographics rights
organization. Inquiries concerning reproduction outside the scope of the above should be sent
to the Rights Department, Oxford University Press, at the address above.

You must not circulate this work in any other form
and you must impose this same condition on any acquirer.

CIP data is on file at the Library of Congress

ISBN 9780197813614

ISBN 9780197813607 (hbk.)

DOI: 10.1093/9780197813645.001.0001

Paperback printed by Integrated Books International, United States of America

Hardback printed by Bridgeport National Bindery, Inc., United States of America

The manufacturer's authorized representative in the EU for product safety is
Oxford University Press España S.A., Parque Empresarial San Fernando de Henares,
Avenida de Castilla, 2 – 28830 Madrid (www.oup.es/en).

Contents

List of Figures

List of Tables

Acknowledgments

As a senior at the University of Texas at Austin, I learned that my senior thesis advisor, Andy Karch, had studied under Theda Skocpol for his own graduate work. I had just read *States and Social Revolutions* and was so excited that I was two degrees separated from the scholar who had written such compelling and fascinating social science. Little did I know, five years later, that I would begin graduate school to work on my own PhD (which would lead to this book) and would collaborate with Theda and invite her to serve as my own dissertation chair. I am so grateful for Theda's high expectations, her unwavering belief in this project and my ability to do hard things, and her investment in sharing the ins and outs of excellent mixed-methods research. Learning from her passion for relevant and precise research using a range of data sources has been a true joy of becoming a scholar.

Thank you as well to Dan Carpenter and Jennifer Hochschild, whose outstanding feedback and encouragement have made this project immeasurably better. This group's collective belief that complicated questions that have the potential to improve the world and address injustice empowered me to embrace a research agenda that I believed in despite the many challenges and setbacks it presented.

Practically, this research would not have been possible without the vision, compassion, and foresight of Kathy Edin, director of the Multidisciplinary Program on Inequality and Social Policy at the time I applied to Harvard. Within a week of learning of my acceptance to the PhD program in Government and Social Policy, I was also asked to serve as the interim high school principal at the school I had taught at for five years. I loved teaching and working at a school that was proactively trying to close the opportunity gap for our students, and my first ever cohort of students would be seniors the following year. I was hesitant to pass up the opportunity to both accelerate this work and to implement new policies and traditions that would bring more joy and rigor to my students' high school experience. When I explained my dilemma to Kathy, I recall that, without hesitation, she replied: "We need more people like you, who care about the world and who have experience in it, doing research. I'll get you the deferral." She did, and I am forever grateful. I hope that this work furthers attention to inequality and social policy as Kathy's has done.

This research and my morale have benefited from an outstanding community of fellow scholars, friends, and family. Amy Lakeman, Meredith Dost, Liz Thom, and Shannon Parker have read many memos, drafts, and one-off questions over the past several years. Their feedback and encouragement always left me inspired and excited to improve this book. Their companionship was invaluable in making the challenges of writing a book tolerable and, on many occasions, enjoyable. Shanna Weitz and Angie Bautista-Chavez also provided extensive feedback on much earlier versions of this project, and their example encouraged me to pursue this project. Political science is lucky to have such a stellar generation of women preparing to join its ranks. I also owe Jaclyn Daumerie enormous thanks for first alerting me to the truancy case study in Texas that inspired the broader project. Thank you to my parents and my brother for supporting and encouraging my work, suggesting new ideas, and making me laugh along the way.

And finally, thank you to my partner, David Henry, who unwaveringly supports and believes in my ability to be an outstanding scholar. His willingness to hear feedback, give advice, share a hug, or take the pack on a hike while I decompressed made the journey of researching and writing this book while becoming a parent, surviving a pandemic, and moving cross country feasible and rewarding. Beacon (our sweet golden retriever), Hazel, and Sadie all joined our family throughout the process of research and writing this book. Their joy, goofiness, and curiosity are welcome reasons to put work aside, and experience the world.

Introduction

> *"There is nothing a government hates more than to be well informed; for it makes the process of arriving at decisions much more complicated and difficult."*
>
> —John Maynard Keynes (quoted in Skidelsky 1986)

> *"When I have fully decided that a result is worth getting, I go ahead of it and make trial after trial until it comes...Results! Why, man, I have gotten a lot of results. I know several thousand things that won't work."*
>
> —Thomas Edison (quoted in Young et al. 2018, 195)

This book began with a puzzling story I heard early on in graduate school. I was speaking with a college friend who had gone on to work in the Texas state judiciary. Knowing that I was interested in education, inequality, and the carceral state (and searching around for a dissertation topic), she mentioned that Texas had just reformed a more than two-decades-old policy called Failure to Attend School (FTAS) that allowed law enforcement officers to ticket and detain young people for skipping school. As a former high school principal (who had had her fair share of trying to support students to maintain consistent attendance), I was stunned by this policy. First, I was floored that anyone with any experience working with students would have thought that ticketing, arresting, charging those struggling with attendance with an adult criminal misdemeanor, and then, in some cases, jailing them would in any way enhance attendance or graduation rates. If nothing else, it seemed absurd to expect students to be able to be in class more often if they now had a slew of court dates to attend.

Second, I knew that research from the past decade and a half or so had also shown profound negative social, economic, and political consequences for young people exposed to the criminal justice system. Criminalizing school-based misbehavior both exacerbated students' inability to make rational decisions and undermined a fundamental purpose of free and public education: instilling civic skills and investment. Education and educational access are supposed to be the great equalizers, though my time in public education has long rid me of such an idealistic notion. However, by channeling

The Politics of Failed Policies. Sarah James, Oxford University Press. © Oxford University Press (2025).
DOI: 10.1093/9780197813645.003.0001

some students (again, mostly those who already face the most obstacles to entering the middle class and achieving financial independence) into the juvenile justice system during the very time in their lives when they are first learning about how who they are and how they fit into their broader communities—a process that often involves making mistakes and learning from consequences—it becomes clear that some policies actually exacerbate the very inequalities education is supposed to solve.

I was also surprised that Texas, a conservative, traditionally tough-on-crime state with an "individual responsibility or take the consequences" worldview, had not only recognized this failure but had also generated substantial political will to revise it. And so began my interest in data, research, and the politics of when and how this information informs policymaking.

FTAS is just one of many policies that, while implemented to address inequality, actually reinforces disparities. Among these policies are those affecting families living on $2 a day, the impacts of welfare work requirements (Edin and Shaefer 2015), subsidized housing policies that ignore the importance of child care for low-income families and punish rather than rehabilitate drug use (Gilmer et al. 2014), abstinence-only education policies that lead to high rates of teen pregnancy and sexually transmitted infections (Kirby, Laris, and Rolleri 2007), as well as tax incentives for businesses that strain state budgets without creating promised economic growth (Jensen 2016). Clearly, public officials cannot be expected to know how these policies will turn out before trying them, and certainly, ideology and deeply entrenched perspectives on the appropriate role of government dictate the perspectives of many public officials on these issues.

Crafting public policy is a complex process. Developing sound public policies that generate the intended outcomes realistically requires figuring out many things that have not worked before, and hopefully, finding something that does. State governments, however, are composed of dozens, if not hundreds, of politicians and bureaucrats, all of whom may have disparate incentives in the discovery process. Further complicating learning from experimentation is an aversion to information (or at least certain kinds of information) from elected officials. As Keynes astutely noted (Young et al., 2002, 218), being more informed about the nuances of policy outcomes does not necessarily make governing any easier. The ideologies, power disparities, resources, and entrenched interests inherent to the American political system obfuscate the translation of data and findings into coherent policy design. And yet, state governments as well as the federal government continue to experiment with new approaches to achieving desirable social and political outcomes. This begs the question:when do the failed experiments get recognized as such?

It seemed that FTAS might be an unexpected example of elected officials learning about policy outcomes, sensing failure, and changing their minds. In an era of intense partisan polarization, it is puzzling that Texas public officials changed their minds about the effectiveness of FTAS. Though elected officials certainly have more data and sophisticated analytical tools at their disposal than at any other point in American history, the pressures of ideological conformity and purity, especially in a conservative state like Texas, didn't seem especially conducive to learning and revising one's opinion. And yet, it had. This case led me to wonder about what conditions will lead public officials to recognize policy failure. And when can they learn about the impacts of the policies and update both their preferences and the policies to match what systematic research tells us about outcomes in the real world, rather than the outcomes that ideological paradigms say *should* result?

Answering these questions offers insight into our understanding of state policymaking, public policy, and the politics of public administration. A Panglossian (and antiquated) view of American politics suggests that when policy failure is sufficiently harmful or intolerable, those affected should demand change. In the 1970s, Albert Hirschman (1970) argued that dissatisfied citizens have three options for instigating policy change: exit, voice, and loyalty. Unfortunately, as has become even clearer in the half-century since Hirschman's writing, members of traditionally marginalized communities do not usually have equal access to all three of these options. Exit can be financially and socially impractical in a society plagued by discriminatory policies intended (at least at one point) to control the movement of Black, Brown, female, and queer bodies (to name a few of the many marginalized groups in American society). Loyalty to this system is an unreasonable expectation for the same reason. Thus, voice remains the critical tool for those most disadvantaged by America's political system. But whose perspectives get taken seriously by people in power? And when can those harmed by policy failure be heard and heeded? As I learned in the FTAS case, parents, advocates, and students had long been decrying the failures of a system that criminalized minors for truancy, and yet the policy remained law for two decades—until, all of a sudden, it wasn't. What had changed? And what lessons can policymakers, advocates, activists, and scholars take from this example about how to elevate the perspectives of those harmed by policy failure?

The research for this book was driven by the questions that arose from my observations in the real world of state politics: What happens when policies fail to produce their intended results? What happens when these failures burden politically marginalized constituencies? When and how do elected officials learn about and respond to policy failure?

This book will show that the capacity to collect data and analyze it—essential prerequisites for evaluating policy—is *itself a political decision.* Even more importantly, it is a political decision that has long-term consequences for the longevity of a policy and for political and economic inequality. We cannot fully understand state-level policymaking or effectively address patterns of inequality until we consider these efforts to evaluate and reform policies.

This book centers on data collection and analysis as essential tools for identifying, communicating, and mobilizing around policy failure. However, of equal importance here is the imperative that we should not be fooled by the seemingly objective nature of numbers. In her book on how numbers affect our perception of what matters, Deborah Stone notes that even counting requires subjective decision making about "what is like what." The stories we tell about numbers are important because they influence how we approach categorizing and counting. Measuring and analyzing complicated phenomena such as policy outcomes involves a series of subjective decisions about "what goes with what" and storytelling. These decisions, like all political decisions, are made by people in power. The goal of this book is not to argue that quantitative data is the infallible authority on reality, but rather to enhance our understanding of the *politics* of policy evaluation and how choices made in the policy evaluation process have long-run political consequences. In addition, hopefully, my findings can help make policy evaluation processes more transparent, equitable, and accessible to a wider group of people.

Findings from three disciplines—public administration, public policy, and political science—together explain *when* and *how* information on policy outcomes translates into the recognition and revision of failed policies. This book also shows that investments in and design of state administrative capacity to collect and analyze data (a topic usually relegated to the public administration literature) have substantial impact on the politics of revision among public officials trying to sort out the merits of public policies.

For scholars studying public administration, my findings center not only on *what* public officials do, but also on *when and how* they choose to do it. In other words, I focus on important concepts from political science such as sequencing, policy feedback, and historical institutionalism in an effort to understand the effectiveness of public administrative decisions. For scholars of public policy, I highlight the political nature of policy evaluation and offer new concepts for parsing when and how political choices affect our ability to understand the impacts of public policy and the politics they produce. Political scientists will find that this book advances our understanding of state politics, policy feedback, and policy learning.

For students and emerging scholars in public administration, public policy, and political science, this book offers the same theoretical advancements described above. Hopefully, too, it can also serve as a model for in-depth comparative case studies and archival research for elucidating contemporary political processes. While advances in causal inference and statistical analysis have contributed immensely to the study of American politics, many questions that elude precise measurement and causal identification remain.

More broadly, this book contributes to the burgeoning literature on the politics of numbers (Best 2012; Gamble & Stone 2006; Stone 2020; Stone 1989), data activism (Milan and Velden 2016), and community-based public research (Atalay 2012; Israel et al. 1998). This literature is interdisciplinary and takes seriously the notion that quantification and measurement are central to power and to decisions affecting present-day Western society and governance. However, this literature moves beyond some of the original assumptions of the evidence-based policymaking literature by complicating the conditions under which quantitative measures can provide value, the ethics of measurement, and the power dynamics inherent in these practices. This book highlights political and institutional explanations for how to meaningfully incorporate policy evaluation into policymaking and when it can distort the preferences and wisdom of the communities that policies impact.

In short, this book analyzes the politics of policy evaluation. This stage of the policy process does not center solely on technical experts' calculations of costs and benefits. Nor is policy evaluation a neatly defined moment in the policy process. The potential for evaluation is the product of political decisions and processes that begin with design of the policy itself. Policy evaluation also involves ongoing struggles over information and analysis that profoundly impact the future direction of public policy. Legislators, interest groups, policy analysts, and policy recipients all play important roles in what information is collected, disseminated, and popularized. Some of these struggles are overt and immediate, but many develop over long periods of time and are hidden from public view. This book aims to make these processes explicit and theorizes about the conditions under which different groups can succeed in putting policy failure on the political agenda.

Looking Ahead

This book is divided into two parts. Part I (chapters 2 through 5) outlines my theoretical contributions, and Part II (chapters 6 through 10) traces the four policy trajectory case studies. Chapter 1 outlines the empiricial and theoretical puzzles that this book aims to answer. Chapter 2 introduces my theory on the policy feedback effects of institutional capacity for data collection and analysis on the persistence of failed social policies. This chapter provides an overview of existing theories of policy learning and policy change and describes how an institutional perspective combined with elite policy feedback theory offers important additions to these findings for explaining the politics of failed policies. Chapter 3 outlines my research design and methods and briefly introduces each of the six case studies that inform the remainder of the book.

Chapter 4 describes data collection capacity in greater depth, delineating features of state policy areas that reflect high data collection capacity. Centrally managed collection plans, clearly articulated definitions, and ongoing and overlapping data collection efforts characterize high collection capacity. Comparisons between states whose elected officials have exhibited even limited acknowledgment of policy failure (Texas and Washington) and states that have not (Wyoming for truancy and Kansas for tax incentives) how that the availability of high-quality data is necessary for any meaningful failure recognition. These data also show that state governments (vs. non-state actors) are uniquely positioned to collect data that can be effectively deployed to highlight policy failures.

Chapter 5 defines analytical capacity. Unlike previous studies of state research capacity, I show that data collection capacity is distinct from analytical capacity. The case studies presented demonstrate both the existence and impact of differing capacities for data collection and analysis. Analytical capacity alone is not sufficient to encourage public officials to acknowledge policy failure. Unlike the case with collection capacity, analytical capacity can be effectively supplemented by nonstate actors.

Part II explores when and how public officials revise failed policies and unlike Part I, which is organized around key theoretical contributions, Part II centers on the narratives of the specific case studies. The cases are examined in order from most to least aligned with the stylized path from policy implementation to revision. This ordering highlights how breakdowns in collection and analytical capacity yield different policy and political outcomes. Chapter 6 details the research and design tax credits in Washington State, in which public officials across both parties and multiple branches of government have responded to clear data and state bureaucracies have conducted meticulous analysis of the failure of the well-intentioned economic incentive program. Failure to Attend School in Texas follows in Chapter 7, showing how strong state-orchestrated data collection paired with credible nonstate organizations conducting data analysis can also highlight failure and empower those most harmed by a policy to demand change. Discussion of Washington's truancy policy, Becca's Bill, follows in Chapter 8. This case demonstrates that many obstacles to policy revision arise when capable researchers in state research organizations do not base their analyses on reliable and consistently collected data.

Chapter 9 focuses on Texas's Ch 313 tax incentives, which represents a case of low collection and analytical capacity. The case of Ch 313 highlights how partisan politics and well-resourced, well-connected interests can dominate the policy conversation in the absence of consistent, reliable findings on a policy's impacts. Also discussed is the role of the original policy context for the likelihood that a failed policy will be revised. Policies created in response to a crisis will be more resilient to revision than those that emerge as a proactive solution. The tenth and final chapter focuses on the implications of my findings for recognizing and responding to policy failure and the impact on persistent inequality moving forward.

PART I
THEORETICAL CONTRIBUTIONS

1

The Tricky Thing about Experimenting

To stay experimentation in things social and economic is a grave responsibility. Denial of the right to experiment may be fraught with serious consequences to the nation. It is one of the happy incidents of the federal system that a single courageous state may, if its citizens choose, serve as a laboratory, and try novel social and economic experiments without risk to the rest of the country.

—Justice Louis Brandeis in his dissenting opinion in *New State Ice Co v. Liebmann*, 1932

In 2005, Utah committed to an audacious and ambitious goal: end chronic homelessness within a decade. By 2015, rates of the unhoused in the Beehive State had plummeted over 90 percent (McEvers 2015). In pursuit of this goal, the state government decided to experiment with a "housing first" approach. As its name suggests, housing first calls for getting people into subsidized, stable housing *before* engaging them in services to address addiction, employment, or health challenges.[1] And, importantly, there are no requirements for maintaining eligibility for housing.

The "housing first" policy contradicts the historical approach to subsidizing housing, and social welfare more broadly, in the United States in the twentieth century. Contrary to the housing first philosophy, most American programs for the unhoused have strict eligibility criteria, including abstinence from substance abuse, which recipients must meet to qualify for and remain in the housing. This alternate approach is known as the "housing readiness" or "treatment first" model. Furthermore, much of the housing assistance offered is temporary and can be revoked at the first sign

[1] Scholars and the media attribute the housing first approach to Sam Tsemberis, a clinical psychologist who experimented with the effects of guaranteed housing in the 1990s and showed an 85 percent retention rate in housing and counseling—a dramatic improvement from the next best models, which showed 60 percent retention, at best (McCoy 2021).

The Politics of Failed Policies. Sarah James, Oxford University Press. © Oxford University Press (2025).
DOI: 10.1093/9780197813645.003.0002

of deviation from expectations or failure to submit proper documentation (Desmond 2016; Edin and Shaefer 2015; Soss, Fording, and Schram 2011).

Initially, many Utah policymakers were skeptical of the housing first approach. Utah is a generally conservative state, though the strong religious traditions (namely, the Church of Jesus Christ of Latter-Day Saints) in the state may have made its residents and public officials more open to experimenting in the name of supporting the poor (McEvers 2015). But what won over many conservatives was the early evidence about the program's cost savings. Initial studies of housing first suggested that the state could save as much as 50 percent by guaranteeing housing for the chronically unhoused. By some estimates, it cost $30,000–$50,000 per person per year to address the emergency needs of the unhoused, while guaranteeing housing cost between $10,000 and $15,000 (McCoy 2021; Rodgers 2021; Woodhall-Melnik and Dunn 2016). This cost savings was on top of evidence that participants in the program were more likely to engage in counseling and addiction treatment programs and even maintain stable employment (Gilmer et al. 2014; Rodgers 2021).

After early adopters of the housing first strategy saw initial success, other states and cities tried the approach as well but with mixed results. New York City has attempted several versions of this concept but continues to experience astounding rates of homelessness. Houston, Texas is often touted as another success story, though the state capital, Austin, only three hours away, has yet to make a significant dent in its homelessness crisis. California—and Los Angeles in particular—has yet to show the same payoff from investing in these policies (Cohen 2022).

As more states and localities have experimented with a housing first approach, more data to assess the program have emerged. These data have revealed more nuance and generated skepticism about whether, when, and how this program works. More recent studies distinguish between the effectiveness of housing first, depending on the substance to which an individual is addicted. People with alcoholism seem to fare better in the housing first model than those with addictions to cocaine or opioids, for example (Woodhall-Melnik and Dunn 2016). We are learning that the programs' cost savings may be dependent on the number of available housing units and market rates for real estate and construction materials. Cities like Los Angeles, with the highest rental costs, are struggling to afford enough available units. These also happen to be the same cities with the highest rates of residents who are unhoused. In other words, the housing first experiment is still running, and the results (i.e., the effectiveness) may well vary by the social, economic, and geographical context. Cities and states may not be able to assess the value of the program simply by looking to their neighbors. They might just need to try it out and carefully observe the outcomes.

The United States' federal structure allows every state in the union to experiment with its housing policy among a plethora of other policy areas. But with experimentation comes the possibility of success *and* failure (and we might even think failure is more likely). States also vary in their capacity to collect information about issues within their borders (Brambor et al. 2020). When do state elected officials recognize that a policy experiment has failed? And what do they do about it? When are public officials willing to recognize policy failure when it contradicts their *a priori* expectations, partisan preferences, or preferences of powerful interests? These are the sorts of questions this book seeks to understand.

Experimenting in an Age of Polarization and Evidence

The trajectory of Utah's journey to end homelessness echoes a long-standing and rapidly increasing interest in evidence-based policymaking in American politics. Indeed, on March 30, 2016, President Obama signed H.R. 1831, the Evidence-Based Policymaking Commission Act, into law, after the House and Senate passed it with overwhelming bipartisan support. This was one of the few bipartisan and unanimous acts passed in an otherwise rancorous year between the executive and legislative branches. (Recall that a few weeks earlier, Senate Majority Leader Mitch McConnell and other Senate Republicans had announced that they would stall nomination hearings for Obama's replacement for Justice Anthony Scalia on the Supreme Court.)[2] House Speaker Paul Ryan, a staunch conservative who actively fought the Democratic agenda, sponsored the bill in the House, while Senator Patty Murray, a Democrat from the progressive Washington State sponsored the bill in the Senate.

HR 1831 was the culmination of decades of effort from social scientists, advocates, foundation leaders, and policymakers to embrace the best social sciences practices in order to evaluate the outcomes of social programs, bolstering those found to be effective and revising or eliminating

[2] HR 1831 was passed by unanimous consent in the Senate and a voice vote in the House. There are no documented objections to the final version in the legislative record.

the ineffective ones. Presaging the bipartisan support for HR 1831, both parties increasingly began referencing evidence and data in their platforms starting in the 1990s. Figure 1.1 shows the rise in the number of times evidence-related terms were mentioned in the Democratic and Republican national party platforms between 1988 and 2022. And although their rationale for passing HB 1831 varied,[3] there was robust support from both Democrats and Republicans during a time of extreme partisan polarization.

This enthusiasm for evidence-based decision making relies, at least in part, on the assumption that once findings are made available, stakeholders will respond uniformly and logically to evidence on policy outcomes. Policy analysis—"identifying relevant social values, crafting alternative policies, predicting the consequences of the policies, and assessing them in terms of the identified values"—provides the foundation for evidence-based

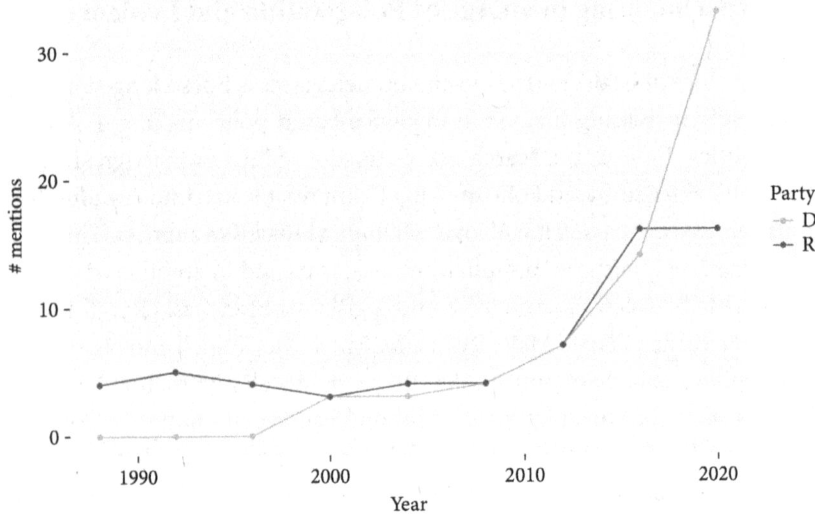

Figure 1.1 References to evidence in national party platforms, 1988–2022

Source: Author's calculations based on keyword searches of national party platforms from 1988 to 2022. Number of mentions reflects a count of how often each platform used the terms *data*, *evaluation(s)*, or *evidence*.

[3] Republicans tended to support the act from the perspective of saving tax dollars and creating more efficient government in the long run, presumably assuming that evaluations would show government to be an inefficient service provider along many fronts. Democrats, on the other hand, tended to support the bill from the perspective of measuring equitable outcomes and proving that government in fact *was* an effective actor in social welfare provision.

policymaking (Weimer and Vining 2007, 19). However, measuring the impacts of policies is a challenging task that is far less objective than we might like to think. Randomized controlled trials (RCTs), the gold standard of determining causal relationships, are expensive, logistically complicated, and, in many cases, unethical to conduct with public policy. There *are* an increasing number of alternate strategies for estimating the causal effects of policy interventions, but these strategies also require making subjective assumptions and research design choices. Findings from RCTs are also vulnerable to criticism; they are time-limited and require people to opt into participating. The myriad judgment calls and decision points involved in policy analysis create opportunities for ideologically fueled dismissal of findings that counter one's partisan preferences (Jenkins-Smith 1988; Kraft, Lodge, and Taber 2015; Strickland, Taber, and Lodge 2011).

Even under less polarized conditions, abandoning or significantly reforming existing policies is a big ask for reelection-minded public officials who gained power under the status quo. Indeed, as early as the 1970s, scholars argued that termination of programs is a rare event in American politics (Kaufman 1976; Patashnik and Zelizer 2013). Even simply changing one's mind or updating one's preferences can result in accusations of being a flip-flopper or ideologically unpredictable (e.g., Baker et al. 2001; Haberman & Parker 2016; Halbfinger 2004; Koerth-Baker 2012). Emphasis on ideological purity and consistency further stymies a political culture in which the elites and the public reward trying, failing, learning, and adjusting. But for evidence-informed policymaking to work, policy evaluations must affect future policy outcomes, and public officials need to be open to adopting evidence-based practices *and abandoning failed ones.*[4] If state governments are to achieve the full promise of innovating policies, experimenting with implementation, and adjusting course, scholars and practitioners alike must understand and account for the politics of failure. This is precisely the contribution of this book.

The following section describes the growing interest in evidence-based policymaking among public officials on both sides of the political aisle and discusses the position of states as laboratories of democracy and the role

[4] Learning from failure is a touted strategy in the private sector (e.g., Bursztynsky 2023; Leak 2021; Maxwell 2007; McArdle 2015), and yet leaders in the public sector face significantly more headwinds in trying to embrace failure as an important leadership and governance strategy. Voters, elites, and fellow public officials often lambaste those who innovate if they do not succeed right away.

experimentation can play in a federal system. This view of American federalism has not fully accounted for what happens with failed experiments—a more likely outcome than successful ones. In addition, I argue that understanding when elected officials recognize and address failed state policies is an important lever for explaining and ameliorating rising inequality. The chapter concludes with a preview of the argument and cases presented in the remainder of the book.

Early Evidence-based Policymaking Efforts

Efforts to employ systematically collected and analyzed data to inform policy decisions are not unprecedented. Early in the twentieth century, policymakers, foundations, and practitioners began to realize the power of data collection and analysis to evaluate the effectiveness of large-scale social programs. In the 1930s, evidence-oriented reformers and public officials attempted small-scale studies of the effectiveness of their social programs. For example, in the Cambridge-Somerville Youth Study conducted in Massachusetts in the 1930s, researchers conducted a small-scale RCT to study the effect of counseling and social activities on the behaviors of adolescent young men considered at risk of delinquency (Baron 2018; Dishion, McCord, and Poulin 1999). Efforts to study policy outcomes increased dramatically in the 1960s and 1970s (think the Perry preschool study or the Manhattan Bail Bond Project; see Baron 2018 and Haskins (2018) for excellent overviews). In 1962, the Federal Drug Administration led the way in evidence-based policymaking by requiring that all drugs undergo rigorous RCTs before the agency would consider licensing a drug.

By the 1980s, other federal agencies and foundations were seeking to bring best practices of data-driven decision making to their work. Notably, under both the George H.W. Bush and the Clinton Administrations, the Ford Foundation, Health and Human Services, and Housing and Urban Development all collaborated to assess the impact of various state-level welfare to work programs, the findings of which later lent political support and credibility to President Clinton's Personal Responsibility and Work Opportunity Reconciliation Act of 1996 (Baron 2018).

The meteoric rise in computing power and in scholars' understanding of statistics and causal inference expanded the possibilities of policy evaluation and evidence-driven policymaking in the 2000s. Education reformers, practitioners, and policymakers demonstrated a particular interest in these practices. In 2002, Congress established the Institute for Education Sciences—a mostly independent research organization housed in the Department of Education—through its Education Sciences Reform Act, which directed RCT evaluations of educational programs whenever possible (see Whitehurst 2018 for education's pioneering adoption of evidence-based practices).

In the last fifty years, nongovernmental organizations also furthered the investment in evaluating policies, with the establishment of the Poverty Action Lab at MIT—a renowned research organization that studies the effects of antipoverty work across the world—and the Coalition for Evidence-Based Policy, which regularly collaborates with Congress and the Executive branch to encourage the use of rigorous evidence in policymaking. Congress continued to support evidence-based policymaking by attaching funding incentives to states that incorporated evaluation into various education and welfare programs. More recently, several major philanthropic research organizations, such as PEW Charitable Trusts and the Arnold Foundation, have invested millions of dollars in both studying policy outcomes and promoting the virtues of evidence-informed policymaking.

Policy wonks, foundation leaders, civil servants, and elected officials are not the only ones who expressed more interest in evidence-driven policymaking in the last four decades. The news media has also adopted the language of evidence and evaluation when discussing policymaking. References to evidence-based policymaking in American media skyrocketed twenty-fold, from fewer than fifty stories in 1995 to more than 7,500 in 2015.[5]

The first Trump administration's skepticism of science, facts, and mainstream institutions temporarily stalled national evidence-driven policymaking efforts.[6] However, in 2022, a week after signing the American Recovery Plan (ARP) into law, President Biden issued a presidential memorandum making it the official policy of his White House to evaluate programs funded through the ARP and to use evidence of informed policy decisions (American Rescue Plan Equity Learning Agenda 2022). Even more unusual, this memo explicitly made equitable recovery across marginalized communities a key outcome for ARP programs. The Office of Evaluation Sciences, which was created in response to recommendations from the Commission

[5] Calculations based on author's analysis of Nexis Uni newspaper and media mentions between January 1 and December 31 of the given years.

[6] The Commission's website was frozen as of Trump's inauguration day in 2017, as his administration no longer supported maintaining its webpage.

on Evidence-Based Policymaking (which was the product of Paul Ryan and Patty Murray's advocacy for HB 1831), now manages dozens of program evaluations and is deploying federal funds in accordance with measurable outcomes.

These investments in policy evaluation have not substantially reconciled or even shifted policy preferences among American partisans. In fact, a closer look at the national party platforms reveals stark partisan patterns showing how the parties invoke evidence in describing their visions for American government. Figure 1.2 shows whether using the word "evidence" *justifies* a preexisting policy preference or calls for systematic policy evaluation and data-informed decision making. Republicans use the term *evidence* largely to justify preexisting policy preferences (e.g., "Given the weight of social science evidence concerning the crucial role played by the traditional family in setting a child's future course, we urge a thoughtful review of governmental policies and programs to ensure that they do not undermine that institution" [2008 Republican Party Platform 2008]), while Democrats are more likely to use the term to call for evidence-based policymaking (e.g.,

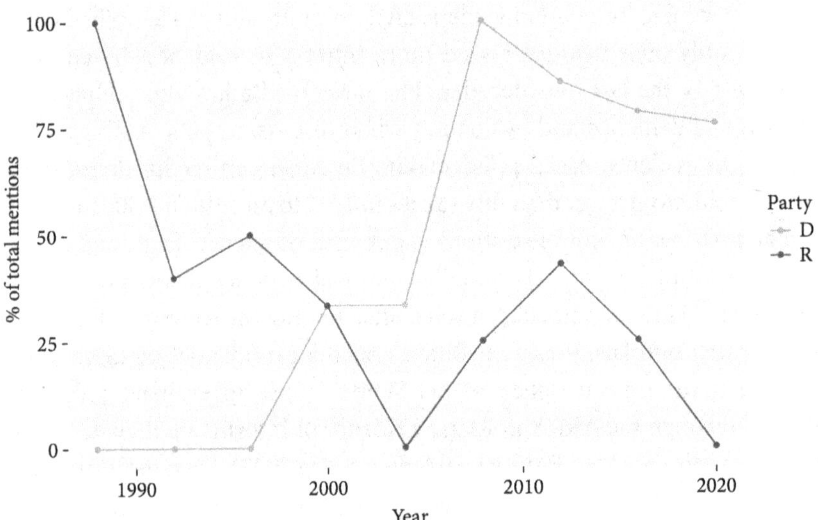

Figure 1.2 References to evidence-based policymaking as a proactive policy approach in national party platforms, 1988–2022

Source: Author's calculations based on keyword searches of national party platforms from 1988 to 2022.

"We will end the Bush Administration's war on science, restore scientific integrity, and return to evidence-based decision-making").

In fact, the 2008 Democratic platform is the first to explicitly mention the full term "evidence-based decision making." The full explanation for these patterns is beyond the scope of this book. However, the fact that both parties recognize the cachet of evidence and data further emphasizes the at least perceived political value of claiming evidentiary support for their policy platform. The variation in *how* the two parties invoke data also suggests that they do so strategically to achieve political goals. The increasingly divergent patterns in how partisans invoke evidence underscores the importance of understanding when, how, and why data can be invoked to draw attention to policy failures. I argue that intentional investment in and strategic design of the procedures, expertise, and resources for collecting and analyzing data has the potential to empower evidence-based policymaking above the cacophony of partisan politics.

Federalism and Laboratories of Democracy

That Utah was able to nimbly implement a radical new approach to sheltering the unhoused is a direct result of the federal design of American government. In American federalism, the fifty states have the authority to make myriad consequential laws and decisions. According to the Tenth Amendment, states have control over any issue that has not been expressly reserved for the national government. And in such a large country with substantial variations in political economies, geography, and cultures, states do indeed choose to implement different policies on everything from taxes (Franko 2021; Jansa 2020) to education (Hartney and Flavin 2011; Manna and Harwood 2011) to water management (Lowry 2005).

American federalism creates a unique opportunity for its subnational units: states can innovate and experiment with new policies without the burdens of instigating nationwide change. This opportunity also, in theory, allows each state to develop policies that are better suited to its specific needs and contexts. In a 1932 case regarding the constitutionality of requiring ice distributors to be licensed, Justice Louis Brandeis saw a threat to this important feature of American government. The courts had ruled that Oklahoma's policy of requiring ice distributors to be licensed violated the equal protection clause of the Fourteenth Amendment. In his dissent, quoted directly in this chapter's epigraph, Justice Brandeis warned against excessive interference with state policy experimentation and the dampening effects for learning and innovation. Although Brandeis was far from the first (or the last) legal voice to value states' dexterity and responsibility for trying out new approaches to governing, his metaphor of the states as laboratories of democracy stuck and has been often cited since.

More recently, politicians have used the laboratories of democracy argument to justify the devolution of the design and implementation of American social policy to state governments (Collins and Gerber 2006; Nathan and Gais 2001; Soss et al. 2001). States now decide who gets access to what levels of state support for everything from health care to tax incentives to criminal justice to housing to education.

The challenge associated with states as laboratories of democracy, however, is that like true scientific laboratories, most public policy innovations (or experiments, if you will) fail. Several estimates suggest that as much as 80 percent of social programs are ineffective (Baron 2013, 2018; Sawhill and Baron 2010). Knowing if a policy has failed is also a complicated question, subject to ideological preferences, availability of information about policy outcomes, and willingness to earnestly compare a policy's goal and its actual outcomes. The evidence-based policy movement aimed to address this gap, marshalling systematically collected and analyzed data to generate objective measures of policy impacts. The excitement over the possibilities of policy evaluation, however, neglects the challenges that arise when those evaluations suggest failure rather than success. The literature on policy diffusion does examine when and how states learn about successful policy experiments and when they adopt policies from other states. And yet important questions about when and how elected officials learn about policy failure remain underexamined and undertheorized. This book seeks to meet this need.

Unequal Guinea Pigs in a Federal System

Making policy is complex: it is impossible to know how a program designed in the bowels of a legislature will interact with the myriad systems, resources, and personalities involved in implementation. Further complicating responsive policymaking is the "upper-class accent" that inflects much of American politics (Schattschneider 1975, 35). In other words, the wealthy and powerful are more likely to have government respond to and reflect their policy preferences (see also Hacker & Pierson 2014 and Gilens & Page 2014). In the U.S. political economy, large corporations are often the most well-organized interests with the most resources and opportunities to make long-term investments in political outcomes across multiple venues (for example, across local, state, and federal governments or in both the legislature *and* the courts) (Hacker et al. 2021). If policies enrich already powerful constituencies—like corporations or the wealthy—then substantial political pressures will be exerted to sustain the policies despite their failures.

There is (and has been) great excitement about the promises of evaluating policy outcomes for ensuring that leaders disseminate policy successes. However, given the high propensity of failure of experiments, it is imperative that scholars and practitioners understand the political response when a new program *does not* work. Failed policies waste scarce resources, exacerbate suffering among recipients of government aid, threaten economic growth. and even undermine government legitimacy (Schuck 2014). Leaving policy failures to fester, especially when the failures harm the poor and marginalized, only exacerbates already rampant political, social, and economic inequality in the United States (Michener 2019).

If states are to benefit from the advantages of being laboratories of democracy, they need ways to consistently and accurately identify when their experiments go awry. If experimentation is going to be a feature—not a flaw—of the American federal system, then we must be intentional about when and how elected officials recognize and address policies that deepen the very problems they purport to solve. When states fail to invest in the capacity for collecting and analyzing data on policy outcomes intentionally, failed policy experiments are going to consistently harm the very marginalized constituencies that the American state has so often neglected.

Policy feedback theory shows that policies make new politics. The creation of new programs changes the distribution of resources, preferences, and power of providers and beneficiaries. Elected officials who participate in the passage of a failed policy may also have substantial reputational stakes in portraying it as a continued success. New programs can create new vested interests that can powerfully advocate for the protection of a policy, even if it is not achieving its intended results. If the policy is not creating harm, then such an event could be a happy accident with unintended, but manageable outcomes. However, if the policy aggravates the very problem it was intended to solve, we may very well be concerned about when and how public officials will come to recognize the failure and address it. As Rom (2006, 259) notes in his study of national government failure that "innovations that are instrumentally beneficial [can be] politically undesirable, and innovations that have negative policy impacts [can be] nonetheless politically attractive. When these combinations occur, it is generally safe to assume that politics trumps policy: the good policies will be neglected, and the bad ones adopted."

When, how, and why do the incentives shift for public officials to recognize and address failed policies, despite the fact that the most resourced and powerful still benefit from them?

In his vision for laboratories of democracy, Brandeis is explicit about the role of the people, saying: "if its citizens choose," their state may serve as a laboratory. According to this logic, and that of pluralism, when a majority is harmed by policy outcomes, it would have the political power to elect representatives supportive of reforms. American democracy, however, is not a fair conduit of the preferences of the majority. As subsequent scholars have argued, American democracy reflects more of an oligarchical than a pluralist tendency (Hacker & Pierson 2011). Money (Gilens and Page 2014), gender (Hennings and Urbatsch 2016; McQueen 2021), race (Schram, Fording, and Soss 2008; Soss, Fording, and Schram 2011), social status (Gilens and Page 2014; Soss, Fording, and Schram 2011), and geography (Gaines and Jenkins 2009) all influence how clearly voices are heard in our political process. Traditionally marginalized communities—those most likely to be harmed by policy failure in our system—are also traditionally the groups with the least political power needed to draw attention to their experiences and to enact their preferences into law. Neglecting a process for when and how to identify policy failure in turn plays a role in the rampant racial and economic inequality plaguing the United States.

The Case for Studying Policy Failure at the State Level

Studying evidence-based policymaking at the state level can offer important insights into state politics. Since the 1930s, an array of national policy evaluation outfits—such as the federal Office of Evaluation Sciences, public policy research institutes at elite universities, and a panoply of think-tanks—have cropped up to document policy outcomes and assess their effectiveness and share the results with relevant agencies and elected officials. But elite, national institutions are not the only ones investing in evidence-based policymaking. Several public state universities—like the Idaho Policy Institute at Boise State University or the Texas Public Policy Research Institute at Texas A&M—house policy evaluation labs that conduct research for the state. State legislatures have also invested in identifying and developing their own internal capacities for policy evaluation, though this investment does vary. All but six states have at least one agency whose mission is, at least in part, dedicated to evaluating and informing policymaking. The modal number of agencies dedicated to policy research and data is one, though twelve states have five or more such agencies.[7]

State legislatures themselves have also shown an increasing commitment to evidence-based policymaking. Since 1991, state legislatures have exponentially increased the frequency with which they include the term

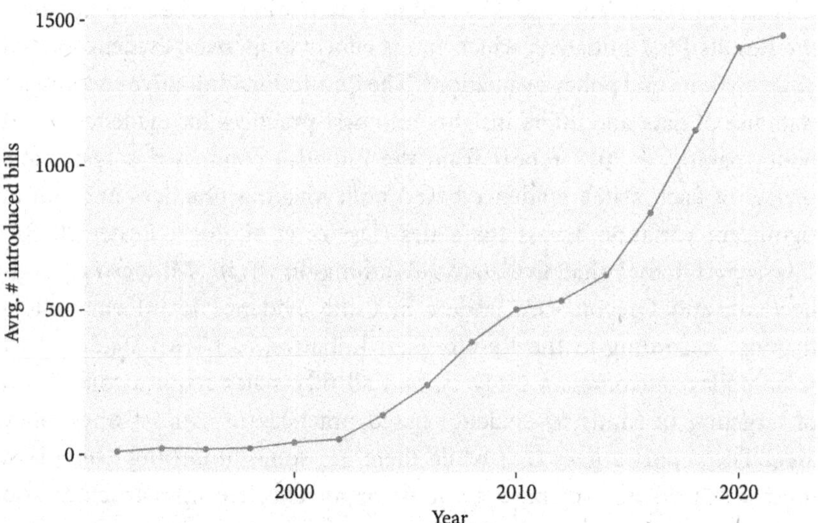

Figure 1.3 Introduced state legislation citing term evidence-based, 1991–2022
Source: Author's calculations based on keyword searches of state legislation through Nexis Uni.

[7] The state agency numbers are based on keyword searches on state agency directories. I counted any state agency that was listed as an independent entity on a state's agency directory that had one or more of the following keywords in its title or mission statement: "research," "data," "review," "statistic," or "audit."

evidence-based in introduced bills (see Figure 1.3). The 1990s saw a total of 207 introduced bills referencing evidence-based policymaking, and only two decades later statehouses brought a whopping 8,322 bills that met the same criteria.

While the overall invocation of evidence-based policymaking has increased over time, this trend has varied substantially across the states. Figure 1.4 shows the percent of introduced bills that contain the term *evidence-based* which were enacted in each state between 1991 and 2022. The exact explanation for this variation is less important for our current endeavor than the evidence that states do indeed vary in their orientation to the value of explicitly naming evidence as an important criterion for effective policymaking. While further research into the explanations for this variation is warranted, a cursory examination suggests partisanship alone does not explain this variation.

Not-for-profits that encourage evidence-based policymaking have also noted an increasing but varied investment in state interest in evaluating policies. Committed to encouraging evidence-based policymaking, PEW Charitable Trusts and the MacArthur Foundation teamed up to form the Results First Initiative, which funds efforts to increase evidence-based policymaking and policy evaluations. The Results First Initiative encourages state use of data and offers insights into best-practices for evidence-based policymaking. A 2017 report from the Initiative conducted a systematic review of each state's evidence-based policymaking practices and found significant variation across the states (Davies et al. 2017; Lester 2018).[8] The report found that five states—Washington, Utah, Minnesota, Connecticut, and Oregon—are leaders in using evidence to inform policymaking. According to the Results First Initiative, forty-two states report *some* policy outcomes in budgets, and all fifty states require some form of targeting of funds to evidence-based practices in at least one policy area. The report argues that while there are some promising exemplars, most states do not yet have a robust or an effective infrastructure and processes or human capital to faithfully or consistently implement evidence-based policymaking. The report also shows that this capacity for evaluating policies varies not only across states, but also within states across policy domains.

[8] The report examines four policy areas: behavioral health, child welfare, criminal justice, and juvenile justice. The findings are based on the Results First Initiative's index of several evidence-based best practices, and the researchers gathered data from publicly available documents and through surveying state policymakers (Davies et al. 2017).

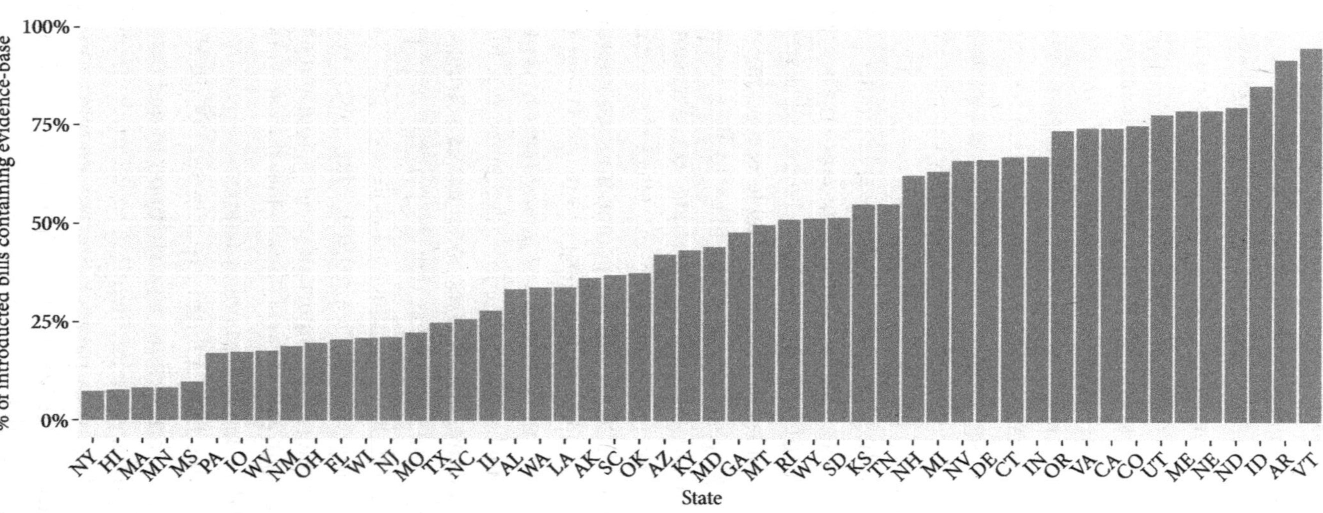

Figure 1.4 Percent of Introduced bills containing "evidence-based" that were enrolled by state, 1991–2022

Source: Author's calculations based on legislation keyword searches on Nexis Uni and state legislative archives.

While policies can fail at all levels of government, state-level policy plays a particularly important role in the rising political, economic, and social inequality endemic to contemporary American society. Understanding the state-level response to policy failure is essential for understanding and addressing broader patterns of inequality. States have increasingly become the designers and implementers of much of our nation's social safety net (Nathan and Gais 2001; Soss et al. 2001). Supporters of this approach suggest this decentralization offers states the opportunities to innovate and tailor their policies to meet the needs of their people. Indeed, this is at the root of Brandeis's defense of states acting as policy laboratories, experimenting with new ideas and passing the good ones along to their fellow states. However, with experimentation comes failure, and failure can exacerbate the very problems elected officials claim to be solving.

While existing political science offers many explanations for when and how successful policy ideas diffuse across state borders (Berry and Berry 1990, 1999; Gilardi 2010), we don't yet understand what happens when an experiment fails. Volden (2016) is a notable exception, showing that more professionalized legislatures are more likely to abandon a policy they observe failing in an ideologically similar state. Eric Patashnik has conducted a series of important studies on the effectiveness of reforms to national laws (Patashnik 2008) and the potential for countermobilization and backlash against existing policies (Patashnik 2023), but these works focus on development of the *perception of failure* regardless of whether or not the policy is actually producing the intended outcomes. In his study of policy learning and failure, May focuses on failure as a "trigger for considering policy redesign" and emphasizes that the perception of policy failure often outweighs the empirically documented realities of policy outcomes in the political process (Ingram and Mann 1980; May 1992). While the perception of failure is absolutely an important political tool and phenomenon, this project is interested in cases in explaining when the perception of failure aligns with *empirically* documented policy failure.

When no one benefits from a failed experiment, the usual channels of political feedback can work well to draw attention to and demand reform of the policy. Public outcry, media attention, social media trends, and lobbying from organized interests have all directed attention to state policies they deemed failures. These strategies, however, are not limited to only addressing objective failures, and not every group can access or employ these strategies as effectively. Engaging in these advertising campaigns about a policy's failure is both challenging and costly. However, policy failures can fail the intended constituency while enriching another. Policy failures that create a beneficial outcome for some groups can in turn can build political support for continuing the policy, even though it is not achieving the intended outcome. Continued support for a failed policy is especially likely when the group benefitting from a failed policy is already highly organized, and the victims of the failure are either diffusely organized or not organized at all.

Scholars of state politics have not sufficiently probed when and how elected officials are willing to acknowledge and learn from failure when the evidence comes from their own constituents' experiences with state-level policies. The present text aims to understand when and how public officials act like responsible scientists, learn about failure, and respond by adjusting course on their policy experiment.

To do so, using a comparative case study of six state policy trajectories, I examine two policy areas in which state authority has substantial influence: truancy policy (which sits at the intersection of education and juvenile justice) and business location tax incentives. These types of policies have profound implications for individuals' access to resources and for the long-term political, social, and economic inequality within a state. For this purpose, I examine truancy policy in Texas, Washington, and Wyoming, as well as business location tax incentives in Texas, Washington, and Kansas. The six policy trajectories represent a range of responses to failure both within and across states. Texas and Washington are especially useful analytical foils because public officials in each state recognize and address policy failure in one instance but not the other. Furthermore, the responses to failure within each state do not reflect simple partisan responses. Chapter 2 offers more detail and justification for each of these selections and the research design.

An Institutional Theory for Addressing Policy Failure

Fundamentally, the availability of credible evidence of policy failure can shift political pressures and incentivize elected officials to address the policy outcomes that they might otherwise have ignored. This book develops a new theory in which state-level institutions and resources are key to explaining when these elected officials will recognize and address policy failure.

A policy is defined as having failed when its measurable outcomes either undermine or contradict its intended purpose. (This definition is elaborated on and defended in Chapter 2.) I leverage policy feedback theory to explain how investments in state capacity have long-term consequences for which interest groups win out in the debate over a policy's failure. Most of the existing policy learning and diffusion literature focuses on individual characteristics that affect public officials' likelihood of internalizing new information and refining their policy preferences. In stark contrast, I take a historical institutionalist approach, which emphasizes the importance of observing political processes over time, the influence of structural constraints on individuals' political behaviors, and the power of carefully selected comparative case studies for systematically observing political change (Pierson 1993). The design, resources, and processes of state-level institutions can systematically influence when evidence can overcome confirmation bias, bounded rationality, and partisan preferences among elected state officials evaluating a policy.

I argue it is important to parse "research capacity"—the existing paradigm in social science for thinking about evidence-based policy—into two distinct features: *data collection capacity* and *analytical capacity.* These two capacities can *vary independently of one another*, and each requires different resources, processes, and levels of state involvement to be able to convincingly highlight policy failure for skeptical public officials. These capacities also vary across states and across policy areas within states. As will be shown, distinguishing between these two features better explains patterns of elected officials recognizing and addressing policy failure.

Importantly, the investment in and availability of these capacities are the products of *political choices* in and of themselves. Whether or not elites choose to invest in data collection and analysis of different policies reflects political preferences and priorities at the start of a policy's trajectory and has long-run consequences whose perspectives are incorporated into policy evaluation years, and even decades, later.

In this book, these novel concepts of data collection capacity and analytical capacity are used to make three arguments about when, how, and why elected officials are likely to recognize and address policy failure. First, the *timing and sources of these capacities influence the likelihood of elites recognizing policy failure.* Establishing data collection capacity early in a policy's trajectory is essential to producing convincing evidence of its failure, while analytical capacity can be generated farther along in a policy's life span. I also show that the state itself is uniquely positioned to gather the most convincing data on policy outcomes. In contrast, I show that, under certain conditions, nonstate actors can effectively supplement analytical capacity.

Second, the power of credible data and analysis lies in their ability to *corroborate the narratives of those harmed by policy failure.* Partisan politics and vested interests often dominate American policymaking. When policies contradict the preferences of the party in power or when they harm well-organized interest groups, the policies usually get changed, regardless of the alignment of the intended and actual impacts. Diffusely organized groups, which too often are also traditionally marginalized groups, harmed by policies struggle to achieve such policy responsiveness. Under certain circumstances, compelling data and analyses can change these dynamics.

Third, the available data collection and analytical capacities within any given state interact with the *context of the passage of the original policy* to influence the likelihood of policy revision once acknowledgment has occurred. More specifically, whether a policy was passed reactively or proactively affects the risk tolerance of public officials and their willingness to abandon an existing but failing policy.

In short, a key finding of this book is that *patterns of acknowledgment and revision will vary as a function of institutionalized data collection and analytical capacity.* The timing of when a state invests in capacity and the features of a policy's original design mediate these effects. Strong data collection and analysis have the potential to disrupt stakeholder dynamics in ways that empower a policy's opponents over its beneficiaries. Revision will also be responsive to elected officials' perceptions of the policy as a proactive or reactive measure.

Conclusion

When Paul Ryan spoke on behalf of the Evidence-Based Policymaking Commission Act (HB 1831) to the House chamber in 2015, he shared his vision for the power of systematically incorporating evidence into policymaking and some of the challenges that had yet to be worked out:

> Let's use the data we're already collecting to improve how government works. How can we use data to evaluate policy? How can we protect people's privacy? How can we get the best results for the American people? If we do this right, we'll stop having debates over what's Republican and

> what's Democrat . . . or what's liberal and conservative. . . . And we'll start having debates over what works and what doesn't work. Those are the kinds of debates we need to have.
>
> (Congressional Record—House 2015, H5488)

It is impossible to know if Ryan thought this Panglossian prediction was likely (or even possible), or if it was a grand rhetorical device to build support for his bill. It is hard to imagine that an experienced politician and dedicated conservative like Ryan would genuinely believe that ideological differences would be overcome by data. Regardless, Ryan reflects some of the naïveté many have exhibited toward evidence-based policymaking. Ryan's comment echoes the fallacy that data collection and analysis is objective, easily conducted free of bias, and immune to the moral and political values of the researcher. Contrary to Ryan's speech, this book shows the inherently political nature and consequences of policy evaluation. Among other things, this book will show that the capacity to collect data and analyze it—essential prerequisites for evaluating policy—is *itself a political decision.* Even more importantly, it is a political decision that has long-term consequences for the longevity of a policy and its effects on political and economic inequality. We cannot fully understand state-level policymaking or effectively address patterns of inequality until we take these efforts to evaluate and reform policies into account. Let us now turn to the theoretical framework that the empirical chapters will corroborate.

2
Policy Feedback, Institutions, and Policy Learning

> *Politics finds its sources not only in power but also in uncertainty—men collectively wondering what to do. . . . Governments not only "power" but they also puzzle. . . . Policymaking is a form of collective puzzlement on society's behalf; it entails both knowing and deciding.*
>
> —Hugh Heclo, *Modern Social Politics in Britain & Sweden* (1974, 305–6)

To successfully innovate, scientists must observe the outcomes of their experiments and compare them to their original hypotheses. Based on a comparison of the predicted and actual result, they may then make tweaks and rerun their study or, in the case of a total failure to produce useful results, fundamentally redesign their experiment. In our federal system, the states can be thought of as fifty different laboratories, their elected and appointed public officials as the scientists, and the array of policies and programs they put in place as the experiments. The process of observing and responding to experimental outcomes, however, is much more complex in our federal system than it would be in a petri dish in a lab.

Few, if any, social policy experiments are as contained and controlled as the conditions found in a well-run laboratory. Even when public officials express interest in evaluating policy outcomes, deciding *how* to measure outcomes as complicated as addiction rates, economic growth, educational attainment, or civic engagement is both challenging and subjective (Deutsch 1966; Stone 2020; Stone 1989). Even when scholars develop reasonable metrics for assessing these outcomes, the challenges of causal inference remain. How can we know for sure that guaranteed housing led to someone becoming sober and maintaining steady employment? Was it really the tax breaks that generated more employment opportunities, or would that have happened anyway because of specific social and political forces within a given

The Politics of Failed Policies. Sarah James, Oxford University Press. © Oxford University Press (2025).
DOI: 10.1093/9780197813645.003.0003

state? What methods for subsidizing a family's food budget are most effective in getting nutritious food to children? Public policies are created to affect people's well-being, and with that comes as many complicating factors as there are people using a given program. Being able to change only one variable at a time and observe the consequences, like a scientist is able to do in a controlled lab experiment, is impossible.

And yet, state legislatures can and do experiment to solve pressing problems, and they cite the importance of evidence and evaluation in policymaking. Truly puzzling over what works and what does not requires a willingness to hear evidence contrary to your own beliefs and preferences and then an openness to governing accordingly. Politics, however, does not often encourage this kind of intellectual honesty or curiosity. This chapter outlines the theoretical framework for when government elites are likely to recognize and respond to failed policies.

My theoretical contribution diverges from existing work on policy learning and research capacity in three key ways. *First, I argue that collecting data and analyzing it are distinct features of a state's institutional landscape and can vary independently of one another.* In other words, just because a state collects data doesn't mean it will be analyzed to inform policymaking. Alternatively, having a cadre of professional researchers is useless if there are no relevant and accurate data to analyze. Both collection and analytical capacity are necessary for recognition of policy failure, and the absence of one or the other results in predictable patterns of the recognition of policy failure. As a result, only when high collection capacity is paired with high analytical capacity should we expect an evidence-driven response to policy failure.

Second, I argue that institutions and their capacity for research are key sources of policy feedback effects for failed policies among elected officials. Consequently, investments in these resources affect the likelihood that elites will recognize failure. When and how much a state invests in its capacity for policy evaluation impacts the possibility for data-driven policy learning, despite entrenched interests or partisan preferences. Understanding whether elected officials are likely to recognize failure requires centering institutions as important sources of elite policy feedback effects. The politics of recognizing and addressing failure are not restricted to the moment the failure is recognized. Investment in state institutions, the landscape of nongovernment research institutions, and the original policy design all generate feedback effects that have long-term influences on the likelihood of addressing policy failure.

Third, the timing of when and how each capacity develops is critical to whether failure is recognized. To enhance the chances that a policy will be fairly evaluated, a clear process for collecting data must be established early in the policy's trajectory. The more credible and compelling the data, the more likely that a policy's opponents will be able to use it on behalf of their policy goals. Analytical capacity, on the other hand, can develop later in a policy's trajectory and still generate credible evidence about a policy's outcomes. The availability of credible data and compelling analysis is so important because it can change the power dynamics between vested interests benefiting from a failing policy and the (usually) less well-organized constituencies being harmed by it. Data can corroborate anecdotal accounts of harm and serve as an organizing tool and clarion call for public officials to reassess their policy perspectives despite ideological or partisan commitments. In other words, to fully explain when and how policy failure gets recognized, we must move beyond behavioral explanations to look at the political, institutional, and economic context of a policy's origins and development.

In what follows, I first define policy failure more precisely and justify my operationalization of the concept. I then present an overview of theories of policy change to highlight how scholars have given an increasingly starring role to information, new ideas, and learning dynamics in how public officials' form policy preferences. Next I define institutions and theories of policy feedback and explain the role that each plays in recognizing policy failure. The second half of the chapter introduces the data collection analytical capacity and explains how they differ from one another. The chapter concludes with an overview of the typology of recognizing policy failure that results from the interaction of these two capacities.

Policy Failure as a Scope Condition

A host of social scientists (not to mention philosophers) have long recognized the inherently subjective nature of knowledge. In his study of political communication, Deutsch argues that "no knowledge is completely 'objective'" because the "knower" has selective interests and uses this information to make decisions about how to summarize, symbolize, and communicate their knowledge (1966, 5–6). Stone echoes this sentiment in a more contemporary study of how we use numbers to make important decisions. She argues that even when we are simply counting, we are "forcing things into categories by ignoring their differences" (Stone 2020, 2). She goes on to say, "Every number is born of subjective judgements, points of view, and cultural assumptions. Numbers are filled with bias through and through, because that's what categories do. Categories are ways of seeing and *not* seeing in the same way a racist sees a skin color without seeing a person" (Stone 2020, 12).

In other words, what we count, how we count, and what we deem unworthy of recognition in our categories are in turn the product of who has power when the counting is taking place. Similarly, whoever has a seat at the table when decisions about policy design and evaluation are being made will affect whose perspectives and biases are ultimately represented in the policy implementation and evaluation processes.

It was therefore unsurprising that a key challenge of this book was how to define policy failure—a not particularly obvious categorization that involves a host of decisions about what counts and what doesn't—in a way that is not simply an expression of political preferences and who has power. Scholars have distinguished between *political failures*—when a policy loses political support due to a change in officeholder, loss of public support, or some other political crisis—and *policy failures*—"when the policy does little to remedy a policy problem or when it brings about significant harmful side effects" (Volden 2016, 47; see also Gilardi 2010; May 1992; Rom 2006). This book focuses entirely on understanding the conditions under which policy failure generates political failure. In other words, when do people in power decide that an empirically failing policy is no longer worthy of political support? Existing definitions do not clearly address the challenge that deciding when a policy "does little to remedy a problem" is itself often a political act. In this book, I define a policy as an empirical failure if it satisfies the following two criteria:

1. The policy has a *clearly advertised intent*[1] explicitly listed in the original legislation.

[1] Policies may list multiple intents. In some cases, the listing of multiple purposes is a delineation of several submetrics relevant to the main goal of the legislation. If a policy is attempting to achieve multiple goals, it is plausible that the policy could fail to achieve one goal while succeeding at the other. Such a case would be a prime opportunity for both supporters and opponents of the bill to craft a narrative about the policy as a failure or success, emphasizing the portion of the policy that aligns with their outlook on the whole thing. Certainly, the politics of a policy with multiple intents will not be as straightforward as one with a single intent, and I would argue that the dynamics of leveraging data to craft credible narratives would still apply.

2. There is *consistent, reliable, scholarly research* demonstrating that the *intent of the law* is either not being met or is being undermined by unexpected consequences.

Following Boswell (2009), I define research as the digestible information produced by individuals and institutions with recognized qualifications to implement logically coherent methodologies that will produce knowledge that meets "certain standards of theoretical and conceptual coherence" (Boswell 2009, 56).[2] In other words, research is the information uncovered through systematic methods of a given discipline and connected to existing knowledge, concepts, and mechanisms. I use findings and consensus from existing scholarly research to identify the types of policies we should expect to fail. This identification qualifies the specific state policy for inclusion in my study. Whether a specific state documents the specific policy's outcomes and recognizes failure is the dependent variable I then observe (or fail to observe) and try to explain.

While any policy can "fail" against myriad post-hoc developed criteria, I am interested in explaining the process whereby public officials recognize failure in outcome-oriented public policies. These are the policies for which we might most expect learning to occur, given that there was a practical incentive for the policy in the first place. Therefore, I narrow my scope to policies whose expressed intent was to produce a particular outcome at the time of passage. This is not to say a policy will not fail to produce a latent intent held by its original supporters. However, I follow the practice of many state courts by interpreting the plain meaning of the language in the original statute (Micheli 2019).

Some may also argue that the intent included in legislation does not necessarily reflect lawmakers' *actual* intent with the law.[3] While indeed there may be multiple intents for a bill, if a piece of legislation contains a clear description of the policy's goal and the bill receives support, then we should take this intent seriously as described in the passed legislation. A statement of legislative intent is a public commitment between the bills' supporters and

[2] This will most often reflect work done by academics, who are trained in research procedures, though there may be some exceptions.

[3] Admittedly, discerning intent is a messy process that has plagued the judiciary for as long as they have sought to interpret the law. Lawmakers can even have electoral incentives to strategically misrepresent their intentions with supporting a particular bill (Calvert and Fenno 1994). Therefore, it is entirely possible, even likely, that lawmakers have multiple intentions for a bill and that the advertised intent included in a bill may not be either the sponsor's or the rank and file's main internal rationale for supporting the bill.

the public regarding the purpose of the law. Consequently, it is reasonable to assume that, even if it is not the only or even the main intention of legislators, the advertised intent is a meaningful bar we can use to measure policy outcomes.

The degree of political contestation and partisan framing associated with different policy areas varies enormously. The extent to which an issue is polarized in turn affects the chances that new information can affect when and how public officials learn about policy outcomes. In discussing the conditions under which policy learning and feedback can occur, Pierson states that the more complex and technical the policy issue, the greater the chance that "social investigation and analysis" can affect perceptions of the policy (Pierson 1993, 618). When policies are more straightforward, "'puzzling' is likely to give way to 'powering'" (Pierson 1993, 618). Pierson argues that learning is much more likely to occur in complex policy areas such as education policy compared to areas in which policy more obviously translates into outcomes, like abortion. Deutsch makes a related argument about the effects of polarization and politicization on the potential for learning. He notes that learning requires some instability of equilibrium such that a potential "learner" is open to hearing new information, "at least some part of the receiving organization must be in a highly unstable equilibrium so that new information can set off a reaction of changes" (Deutsch 1966, 147).

Intense political polarization of a particular issue can provide a stabilizing force that can significantly reduce the chances of learning. These findings lead to a reasonable conclusion, especially in today's political climate: for policies that are at the height of their politicization and polarization (e.g., abortion, prayer in schools, gun control), party politics and existing power dynamics will likely drive the framing of the policy outcomes, regardless of empirical data. However, there are plenty of other important, and more complex, policies for which we might hope and expect learning can occur. These types of policies are at the heart of the present study.

The extent to which a particular policy domain is polarized waxes and wanes over time—think abortion (Hout 1999), temperance (Andersen 2013), or the Second Amendment (Lacombe 2019), to name a few. I suspect no amount of data (at least in the short run) will alter the political calculation of the supporters and critics of such policies. Thus, I study policies for which positions are less calcified during the period of study. My findings, therefore, should be applicable to a range of policy domains that may have clear alignments with partisan preferences but are not the most salient, hot-button issues of the day. And even for the most salient, polarized issues, we should expect their salience to change over time, at which point my findings may more readily apply.

While partisan politics certainly influence all levels of policymaking for all types of policies, of greatest interest here is in explaining when elite perception of failure aligns with empirically documented failure. In other words, this book examines the way politics intermingles with data analysis, public administration, and policy learning. Political scientists have documented myriad ways in which party politics influences ideologically salient policies and issues. What we understand less clearly are the ways in which politics seeps into and shapes the supposedly more objective processes of evidence-informed policymaking. This book is an attempt to examine how the decision to invest in creating policy knowledge is a political choice unto itself, with downstream consequences for future political conflicts. I argue not that data and analyses eradicate politics but rather that the availability and quality of the data and analyses are the results of political decisions themselves that have downstream political effects. Furthermore, these capacities interact with existing political dynamics to constrain and motivate public officials' future political calculus.

Policy Change, Information, and Learning

Explaining policy change is a core task of political science. Conflict-oriented theories dominated early explanations of policy change, ignoring the agency and preferences of individual policymakers (see Bennett & Howlett 1992, for an excellent overview). Robert Dahl (1961), in the pluralist tradition, canonically argued that it was coalitions that cooperated to bring about their desired policies. According to this view, policy change takes places when sufficiently resourced and vocal groups impose their will on a relatively passive government (Nordlinger 1982).

More recent scholarship, however, acknowledges that policymakers and bureaucrats have ideas and preferences of their own and can act to implement them separate from any demands from their constituents. In 1974,

Walker argued that civil servants and other policy specialists played a critical role in policy change, given "their ability to shape the intellectual premises and performance measures employed by policy-makers" (Walker 1974, 3). Hugh Heclo, in his seminal study of Swedish and British social policy, further emphasized the influence of ideas on the development of social policy. Heclo argued that theories of policy change focusing exclusively on constituent demands were incomplete: they ignored the role that new ideas could have in how legislators chose to design their policies (Heclo 1974). Instead, he emphasized the importance of knowledge acquisition and utilization. As described in this chapter's epigraph, it is the uncertainty about what to do, the "collective puzzlement on society's behalf," and the ideas that public officials bring to bear on this puzzlement that influences what slate of policies get enacted (Heclo 1974, 305).

A decade later, in the 1980s, John Kingdon's innovative metaphor of policy streams highlighted the importance of public officials having and using information for explaining policy change. Kingdon (1984) argued that policy change happens when three "streams"—the policy stream, the problem steam, and the politics steam—intersect. The policy stream, according to Kingdon, represents the regular flow of ideas coming from "policy entrepreneurs," that is, researchers, legislative staffers, advocates, and engaged citizens, who determine which policies should be implemented. From this ubiquitous "primordial soup" of ideas, policymakers can develop concrete policies. When a particular problem becomes salient, policymakers can then match their policy solution to the idea, marking the convergence of the policy and problem streams (Kingdon 1984). But only when the political context (or stream), which can be the partisan control of government or the timing of impending elections, aligns with the other two does policy change come about.

Subsequent research corroborates the importance of ideas and information in the policy change process. Scholars have identified several different types of this "experience-induced policy change," often called policy learning (or some variant thereof), using overlapping and sometimes contradictory definitions. For my purposes, policy learning is what May (1992, 331) refers to as "instrumental learning," which occurs when new information about outcomes changes public officials' beliefs about a policy's effectiveness. Dynamics internal to a state, such as bureaucratic feedback, state policy history (Rose 1991), or policy entrepreneurs and interest group demands (Rose 1993) can spur learning.

In his 1993 study of policy learning and policy feedback effects, Paul Pierson laments the lack of theoretical clarity regarding exactly who does the learning in policy learning, when we should expect learning to result in incremental or reactive policy shifts, and how frequently learning should occur (Pierson 1993, 615). Policy learning theories all suggest some process through which policymakers adjust their present actions and preferences based on acquired information about existing policies. However, there is substantial variation in the actors, mechanisms, intentionality, and timeframe that scholars place at the center of these explanations. Existing theories range from intentional "social learning" in which governments adjust their goals and techniques to improve governance (Hall 1993), to more passive "policy learning" about the causes and effects of policies in different political climates that result from experience in government (Heclo 1974), to the individual "policy-oriented learning" in which individuals have "enduring" changes in belief systems based on experience in government (Sabatier 1987, 1988).

In addition to the conceptual opacity of what exactly policy learning is, there are conflicting perspectives on *who* does the learning and *why* they might do it. Bennett and Howlett (1992) provide an excellent overview of this work, but it is worth recapping the highlights briefly here. Heclo (1974) argues that "policy middlemen" influenced by societal forces—such as economic development, elections, interest group pressures. and administrative expertise—bring new ideas to policymakers, which in turn can make their way into policy. Exactly who these policy middlepersons are though remains unclear (Bennett & Howlett 1992). Others have emphasized the preeminence of the formal state institutions (Skocpol et al. 1985) and the relevant bureaucrats (Etheredge 1981) as key actors in the learning process. These theories of learning provide an important foundation for considering the role of ideas and information in the policymaking process. However, they deserve revisiting in light of three monumental developments in the last three decades: first, the revolutionary advances in technological capacity to collect, store, and analyze big data (Brady 2019); second, the increasing devolution of social policies to state governments (Soss et al. 2001); and, third, the meteoric rise in affective partisan polarization (Iyengar et al. 2019). This book contributes to the literature on policy learning by focusing on acknowledging failure as a critical facet of learning, centering government elites as the learners, and identifying institutional capacity as a critical resource for catalyzing learning.

Policy Learning in a Federal System

State politics scholars began to take an interest in the role of information and learning in the late twentieth century, as they observed state governments imitating policies passed by other states, a process known as policy diffusion. The diffusion literature emphasizes that policymakers themselves, together with their relationships with other political elites, are key drivers of policy change (Mintrom and Vergari 1998). Policy diffusion studies show how lawmakers look *outside* their borders for information about ideal policy options, using others' experiences with a policy to determine its appropriateness in their own context. Geographic proximity, a state's reputation as a policy leader (Walker 1969), frequency of prior adoptions (Gray 1973), policy entrepreneurs (Balla 2001; Mintrom 1997), and ideological alignment between states (Volden 2016; Volden, Ting, and Carpenter 2008) can all impact the likelihood of policy diffusion.[4] Finally, the diffusion literature by and large assumes that successful policies spread from one state to another, leaving many unanswered questions about the dissemination, adoption, and abandonment of failed policies. (See Volden 2016 for an important exception, though this study too relies on individual features of elected officials as an important explanation of policy abandonment.)

Theorizing about an idyllic process of learning from new experiences and information can seem quaint in our current era of vitriolic and polarized politics. Today when elected officials stray too far from the party line, they regularly face more extreme primary opponents sponsored *by their own party* (Boatright 2013). In their study of conservatives' support for addressing mass incarceration in Texas, Dagan and Teles (2016) offer us some hope that entrenched partisans *may* change their minds. They find that, in response to negative personal experiences with a policy, policy entrepreneurs can initiate negative policy feedback cycles, cutting ties between ideology and specific policy positions and, in turn, decreasing political support for a particular policy position. Relying on the coincidence of personal experience and political opportunities in today's politics, however, does not promise regularly responsive governance.

[4] Diffusion can explain policy implementation, as well as reversal (Lowry 2005), though the dynamics differ slightly. Lowry (2005) argues that the diffusion of policy reversal relies more heavily on a state's fiscal health and interest group position-taking. Furthermore, he suggests that policy reversal diffuses more slowly but across a wider geography than policy adoption.

Short-term political interests often dictate policymaker decision making, with limited regard for long-term consequences (Hayek 1973; Jervis 1998; Pierson 2000). Elected officials might often have incentives to turn a blind eye to a policy failure to appease a powerful constituency or to avoid accusations of flip-flopping or, even worse, ideological impurity. What this book examines is a specific type of policy learning that works against this myopia: when are elected officials responding to information about the outcomes for a policy that is already on the books? In other words, when do elected officials acknowledge evidence that existing policies are failing and decide whether to continue supporting them? In the end, what matters for enacted policy is to know when the elected officials are willing to adapt their preferences to credible information about policy outcomes.[5]

Learning about Failure

The diffusion literature generally assumes that elected officials experiment to improve their policies—whether that be better aligning policies with their own ideology or better meeting some policy goal. This literature almost exclusively deals with successful experiments and the subsequent politics (Berry and Berry 1990; Godwin and Schroedel 2000; Volden 2006). While there are many discussions of policy failure and how learning might ensue (May 1992), few empirical studies have been done on the politics of policy failure. Volden (2016) is a notable exception: he finds that legislators tend to look to ideologically similar and geographically proximate states to gather evidence about whether a policy might fail in their own state. Scholars have not systematically documented what happens when experiments fail, and yet failure is an important and likely outcome in the experimental process (Baron 2013, 2018; Sawhill and Baron 2010), despite elected officials' intentions.

Relying on individual elected officials to receive and embrace information from a primordial soup of ideas about failed policies is not sufficiently systematic to inspire much hope for addressing policy failure in any predictable way. Existing work on state politics identifies ideology (Butler et al. 2017), partisanship (Volden 2016), geography (Haider-Markel 2001), and

[5] I am not concerned with whether officials' private personal preferences change, but whether their publicly expressed opinions and votes do because this is what matters for public policy.

personal relationships (Mintrom 1997) as key influencers of what ideas public officials are exposed to and eventually adopt. Further complicating things, scholars have documented myriad ways in which organized and well-resourced interests have developed an outsized influence on policymaking. For example, Bawn et al. (2012) argue that highly organized and well-resourced interest groups can take advantage of the public's "electoral blind spot," or their inability (or aversion) to paying attention to the minutiae of policymaking to implement policies that benefit the most powerful.

Hacker and Pierson (2011) have shown how the winners in American capitalism (think corporations and the super-rich) have leveraged their resources to rework policies to further benefit their pocketbooks (or perhaps Swiss bank accounts is a more apt description). For example, Balla (2001) finds that interstate professional associations can influence the adoption of new policies. And, in education, Terry Moe shows how teacher unions, which are Goliaths of power with their influence over teachers' policy preferences and financial resources, especially compared to students and families, have successfully blocked substantial reforms for decades (Moe 2011, 2019). In other words, elected officials have a substantial incentive to recognize policy failure when it harms well-resourced and highly organized constituencies, but otherwise may simply engage in what May (1992) calls political learning—updating your strategy and narrative to build more support for an otherwise failing policy. When those in power change their narratives about a failed policy, popular *perceptions* of the failed policy may shift but do nothing to mitigate the impact of failure on policy beneficiaries. This leaves scholars without a clear understanding of how the groups disadvantaged in the American political economy (e.g., the middle class, the poor, or racial minorities) can trigger recognition of policies that fail them.

As I will show in Chapter 3, the aforementioned individual, political, and geographical explanations for policy learning and change do not account for the patterns of recognizing policy failure that I observe in my cases. Nor, normatively, might we want them to. If partisan politics (Coffey 2011; Cohen et al. 2009) and powerful interest groups (Bawn et al. 2012; Hacker et al. 2021; Hacker & Pierson 2011), both of which are enormously powerful in contemporary American politics, cannot (and perhaps should not) fully explain when state legislators recognize and respond to policy failure, then what does? My answer: institutions and institutional capacity.

The landscape of state institutions—such as state bureaucracy, research-oriented agencies, state universities, and respected nongovernmental research-oriented advocacy organizations—and their capacity for collecting and analyzing data offer greater insight into when policy learning about failure occurs but also suggests some hope for ensuring more responsive policymaking. This theory builds on a significant body of work that emphasizes institutions not as static artifacts but as important prizes of political contestation that have substantial impacts on politics (Hacker et al. 2021; Mahoney & Thelen 2010; Sheingate 2014; Skocpol 1995; Thelen 2004). It also corroborates a core contention of the burgeoning American political economy literature that the design and purpose of institutions shape which groups organize and the issues around which they organize (Hacker et al. 2021). These patterns of organization, in turn, are critical for fully explaining long-term policy developments and political processes.

Policy Feedback, Institutional Capacities, and Negative Policy Feedback Cycles

Learning is an individual experience and endeavor. Why and how are institutions important agents in this process? The answer lies in the power of institutions to codify practices into long-term "rules of the game" and to alter and cement new administrative capacities within the state. This in turn produces policy feedback effects for elected officials as they consider and reevaluate policies after their implementation. In what follows, I introduce policy feedback and describe the connection between institutions and policy feedback effects for explaining how the politics of failure play out.

Theories of Policy Feedback

Scholars have long argued that the enactment of a new policy is not the end of political contestation—it simply changes it. As Schattschneider said almost a century ago, "new policies create a new politics" (Schattschneider 1935, 288). Once a new policy is enacted, it alters the resources, incentives, power dynamics, and available information for those affected and, in turn, changes how different actors can and want to access the political system. Scholars call this phenomenon policy feedback (Pierson 1993).

In his seminal work on policy feedback theory, Paul Pierson identifies two key pathways for policy feedback: resource (or incentive) effects and interpretive effects. Building on the work of Skocpol (1995) and Weir and Skocpol (1985), Pierson describes how "policies can provide both incentives and resources that mutate or inhibit the formation or expansion of particular groups" and can then change their engagement with and demands on government (Pierson 1993, 599). Even more basically, policies can produce resources—such as access to power or material benefits—that influence the incentives for elites, interest groups, or the mass public to take action. For example, Suzanne Mettler's canonical study of G.I. Bill recipients in the wake of World War II shows how increased access to education and financial stability spurred civic participation among veterans, as they saw themselves as increasingly deserving and empowered political actors. When considering government elites more specifically, policies can generate resources through altering available administrative capacities.

Interpretive effects, on the other hand, occur when policies influence how the actor interprets and makes sense of the social and political contexts (Pierson 1993, 611). The benefits of the G.I. Bill not only conferred resources, but also led beneficiaries to view themselves as important stakeholders in government and public programs (Mettler 2005). Policy feedback effects can also deter participation. Joe Soss, Vesla Weaver, and Amy Lerman, among many others, have shown how demeaning interactions with the state—through welfare offices or police encounters—can erode trust in government and in turn depress political participation (Soss 1999; Soss and Weaver 2017; Weaver and Lerman 2010).

Through the creation of procedures, commitment of funding and personnel, and codification of expectations around dissemination of information, the formalization of a state's capacity to collect and analyze data creates new resources and incentives for government elites to respond to policy failure. For example, once a state agency is staffed with career researchers, they may advocate for an expanded role in the policy evaluation process, or they may advocate for preserving their jobs and agency in the event its value is questioned.

Institutionalized collection and analytical capacity also democratize access to information about policy outcomes. This access is unevenly distributed (see Pierson 1993) and is an important resource in the recognition of policy failure. Armed with coherent and systematic information about policy outcomes, interest groups, advocates, and skeptical public officials can more credibly and confidently place a policy's failure on the political agenda. For interest groups that are already experiencing failure but may lack systematic and convincing evidence that failure is widespread, state collection and analysis of data can corroborate their perspectives.

Investments in state capacity for data collection and analysis can also induce interpretive effects (how actors make sense of their political context). Knowing that policy evaluation regularly happens may affect elected officials' narratives of the policy effects. Having access to credible research on policy outcomes may also influence the decisions of those harmed by a policy to coordinate with others or to advertise their experiences as being more widespread than their individual perspective.

The Role of Institutions

There are almost as many definitions of the term institutions as there are studies of it. In this book, I use the term to refer to time-durable features of state government and elite political culture, notably, organizations like state universities and nongovernmental research and advocacy organizations, state agencies, or the norms and habits that those organizations might perpetuate. Institutions are important to understanding politics because they enshrine procedures, resources, norms, and expertise into regular features of political interactions (Hacker et al. 2021). Institutions are dynamic: their resources, personnel, political and economic context, and mandates can all evolve (Pierson 2011; Skocpol 1995; Thelen 2004). Even with the evolving nature of institutions, they can provide a durable source of state capacity for evaluating policies. This institutional approach stands in contrast to *behavioral* explanations (like ideology, individual experience, or curiosity about new ideas) for policy change outlined elsewhere in this chapter.

Institutions also offer insight into the study of policy learning and response to failure because they can provide expertise and resources to execute tasks important to the state like evaluating and revising policies. Perhaps even more importantly, institutionalized procedures, expertise, and resources for policy evaluation can constrain public officials' reliance on vested interests and partisan ideology when updating policy preferences. This in turn facilitates a state's ability to fulfill its commitment to evidence-based policymaking. In this case, we can think about it even more specifically as having the resources, motivation, and mandate to conduct a given task. In the case of experimental (or new) policies, state institutions that have the resources, personnel, and procedures to collect data and analyze it in turn enhance the state's capacity for policy evaluation.

Institutions are also important because they can insulate the data collection and analysis processes from partisan interference, and as shown in the Introduction to this book, there are some stark partisan patterns showing when and how the two parties invoke evidence-based claims. Career bureaucrats and trained researchers, while not free of bias, are more likely to be systematic in their evaluations and to be seen by elites as being objective (Doberstein 2017). Except for agency heads, bureaucrats and researchers rarely change with the switch of partisan control in state government, giving both groups an air of credibility that elected officials lack when conducting research. We also know that bureaucrats have incentives to preserve their autonomy (Carpenter 2001) and their reputation for competence and vigilance (Carpenter 2014), further encouraging more objective analysis than that presented by partisan organizations. Trained researchers may also be concerned about their reputation among their peers. If researchers try to publish their government research, they must also undergo a peer-review process that puts at least some guardrails on the methods and subsequent claims that they can credibly employ.

Finally, elected officials seek out information to enhance their credibility on specific policy issues (Boswell 2009). After doing so, they may also more reasonably shift the blame of "recognizing" the failure to the research institution, making their updated stances more politically palatable to their constituents. Thus, institutionalized data collection and analytical capacity are more likely to have the credibility to interrupt politics-as-usual, whether that be partisan allegiances or pressures from vested interests, as well as to facilitate acknowledgment and revision of failed policies.

Positive and Negative Policy Feedback Cycles

Positive policy feedback cycles occur when the resulting political context reinforces the viability of an existing policy. Andrea Campbell (2003) offers a classic example of these cycles with her study of senior citizens and Social Security. As beneficiaries of this generous federal program, senior citizens have become a well-organized and consistently active constituency that mobilizes to protect their benefits. In turn, public officials have learned that threatening Social Security or Medicare is a political nonstarter, and these policies in turn have become more entrenched, despite ideological opposition from the right. Negative feedback occurs when policies fail to generate political support or inspire robust political backlash; thereby eroding elite support for the policy. At the federal level, Patashnik has shown that frustration with policy outcomes (2008) and strategic mobilization against policies (2023) can instigate negative policy feedback cycles, resulting in reform or repeal. These studies, however, are agnostic toward the empirical outcomes of the policies in question. My contribution is to assess when the political support erodes (aka when negative policy feedback cycles begin) in response to empirical evidence about policy failure.

Policy feedback scholars by and large have focused on mass feedback effects among groups such as senior citizens and welfare recipients, but policy feedback effects occur among political elites too (Derthick 2011; Heclo 1974). Systematic research on elite feedback effects is far less developed than its mass counterpart (Karch and Rose 2017). The present book is concerned with the latter.

Karch and Rose (2017) provide a notable exception with their study of how federal programs affect the incentives and resources of state public officials. They show how the design, timing of adoption, and interactions between the two in federal–state policies (like Medicaid and unemployment insurance) generate strong feedback effects for elites. This book furthers what little we know about elite feedback effects and the pivotal role that institutions and their capacities play in catalyzing them.

The availability of credibly analyzed data is a necessary condition for the evidence-based recognition of policy failure among elected officials. The institutionalization of the data collection capacity plays a central role because of its potential to catalyze policy feedback effects. Information both conveys authority (Boswell 2009) and is an important resource in political contestation (Pierson 1993). Even when failed policies harm one constituency, they may also generate positive feedback effects for other stakeholders who can advocate on behalf of the failed policy. My theory offers insight into when and how elites find it politically expedient to recognize the failures, despite the fact that powerful constituencies (such as companies, unions, or other highly organized groups) benefit from the policies. Karch and Cravens (2014) offer an example of this in their study of three strikes laws. They show that the beneficiaries of these laws—namely, private prison operators and prison officer unions—stymied the modification and retraction of the three strikes laws (which I believe is yet another example of a failed policy). Interrupting the political power of vested interests of unions, corporations, or interest groups can be challenging. However, credible information that undermines the narratives of policy beneficiaries can kickstart negative policy feedback cycles among elected officials.

The mere existence of institutions focused on policy evaluation or research does not necessarily mean they will effectively draw attention to policy failures. What institutions also need are established resources and the authority to accomplish their missions and tasks—otherwise known as capacity. The following section describes the existing concept of research or informational capacity (Brambor et al. 2020; Lee and Zhang 2017) in the literature on public administration and state politics. This broad conceptualization of capacity misses important realities about how policy evaluations are conducted and how the findings subsequently affect politics. Instead, it is important to study the capacity to collect and analyze data as distinct features of the state's institutional landscape.

Parsing Research Capacity

Capacity is an oft-cited explanation for a range of political outcomes, covering everything from wealth and standards of living (Robinson and Acemoglu 2012) to the enactment of model legislation (Hertel-Fernandez 2014) to the adoption of new technologies (Acemoglu, Moscona, and Robinson 2016) to the strengthening of state power (Skowronek 1982). Broadly speaking, capacity refers to the state's ability "to get things done" (Lindvall and Teorell 2016, 6). More specifically, state capacity can be described as "the degree of control state agents exercise over persons, activities, and resources within their government's territorial jurisdiction" (McAdam et al. 2001, 78). Scholars of policy diffusion and state politics have found relationships between legislative capacity and emulation of successful policy experiments in other states (Shipan and Volden 2014). The availability of information and expertise is also an important resource for public officials, especially legislators (Krehbiel 1992). In their study of collective action and contentious politics, McAdam et al. (2001) show that state capacity is an essential feature of the state that can influence the success and timing of social movements.

Research and research organizations may of course impact elected officials' decision making or the mobilization of political dissent. As early as the 1970s, scholars noted the state's capacity for gathering information as an important input to the policymaking process (Heclo 1974). More contemporary work continues to recognize a critical role for information in the policymaking process (e.g., Bennett & Howlett 1992; Brambor et al. 2020; Lee & Zhang 2017). Nor is it groundbreaking to suggest that the capacity to gather and process data is an important responsibility of the state. Albeit in a comparative setting, Scott (2008) argues that "the breadth and depth of a state's knowledge about its citizens and their activities is an important component of state capacity" (quoted from Lee & Zhang 2017, 118). Brambor et al. have developed a measure of "information capacity" or a state's ability to "collect and process information about themselves, their territories, and their populations" (2020, 175). They find that higher information capacity is associated with the expansion of suffrage. In fact, the importance of a state's capacity to produce knowledge by gathering data and effectively analyzing it is in line with Heclo's (1974) argument that "the administrative research capacities of administrators influence the degree to which they inform and shape the development of policy itself" (Heclo 1974, 302).

This body of work, however, regularly conflates the resources and procedures for collecting data with those needed to analyze it. Even when scholars acknowledge that these tasks are distinct, they tend to assume that they co-vary. Heclo, for example, conflates research capacity with data availability when he describes Sweden's "strong bureaucracy" that facilitated information gathering, while he laments Britain's haphazard system that relied on "multiple nondata-oriented sources" (Heclo 1974, 302). In their work on research expertise, Heintz and Jenkins-Smith also conflate data availability and theoretical foundations for conducting research when they emphasize the importance of analytical traceability, which occurs when "the issue under debate has well developed theory; is well conceptualized and operationalized, and adequate data exists" (1988, 269). More recent studies also tend to lump data collection and analysis together under the label of "research" (Reckhow, Galey, and Tompkins-Stange 2018). Some public health scholars (e.g., Brownson et al. 2009) have acknowledged the important difference between data collection and data analysis for understanding public health outcomes. My work confirms the importance of this difference for understanding systemic *political* outcomes that impact when and how policy change happens.

While existing work accurately describes the politics surrounding policy analysis in the twentieth century, the explosion in data availability, the popularity of big data, and new analytical tools and strategies warrant a revision of

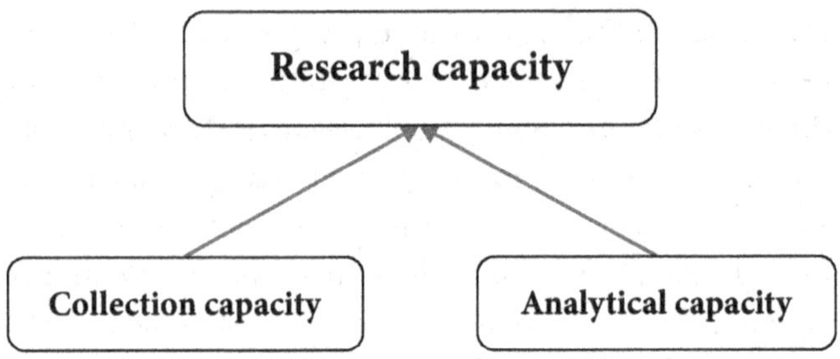

Figure 2.1 Components of "research capacity"

this feature of a state's research capacity. I contribute a theoretical parsing of this concept of research capacity. Conceptualizing research (or information) capacity as the amalgamation of collection and analytical capacity offers more explanatory leverage of when and how a state can produce convincing findings about policy outcomes.

My contribution is to *center the institutional feedback effects for policymakers of investing in both data collection and analysis intentionally and early in a policy trajectory as a key explanation for when policy failures are recognized.* My theory advances studies of state politics and state capacity by separating out two specific characteristics of "research capacities"—data collection and analytical capacity—which influence a state's ability to evaluate its policies (see Figure 2.1). To fully understand the reactions to policy failure, we need to examine the state's capacity to collect data as distinct from its capacity to analyze it. Doing so provides the conceptual clarity needed to understand how one of these two capacities may become institutionalized within the state early in a policy's trajectory, while the other may be neglected. The pattern of interactions between these two capacities has long-term consequences for how the politics of failure play out. Let us now turn to a more detailed description of these two capacities, with even more detail presented in Chapters 3 and 4.

Collection Capacity

As any reasonable social scientist will admit, the range of questions we can answer with our research depends almost entirely on the alignment between our data and the concepts we hope to measure. In fact, the refrain "garbage in, garbage out" reminds researchers that, regardless of how sophisticated their statistical chops may be, their findings are only as good as the data they put into their models. This logic lies at the core of my argument for the importance of data collection capacity in spurring the recognition of policy failure.

Data collection capacity refers to the willingness, resources, and expertise to collect usable data that can inform credible evaluations of a policy's outcome. Clear definitions and state-orchestrated, centralized, and preemptive data collection plans characterize high collection capacity for a given state policy.

The state's investment in collection capacity is essential because, as the designer, implementer, and monitor of public policy, the state is best suited to efficiently observe widespread policy outcomes. In part, this is because the state is best situated to gather information on individuals before and after establishing a new policy (see Brambor et al. (2020) and Schuck (2014) for more discussion of government and data collection). Governments also have an inherent interest in making their practices "legible," which involves both having information about local conditions and practices and presenting the information in standardized forms that public officials can easily digest (Scott 2008).[6] Lee and Zhang (2017), in turn, argue that having legible information is crucial to state capacity. More broadly, institutionalizing procedures and resources for evaluating policies adds legitimacy to the policy efforts (Hall and Taylor 1996; Pierson 2000).

Policies vary in their traceability—how easily outcomes can be linked to government policy and thus be linked to someone to blame—and visibility—how many people experience the policy so that they know to put it on the political agenda (Pierson 1993). Relying on people experiencing a policy's effects to draw attention to failure is complicated because *who* experiences the fallout of failing policies will impact the effectiveness of their political voice. Marginalized groups in American politics often face more challenges in incorporating their concerns and preferences into the political agenda (e.g., Gilens 2009). Data collection creates a potential for traceability by documenting a policy's impacts.

As is true of many matters of policy design and policymaking, sequencing and timing matter enormously to developing data collection capacity (Jenkins-Smith 1988; Karch and Rose 2017; Pierson 1993, 2011).

[6] In his work, Scott studies the development of authoritarian states like Soviet Russia and Tanzania, but his general argument is widely applicable.

Establishing this capacity early on in a policy trajectory enhances the possibility that failure will be recognized. Longitudinal, individual-level data is the gold standard for assessing changes over time. Unfortunately, once a policy is suspected of failing, it is too late to collect credible information about the experiences of policy recipients *before* the policy was put into place. While scholars have developed some statistical strategies for circumventing this limitation, such analyses may be politically more vulnerable than those based on more direct comparisons of individual experiences with a policy. In other words, no amount of money or expertise can go back in time and collect data on past policy outcomes, highlighting the impotence of nonstate actors to supplement data collection efforts.

Analytical Capacity

Robust data collection capacity can produce terrabytes of interesting and usable information. But in the absence of a coherent and credible analysis of this information, the data will be unlikely to influence policymaking. No expert, let alone a busy and distracted policymaker, can derive meaning from millions of individual data points (Jones & Baumgartner 2005). Thus, having the resources, expertise, and mandate to draw scientifically valid inferences from data—which I call analytical capacity—is also essential to spurring recognition of policy failure. This includes having the human capital, technological, and financial resources to conduct accurate statistical tests and develop meaningful models using collected data. High analytical capacity may stem from state-sponsored research institutions, professionalized researchers, and established reporting schedules. Clear and coherent analysis that gets communicated effectively is also essential to the possibility that elites, activists, and interest groups will connect negative outcomes to specific policies and political choices (Greenberg and Robins 1985; Pierson 1993).

Analytical capacity is agnostic to the timing of policy implementation, at least in comparison to collection capacity. The ability of researchers to credibly analyze data is not dependent on *when* they choose to do so (assuming enough time has passed for them to observe relevant outcomes) as long they have access to high-quality data.

This also means that nonstate actors can more credibly supplement state analytical capacity. Professional researchers from established research organizations with reputations for credible, nonpartisan analysis can evaluate state-collected data when they have an interest, mandate, or other incentive to do so. This flexibility stands in stark contrast to collection capacity, in which it would be nearly impossible for a nonstate actor to collect usable data once policy failure has become salient and politicized. When nonstate research organizations can also convincingly report on clear findings, then elected officials may well take notice of policy failure.

While fully funded and institutionalized agencies would be the zenith of capacity, such gargantuan commitments (and expenditure of resources) is not imperative for identifying failed policies. Following the scholarship on historical institutionalism, we see that even small investments in these capacities can self-reinforce over time to yield valuable information for future policy evaluations (Mahoney and Thelen 2015; Pierson 1993; Thelen 2004).

The Intersection of Collection and Analytical Capacity

Distinguishing between collection and analytical capacities and determining the importance of each in laying the foundation for instigating negative policy feedback cycles that spur the acknowledgment of policy failure yield a series of testable expectations. High collection capacity paired with high analytical capacity is most likely to lead to elected officials acknowledging failure, given the clarity of findings that will likely result from a highly centralized and expertly trained policy evaluation process. Credible information may combat the power of vested interests and partisan preferences. On the other extreme, we should not expect any evidence-driven acknowledgment of failure for state policies with low collection and analytical capacity, given that there is no information that will educate public officials. This is not to say that public officials will not argue that a policy without clear outcome evidence has failed, but rather we should expect these claims to occur when it is ideologically expedient to do so rather than in response to evidence.

To highlight the extent and value of my contributions, Figure 2.2 shows the typology of how collection and analytical capacity interact to produce negative policy feedback cycles among elites. Separating out collection and analytical capacity reveals that having a robust network of research

Collection capacity

Analytical capacity	High	Low
High	**Clear cut** • Evidence-informed acknowledgement • Revision likely, but dependent on available alternatives	**Hollow** • Limited acknowledgement • Revision unlikely without single party control
Low	**Treasure trove** • Widespread acknowledgement dependent on non-state actors conducting analysis • Revision possible with coalition building	**Status quo** • No evidence-based acknowledgement of failure • No revision

Figure 2.2 Typology of responses to failed policies

organizations is not sufficient to ensure that policies can be effectively evaluated. In fact, my cases show that data collection capacity is the key component of policy evaluation that the state must orchestrate to enhance the likelihood that public officials will acknowledge policy failure. The following introduces this typology and explains the stylized dynamics that result from each of the four cells.

The Clear-cut Case: High Collection and High Analytical Capacities

In the event of high collection capacity and high analytical capacity for a given state policy, we should expect elected officials to acknowledge failure and engage in a meaningful revision effort. When trained research professionals analyze reliable and accurate data, they can often produce valid findings in which the average individual and elected official will have confidence. The strength of the data and the findings that emerge from a state policy area that benefits from high collection and analytical capacity leaves less room for partisan-inspired disagreement or vested interests to shape the narrative of the policy's success (or failure). Because information confers authority (Boswell 2009), clear findings may boost the efforts of those harmed by the policy to persist in their demands for reform. It may also offer elected officials tools for convincing constituencies of the value of their updated perspectives. Clear evidence resulting from a transparent and robust collection and analytical effort makes it more likely that a social problem will become a policy issue: as "new concepts and data emerge, their cumulative effect can be to change the conventions policymakers abide by and reorder the goals and priorities of the practical policy world" (Weiss 1977, 544). In other words, clear evidence can corroborate and legitimize perspectives among a sea of competing claims about policy outcomes (Jenkins-Smith 1988).

While revision should *most* likely follow acknowledgment of failure in these cases, it may not do so all the time. Offering alternate narratives to explain the policy's outcomes remains a powerful strategy for those opposing revision, even in the face of clear evidence (e.g., Schattschneider 1975, 68).

The Status Quo Case: Low Collection and Analytical Capacities

If the clear-cut case is the ideal case, the lower right-hand corner is the least likely scenario for elites to recognize policy failure, largely because there is no foundation for a credible policy evaluation. When a state lacks the capacity to collect or analyze data, we should not expect public officials to acknowledge or revise failed policies. This is simply because without systematic information, any "failure" label can be deemed the outcome of partisan politics or interest group dynamics in which the narrative is often dominated by the most politically powerful group.

Under these conditions, it is also more plausible for partisans to frame policy debates in terms of morality or values (Greenberg and Robins 1985), thereby heightening the potential of polarization or stalemate. Without usable data or credible analysis, a handful of public officials may still acknowledge failure in response to suggestive reports saying as much, but they will be unable to rally widespread support among elected officials for greater recognition of failure, let alone policy revision. Furthermore, without stable collection or analytical procedures in place, each new administration and legislature can request new collection and analysis efforts that produce findings that might coincide with the existing official's opinion. This in turn reinforces partisan and ideological interpretations of the validity of the analysis and gives public officials permission to ignore inconvenient findings.

The Treasure Trove Case: High Collection Capacity and Low Analytical Capacity

A state can have high data collection capacity but low analytical capacity for a given policy area if the state systematically collects data about a policy's outcomes or recipients but does not require regular analysis and reporting or does not designate an organization in charge of the analysis. This scenario will most plausibly occur when the agency responsible for implementing the policy systematizes data collection without either a plan or the resources to analyze it. However, this could also occur if implementation of a policy inherently generates usable data regarding a policy's outcomes and recipients. Importantly, a state agency can collect data independent of its ability, or even desire, to analyze it. The raw materials of policy analysis—data on policy outcomes—exist in these cases. However, without professionals to analyze the data and disburse findings, we should not expect public officials to acknowledge failure or revise the failed policy because the treasure trove of data would go unanalyzed and therefore would be unable to impact political narratives and incentives. Furthermore, the absence of compelling analysis of existing data leaves the door open for the most powerful groups to dictate the policy narrative that is most beneficial to their interests (Greenberg and Robins 1985).

The involvement of nonstate actors capable of validly analyzing data, however, *can* eventually result in public officials acknowledging failure. Research universities, nonpartisan think-tanks, or foundations can all provide (or supplement) the analytical capacity to draw conclusions from state-collected data. If a nonstate actor steps in to analyze data and has an explicit or implicit ideological leaning, then we should expect public officials affiliated with that ideology to be more likely to acknowledge failure and call for revision. The more credible and nonpartisan the research institution (i.e., a university might be more credible than a think-tank), the more likely it would be for public officials from a range of ideologies to accept the findings, as they would be harder to dismiss as inaccurate. In other words, if nonstate actors can supplement analytical capacity, the case becomes more akin to the clear-cut case.

When a nonstate organization that is not a regular part of the state policy analysis apparatus suggests a policy is failing, public officials inclined to support policy reform may be successful in doing so if they can build a coalition for reform. Because an institution or researcher performing a one-off, or even a poorly executed, analysis on state data may face suspicions of external validity, political bias, or ineptness, such findings could be more easily politicized (see Burstein 1991). In the treasure trove case, there is hope of convincing policy evaluation and subsequent recognition of failure given that the state has already invested in quality data collection.

The Hollow Case: Low Collection Capacity and High Analytical Capacity

Finally, a state may have an established research bureaucracy capable of conducting valid analysis of data, but the data from a given policy area may be low-quality due to imprecision, inaccuracies, or a limited scope of collection. While statistical techniques can greatly enhance the ability of researchers to draw valid inferences from imperfect data, the fact remains that the quality of the data substantially restricts the validity of the subsequent analysis. While this pairing seems unlikely—why wouldn't the research experts who make a state high on analytical capacity inform agencies and policymakers about the qualities of usable data?—it does occur. For example, decentralized data collection and reporting reflects low collection capacity and could significantly impact the possibility of valid findings if the different databases relied on different definitions, formatting, or variables (see Stone 2020 for a broader discussion of this phenomenon). Alternatively, irregular and inconsistent data collection could also hamper the ability of researchers to make meaningful sense of a policy's outcomes in the hollow cases.

Lack of reliability in the data collection phase, in turn, opens the opportunity for skeptics to reasonably question whether a policy is *actually* failing. As Greenberg and Robbins note in their study of social science research in the policy process, the availability of at least some seemingly "scientific evidence shifts attention to methodological issues, which are usually more complex in nature and generally have no clear cut solutions" (1985, 345). This in turn creates a ripe political opportunity to frame an issue in terms of morality or values, rather than empirical outcomes, and can significantly slow or derail the policy change process (Greenberg and Robins 1985). Morality- and values-based arguments are, in turn, much more challenging to refute, especially in a highly polarized political climate. In this context, public officials acknowledging failure will likely fall along ideological lines, possibly precluding policy revision.

Policies emblematic of the hollow case are similar to the status quo case in terms of their susceptibility to the resources and strength of organized policy demanders and the perception of the policy's original purpose. If those supporting the continuation of the policy are more wellresourced and politically empowered than those supporting revision, we should expect the status quo to continue.

Conclusion

To be clear, data alone may not be sufficiently convincing to change elected officials' preferences in view of the maelstrom of electoral incentives, partisan preferences, and group pressures they face. However, together, data and analysis can change the second face of power calculation by changing which reactions elected officials anticipate from their various constituents. This argument also echoes Hall's contribution that the process whereby one policy paradigm comes to replace another is likely to be more sociological than scientific (Hall 1993, 280). The credibility and availability of research can alter public officials' view of which perspectives on policy outcomes are legitimate and worthy of political attention. Furthermore, the decision to invest in these capacities is a political act onto itself. Understanding the landscape of data and analysis of a particular policy's outcome can help explain the types of politics necessary to achieve public officials' acknowledgment of failure and the likelihood of passing reform measures.

In their work examining the changing conservative perspective on tough-on-crime policies in Texas, Dagan and Teles make the following apt statement:

> How a political system processes evidence of policy failure is one of the most important measures of its quality of governance. It is impossible for any policy process to anticipate all possible negative consequences of public policies, but an ability to recognize and respond to problems when they emerge is a reasonable measure against which to judge political regimes. And if we wish to improve our own political system, a good place to start is by understanding the pathways through which previously taboo information manages to break through the daunting obstacles of party politics and biased information processing. (Dagan and Teles 2015, 128)

This book expands on precisely these ideas that Dagan, Teles, and several others have begun to explore. My focus is on how the capacity of state institutions can influence when and how information can maneuver through party politics and biased cognitive processing to generate genuinely evidence-informed policymaking. The next chapter outlines the methodological approach and introduces the six cases that form the empirical basis for this book.

3
Methodological Approach and Case Selection

Exploring the politics of phenomena that have not yet been clearly defined or carefully analyzed in the existing literature—like policy failure or research capacity—requires asking broad questions and maintaining an openness to a range of possible answers. (For the importance of this approach to studying politics, see Michener 2018, Hacker & Pierson 2014, Hacker et al. 2021), and Grumbach 2022). Answering these sorts of *big questions*, as Grumbach (2022) and others have put it, presents challenges. These questions are not always easily studied using traditional research designs and precise causal inference. The myriad overlapping causes and consequences that characterize the realities of policymaking (and policy reforming) require a range of analytical tools to uncover and assess the relationships among actors, events, and institutions. Relying on inductive research through process tracing was especially appropriate for my research questions because state politics scholars have not settled on detailed and consistent definitions of important concepts such as policy failure and research capacity, which are at the core of this book. In fact, a key contribution of this book—the importance of distinguishing between data collection and analytical capacities—resulted from adopting an open approach to understanding how states conduct and disseminate research. Initially, I thought of research and scholarship as a single resource that varied in availability across policies and states. However, in speaking with researchers and policymakers, examining legislative archives, and tracking the sequencing of developments in policy change, it became apparent that more refined concepts better explained the outcomes I observed (see Gerring 1999 for the importance of concept formation).

Thus, this book embraces methodological pluralism and in-depth case studies as essential tools for understanding the long arc of implementing, evaluating, and reconsidering policies. I leveraged methods that were most appropriate to answering the myriad theoretical and practical questions that emerged throughout the project. These methods ranged from transcribing

The Politics of Failed Policies. Sarah James, Oxford University Press. © Oxford University Press (2025).
DOI: 10.1093/9780197813645.003.0004

and coding legislative hearings to interviewing researchers to systematically collecting media stories and organizational reports. As Michener (2018) says in her illuminating study of federalism, Medicaid, and policy feedback, "the methods I employ are a function of the questions that motivate the research and the answers that unfold as the research progresses" (6).

Methodological Approach

One contribution of this book is its comparison of *policy trajectories*—the following of policies and their politics over time. Emphasizing change over time (as opposed to snapshots in time) engages a core contention of policy-focused analysis (Hacker & Pierson 2014) and the burgeoning literature on the American Political Economy (APE) (Hacker et al. 2021). These thought traditions emphasize that "political processes can be best understood if they are studied over time; that structural constraints on individual actions, especially those emanating from government, are important sources of political behavior, and that the detailed investigation of carefully chosen, comparatively informed case studies is a powerful tool for uncovering sources of political change" (Pierson 1993, 596). Many studies of policy feedback and policy failure focus on snapshots at important moments in a policy's trajectory (Pierson 1993). These studies have provided invaluable insight, but, as Hacker et al. (2021, 7) note, "critical actions rarely occur simultaneously or instantaneously, and most of them have long legacies." This requires analyzing the full life of a failed policy to understand how, when, and why it might get fairly recognized as such.

Six cases of multi-decade policy trajectories inform this book's core empirical and theoretical findings on the politics of failure, data, research, and policymaking. All of these cases failed to produce their intended results, but they vary in the degree to which public officials recognized the failure. Process tracing—the systematic study of intermediate steps to make inferences and hypotheses about how and why different sequences and events take place (Bennett & Checkel (2015, 6); see also Collier (2011))—helped uncover the role that various institutions, actors, and events play in instigating elected officials' recognition and response to policy failure. My process tracing relies on systematically collected state histories, legislative archives, key-informant interviews, and news stories, among other data sources, "to see whether the causal process a theory hypothesizes or implies in a case is, in fact, evident in the sequence of and values of the intervening variables" (George & Bennett 2005, 6).

I systematically collected all legislation and legislative documents relating to each policy case, and I also watched and transcribed speeches, committee hearings, and testimonies on the policies over time. I triangulated elected officials' positions and rationales using their public statements, interviews (in some cases), and legislative documents and roll call votes. The Appendix describes each of these in more detail.

Both across-case (King et al. 1994) and within-case comparisons (Fairfield & Charman 2022) inform my theoretical contributions about the politics of failed policies. Comparative case studies lend themselves to in-depth explorations of concepts that the existing literature has not fully conceptualized and that are not easily measured—in this case, policy failure and state capacity for data collection and analysis. In-depth study of each case allowed precise identification of cases of failure to build and test theories about when and how failure gets recognized. In other published work, I leverage quantitative measures of some of the concepts developed here (James, Tervo, and Skocpol 2022). But the work in this book to identify and refine concepts such as policy failure, collection capacity, and analytical capacity is an important first step in these quantitative analyses (see Gerring 2012, Chapter 5).

Research Design

This book relies on a comparative case study of six multi-decade trajectories of failed policies. This menu of cases presents important within- and across-state variation in the degree of acknowledgment of failure among public officials and attempted policy reform (my dependent variables) that facilitate meaningful comparison and process tracing (see Table 3.1). This design allows comparisons across three important dimensions. First, I can compare the politics of policy failures within states over time. Observing the context for when the recognition of failure happens and comparing it to other points in time when elected officials ignore or address failure can provide important information for the necessary conditions for instigating these politics (Birkland 1998; Jenkins-Smith 1988). Second, I can compare the politics of disparate policies within the same state. This allows me to hold state politics, culture, and histories (relatively) constant to assess the common factors that impact when and how failure gets recognized and when elected officials

Table 3.1 Case studies and outcomes on the dependent variable

	Policy	
State	**Truancy policy**	**Business tax incentives**
Kansas	—	No acknowledgment No action
Texas	Widespread acknowledgment Successful revision	Partial acknowledgment Attempted revision
Washington	Partial acknowledgment Attempted revision	Widespread acknowledgment Successful revision
Wyoming	No acknowledgment No action	—

Source: Author's summary of archival material and policy trajectories.

can credibly ignore signs of failure. Third, I can compare the trajectories of similar policies across different states. Together, these cases allow within- and across-case comparisons of most similar and most different cases (Seawright and Gerring 2008). The suite of cases allows both within-state and across-state comparisons, which means that I can more credibly assess the role of partisan politics, state culture, and state institutional investments as key explanatory variables.

More specifically, comparing policies within and across Texas and Washington gives me valuable within- and across-state comparisons for conducting meaningful process tracing. Texas and Washington both have one policy that becomes recognized as a failure and one that achieves only partial recognition, which suggests that state political culture, economy, and history are not meaningful explanations for failure recognition. Importantly, in the truancy policy case, the recognition of failure goes against what existing state politics theories on partisanship and state capacity would suggest.

Case Selection

Studying the more than two-decades-long trajectory of Texas's truancy policy would certainly be interesting and would help clarify what happened in that specific case, but it would offer only limited insight into how the politics of failure operates more broadly. Including additional cases was essential for developing a more widely generalizable theory. One option—one that many scholars take and one that I adopt in other studies—would have been to compile a large dataset of the universe (or some systematic subset of one) of failed state policies for precise quantitative analysis. But, as Shuck astutely notes in his own study of government failure (albeit federal), such a compilation would have been nearly impossible:

> [W]ithout assessing all programs, no one can say for sure whether the ones I discuss are representative, and because programs differ along so many different dimensions—substantive content, animating theory, legal requirements, leadership talent, bureaucratic talent, congressional support, interest group dynamics, market conditions, implementation obstacles—no sampling technique could possibly meet rigorous social science standards. What I can say is that the programs I do discuss are particularly important by reason of their budgetary size, prominence, durability, and political support. (Shuck, 2014, 24)

Thus, I rely on a comparison of six policy trajectories—three truancy policies and three tax incentive policies—across four states. The specific state policy cases chosen are relevant because of their documented misalignment of goals and outcomes and substantial cost to the state.

In picking the cases, I relied on broad scholarly evidence suggesting the policy approach *should* fail. Once I investigated the cases, I evaluated whether elected officials recognized the failure and what sort of internal evidence the state itself generated. My cases also bring important within- and across-state variation in my dependent variables that facilitate meaningful comparison and process tracing.

I first identified the criminalization of truancy as a failed policy approach (a conclusion that I justify in the following section). To find a second policy type, I looked for additional policy domains that have clear policy intents but that scholarly research suggests should fail. I considered abstinence-only education policies, three strikes laws, restrictions on accessing public housing, and business location tax incentives, among others.[1] Of these options, business location tax incentives emerged as an analytically useful foil to the truancy cases for two reasons. First, business location tax incentives both

[1] See Santelli et al. (2017) for an overview of research showing that these programs are correlated with higher teen pregnancy and sexually transmitted infection rates. Woodhall-Melnick and Dunn (2016) write about housing first programs.

represent a clearly distinct policy domain[2] and have generated consistent scholarship, suggesting they do not produce the intended results (e.g., Bartik, 1992; Buss, 2001; Jensen, 2016; Mitchell et al. 2019). Second, the politics of tax incentives invokes radically different interest group dynamics and political-economic considerations. If I were to observe politics of responding to failure that were similar across truancy and tax incentives, I could be more certain that they are not the result of the peculiarities of one type of policy or the other.

Truancy and Tax Incentives as Failed Policies

Extensive scholarly evidence documenting the disparities between the stated purpose of the policy and its actual outcome is the scope condition for inclusion in this project. Assessing whether states themselves recognized the failure is the outcome of interest. After learning about the Texas Failure to Attend School policy, I confirmed that the scholarly literature corroborated my instinct that this program should indeed fail to increase attendance and graduation rates. I then turned to strategically adding more cases to make it most likely that my theories would be generalizable across different policy domains and states. The following introduces the two policy domains, including an overview of the scholarly literature that justifies labeling the criminalization of truancy and business location tax incentives as failed policy approaches. I then briefly introduce each of the state case studies.

Two types of evidence suggest that imposing increasing consequences, like detention and criminalization, for truancy does not result in greater attendance or high school graduation. First, studies show that punitive policies do not effectively alter adolescent behavior. The logic for leveraging the criminal justice system against truants suggests that if students are sufficiently afraid of the consequences of skipping school, then they will change their behavior. There is a robust literature on the ineffectiveness of zero-tolerance policies (e.g., Insley 2001; Martinez 2009; Mongan & Walker 2012;

[2] The other policy domains I identified were too similar to the truancy policy to provide meaningful comparison. Studying abstinence-only programs would have invoked the politics of education, and I wanted to develop a theory that was generalizable beyond any specific policy domain. Three strikes laws posed both of these problems. They invoke the politics of the criminal justice system, and the truancy policies sit at the intersection of criminal justice and education. The well-documented origins of punitive carceral policies, like three strikes laws, and racism make assessing the intentions of elected officials complicated.

Skiba 2000) that mandate suspension or expulsion for specific behaviors (e.g., "Opportunities Suspended," 2000). While the truancy policies in question in Texas, Washington, and Wyoming enforce different punishments—criminal misdemeanors, court appearances, and detention—a similar logic applies. Teenage decision making is often very short term (Defoe et al. 2015), which in turn makes it less likely that the discomfort, inconvenience, or even devastation of a misdemeanor, court appearance, or jail time may not be enough to override the lure of more short-term benefits, such as avoiding a challenging class or spending more time with friends outside of school.

Second, studies on the causes of truancy identify several contextual factors, rather than adolescent decision making, as predictive of absenteeism. Research suggests that low parental involvement, academic struggles, drug use, and exposure to violence and trauma all predict higher rates of truancy (see Teasley 2004 for an overview of these studies). Mentoring, peer tutoring, and other multidimensional supports can be effective in getting families, students, and schools on the same page regarding expectations and positive patterns of attendance. Importantly for this study, the complexity of reasons that likely underlay most students' decisions to skip class suggests that a multidimensional set of preventive supports, rather than the threat of a criminal record or jail time, is most effective in keeping students in school through high school graduation (McCluskey, Bynum, and Patchin 2004).

Business location tax incentives have a similarly clear research record of failing to produce their promised outcomes. Scholars have consistently noted the United States' unique use of its tax code to both redistribute (e.g., the Earned Income Tax Credit) and incentivize (e.g., health savings accounts; Howard 1999). States, in particular, have a history of leveraging their tax codes to encourage businesses to locate within their borders. These tax incentives often put significant dents into a state's annual revenue, but public officials justify the tax breaks as short-term sacrifices for long-term gains (e.g., Adolph 2016; Jensen 2018). In theory, bringing in more businesses to a state creates additional employment, higher paying positions, and a range of peripheral business opportunities to support newly relocated employees and their families. However, a significant body of economic, political science, and public policy research shows that these long-term benefits rarely accrue (e.g., Fullerton & Aragones-Zamudio 2006; Jensen 2016; Jensen, Malesky, & Walsh 2015), and the sacrifice in tax revenue can significantly hinder a state's budget and service provision (e.g., Eullit 2016). In recent years, state legislators have increasingly questioned the tradeoff with tax incentives (*Washington Post*, July 19, 2021), though, as of 2021, forty-eight states continue to provide these opportunities for businesses at a collective loss of more than $17 trillion to state budgets (Tax Break Tracker 2023).

Both truancy and tax policies are also substantively important because of their widespread impact on the American public. Furthermore, both policies also represent common policy approaches among states seeking to address pressing public policy problems. All children are required to attend school, and attendance at public schools is a core component of school funding formulas. Understanding how states experiment, evaluate, and revise such policies has the potential to impact the educational experience of students and families. Understanding the politics behind the failure of punitive truancy policies is also important because of the approach to public policy that it represents. State and federal governments have increasingly turned toward punitiveness and an emphasis on individual responsibility in social policies (Fording, Soss, and Schram 2007; Schram, Fording, and Soss 2008; Soss, Fording, and Schram 2011). Like the effects of the truancy policies featured in this study, these social policies tend to exacerbate inequality rather than addressing it.

Nuanced tax policies are a key tool for redistribution and welfare provision in the United States (Hacker 2002; Howard 1999). Tax incentives for businesses represent between $45 billion (Bartik 1992, 2017) and $90 billion (Story, Fehr, and Watkins 2012) of annual spending (see also Parilla & Liu 2018). All fifty states offer some form of corporate tax incentive. Taxes also are a key source of contention and compromise between government and business in American capitalism. Understanding how and why someone *other* than businesses benefiting from tax breaks can influence the politics of these policies represents an important insight that can help address rampant inequality and ongoing support for businesses at all costs. Like punitive consequences for truancy, business location tax incentives have roots in a particular ideological approach to economic development. Based in the neoliberal logic of trickle-down economics from the Reagan-era tax cuts, supporters of tax incentives claim that the cost savings provided to companies will flow into cost savings for consumers and additional financial flexibility for companies to hire more workers. However, scholars have yet to provide consistent findings corroborating this justification for such programs.

Why These Specific Programs in These States?

Once I identified the most appropriate policy domains, I needed to identify specific state programs to study. Identifying the truancy cases was relatively straightforward. As mentioned at the beginning of this chapter, the Texas truancy case was the case that first piqued my interest. I then chose the additional two cases (Becca's Bill in Washington and the Juvenile Justice Act in Wyoming) based on their similarities in policy goals, policy design, and timeline. While all states had some form of punitive response to chronically truant students, Texas, Washington, and Wyoming are unique in the targets of their truancy policy. These three states were the *only* ones to target these consequences for *the students* themselves rather than the parents. These three states also present variation in the recognition and reform of failure in these cases.

I then chose tax policies in Texas and Washington to create the opportunity for within-state, across-policy comparisons that were implemented around the same time as the truancy policy. The juxtaposition of the Texas and Washington policies is useful because these two states have different levels of professionalized legislatures, different political cultures and partisan patterns, and political economies—all variables that state politics scholarship finds are important factors in explaining political outcomes.

Washington's R&D tax credits and Texas's Economic Development Act (often called Ch 313 for its location in the tax code) stood out because they both garnered significant budgetary resources and media and political attention. Both states are also important economic hubs, albeit for different industries. Texas has a long history with oil, gas, and other extractive industries (e.g., Exxon and Valero), whereas Washington State has incubated some of the most successful technology companies (e.g., Amazon, Boeing, and Microsoft). In both states, companies regularly took advantage of these programs, and journalists and scholars had questioned the wisdom of maintaining the programs.

Included here are four cases in which failure does go unrecognized—the tax incentives in Texas and Kansas, and the truancy policy in Washington State and Wyoming. This research design echoes Leah Stokes's (2020) study, *Short Circuiting Policy*, which examines the role of interest groups in policy change. To explain the limits of existing theories of path dependence Stokes uses process tracing of five case studies of energy policy. These cases met her scope condition (in her case, retrenched clean energy laws), and they also represent variation in their deviance from the expectations of existing theories of interest groups and path dependence (Stokes 2020, 67–70). Similarly, my cases represent different state programs that meet the scope condition and vary in how closely they adhere to the expectations of existing theories of policy learning and policy change.

Data Sources

In order to develop the policy trajectories that are at the foundation of this book's analysis, I systematically collected an array of data. The Appendix offers a detailed account of my data collection and analysis strategies. Following is a brief summary of my approach.

I began with news stories of legislative action and public reaction to the policies in question. I then scoured the legislative archives in the relevant states to construct a detailed timeline of all actions associated with the policies in question. This included both introduced and failed legislation, committee hearings, written testimonies, floor debate, and dozens of revised versions of each bill. I also examined the histories, research papers, and policy briefs of state-run and private research organizations that studied each of my policies. Finally, I conducted almost three dozen interviews with public officials and researchers that participated in the passage, evaluation, or reform of the six policies.

I examined the legislative archives for each state policy to understand the policy history, sequence of policy changes, and policy intent. Using keyword searches in each state's legislative archives, I acquired the text of all legislation associated with each policy. These records capture all proposed legislation, including that at the committee level, and show any changes made in the bills from introduction to passage (or defeat).

Witness lists, which include organizational affiliations, delineated the groups and individuals that acknowledged failure and supported (or opposed) policy revision. Over 500 hours of audio and video recordings of public testimony in legislative committees on proposed legislation offered insight into the rationale leveraged by supporters and opponents of a given policy. These legislative archives are also valuable given the popularity of testifying in front of legislative committees as a lobbying technique and the accessibility of public testimony to groups that may not have established personal connections with political elites (Davidson and Oleszek 1994, 298).

The discussion between legislators and the public that occurs in committee meetings also shed light on the priorities, biases, and logic of public officials as they processed information about policy outcomes. Also observed were various political tactics at work as the public and public officials attempted to win support for their view of the given policy's outcomes.

Primary source materials from both state and nonstate research organizations allowed me to trace the sequencing of the available information on policy outcomes. Furthermore, these reports and related press releases often describe the organization's perspective on the quality of the information available to public officials.

With regard to interviews, while I do speak with many of the people involved in each of these policies and their reform attempts, interview data is not the main source of information in the book. People are notoriously unreliable in their recollections of past events, especially when they need to recall their logic or motivations (vs. their actual actions) (Conway and Pleydell-Pearce 2000; Gardner 2001). Memories of past events are fluid, being subject to change as people revise their perspectives, reevaluate their assumptions, and reassign accountability for things that happened (Keightley and Pickering 2013). While my interviews were invaluable in providing insights into the more subtle tensions and debates in the policy process, when at all possible, I looked to the archival record—such as testimony or written documents—created in the moment as the most credible source of information about what, where, and why people acted the way they did.

To ensure that I was analyzing comparable information for each policy, I created a policy "questionnaire" that I completed for each. These questionnaires (see the Appendix for the template that I used across all cases) probed key information about the timing, context, and actors involved in each policy. Documenting the answers to these questions across all cases made developments easier to compare.

Together these rich sources informed the construction of detailed policy trajectories or timelines for the policies and the actors driving and reacting to each change. A comparison of these trajectories is the foundation of this project.

Introducing the Cases

The next section of this chapter presents a brief introduction to the specifics of the six state policies that serve as the empirical foundation for the remainder of this book. Included are the legislative intent of each policy and a discussion of whether elected officials have recognized or addressed the policy failure.

Truancy

All states have policies requiring school-age children to attend school. Most states aim the punitive consequences of truant students at parents, which aligns with research that teenagers are notoriously short term in their decision making (Defoe et al. 2015) and that students' home environment is a key driver of attendance (Teasley 2004). However, the focus here is on three states—Texas, Washington, and Wyoming—that enacted especially stringent policies specifically targeting students through criminalization or detention as a consequence of truancy. In all three of these states, a large number of children are subjected to detention or criminalization through their truancy policies (for examples, see Santos 2015 for Washington State, Angelone 2010 for Texas, and McCarthy 2008 for Wyoming). While there is a legal, meaningful distinction between receiving an adult criminal conviction and processing in the civil court system, these policies have a comparable effects on youth. Even minimal time in detention can influence the individual's long-term civic, social, and financial outcomes.

Texas: Failure to Attend School

Texas incorporated the Failure to Attend School (FTAS) provision into the state's education code in 1995 (Texas Education Code Section 25.094). The policy allowed schools to ticket and charge students with an adult Class C misdemeanor for surpassing ten unexcused absences in a school year.[3] The 1995 Education Code outlined multiple objectives for its provisions, notably that the state aimed to increase high school graduation rates and provide all

[3] There were additional breakdowns of number of absences during shorter timespans (i.e., a month or a semester) that could trigger FTAS, but the ten absences per year dominates most of the FTAS discussion.

students with the opportunity to fully participate in social, economic, and educational opportunities (see Table 3.2). By 2013, a bipartisan majority in the Texas legislature, the Chief Justice of the Texas Supreme Court, and the Republican governor had publicly acknowledged the failure of FTAS. In 2015, the Texas legislature revised FTAS, decriminalizing truancy and emphasizing preventive measures for addressing chronic absenteeism in Texas public schools.

Washington: Becca's Bill

Washington State passed Becca's Bill—named after a murdered teenager who had struggled with truancy—in 1995. In addition to giving parents additional rights in cases of runaway or substance-abusing children, the law required schools to file a truancy petition with juvenile court after seven absences in a month or ten in a single school year. Judges hearing the truancy petitions were to conduct a fact-finding hearing and then order students to return to school. However, if a student violated this court order, she could be placed in a detention center for contempt of court (Burley and Harding 1998). The original legislation stated its purpose as giving parents and students tools to address mental and physical health issues and to reduce truancy and increase high school graduation rates (see Table 3.2). Despite complaints from advocates, youths, and some public officials, in 2015, a bill to remove detention and require preventive measures failed to leave the Senate Human Services, Mental Health & Housing Committee in the Washington legislature.

Wyoming: Juvenile Justice Act

In 1997, the Wyoming legislature updated its 1951 Juvenile Court Act, including changing its name to the Juvenile Justice Act and updating the statement of legislative intent (see Table 3.2). Like Texas and Washington, Wyoming reiterated its intent to facilitate the care, protection, and development of Wyoming children.

In practice, the changes did little to alter the structure of juvenile justice in Wyoming courts. Judges retained their discretion to decide whether to hear delinquency cases, of which truancy is a major component, under their juvenile judge capacity or their adult district court capacity. In some counties in Wyoming, up to 95 percent of youth are tried in adult courts (Arthur, Rabinowitz, and Horvath 2010). As in Texas, trial proceedings in adult criminal courts can result in fines and jail time. The state did create

Table 3.2 Policy intent and outcomes for truancy cases

State	Year	Policy	Policy intent	Acknowledgment	Revision
TX	1995	FTAS	The mission of the public education system of this state is to ensure that *all* [emphasis added] Texas children have access to a quality education that enables them to achieve their potential and fully participate now and in the future in the social, economic, and educational opportunities of our state and nation. Objective 3: Through enhanced dropout prevention efforts, all students will remain in school until they obtain a high school diploma.	Widespread by 2013	Yes, in 2015
WA	1995	Becca's Bill	The legislature intends to provide for the protection of children who, through their behavior, are endangering themselves. The legislature intends to provide appropriate residential services, including secure facilities, to protect, stabilize, and treat children with serious problems. The legislature further intends to empower parents by providing them with the assistance they require to raise their children. "The truancy petition process is intended to improve educational outcomes for students with excessive unexcused absences. This study examines whether the Becca law improves the chances that truant students will stay enrolled in the following school year." (Truancy Petition Process 2).	Partial	Attempted revision in 2015

Continued

Table 3.2 *Continued*

State	Year	Policy	Policy intent	Acknowledgment	Revision
WY	1997	Juvenile Justice Act	This act shall be construed to effectuate the following public purposes... a. To remove, where appropriate, the taint of criminality from children committing certain unlawful acts; and b. To provide for the care, the protection and the wholesome moral, mental, and physical development of children coming within its provisions.	No	No

Sources: FTAS language comes from SB 1 Section 4.001, 73rd Regular Session (Texas 1995). This bill can be accessed through the Texas state legislative archives at https://capitol.texas.gov/billlookup/text.aspx?LegSess=74R&Bill=SB1. Becca's Bill language comes from SB 5439 Ch 312, 54th Legislature, 1995 Regular Session (Washington State 1995). This bill can be accessed through the Washington State Legislature at https://app.leg.wa.gov/billsummary?BillNumber=5439&Year=1995&Initiative=false. The second purpose statement is taken from the Washington State Institute for Public Policy's first report "Truancy: Preliminary Findings on Washington's 1995 Truancy Law," on Becca's Bill (Webster, 1996 5). The report can be accessed at http://www.wsipp.wa.gov/ReportFile/1217/Wsipp_TRUANCY-Preliminary-Findings-on-Washingtons-1995-Law_Full-Report.pdf. Juvenile Justice Act language comes from Wyoming Statute WY 14-6-201, 1997 Session Law Ch 199. This statute can be accessed through the Wyoming legislative archives at http://pluto.state.wy.us/Library6/1997%20GENERAL%20SESSION%20PDF/pdf/CH0199.pdf.

an Advisory Council on Juvenile Justice in 1996, which published several reports recommending amendments to the Juvenile Court Act. As of this writing, however, policymakers have yet to introduce, let alone adopt, any major reforms addressing the trial of young people in adult courts.

Business Location Tax Incentives

Despite increasingly clear evidence that tax incentives do not provide the economic benefits that elected officials promise (Buss 2001; Jensen 2016), forty-eight states offer some form of tax incentive (Tax Break Tracker 2023). Three specific programs—Texas's Ch 313 property tax breaks, Washington's Research and Development tax incentive program, and Kansas's Promoting Employment Across Kansas incentive—promised companies substantial property and capital goods tax breaks to (re)locate within their state borders. In all three cases, activists from public sectors such as education and social services protested the continuation of tax breaks because of the burden they placed on the state budgets. While the nuances of the tax programs and their intended targets do vary, each of the three cases represents one of the largest tax break programs for their respective state.

Texas Ch 313

With the 2001 passage of the Texas Economic Development Act, also known as Ch 313 for its location in the tax code, Texas put its school districts in charge of deciding which corporations could benefit from tax breaks. Ch 313 allows school districts to offer property tax incentives to businesses that locate within their borders. The state refunds the school district for any loss in revenue experienced because of the tax break. The legislation cited the state's high ad valorem tax as limiting their competitiveness with other states for new capital projects and manufacturing businesses and pointed to encouraging new investment and creating new high-paying jobs as the policy's key goals (see Table 3.3). The policy was set to expire in 2007, but, the Texas legislature voted twice to extend the program[4]. Both Democrats and Republicans have made several attempts to revise Ch 313

[4] In late 2024, the Texas legislature replaced the Texas Economic Development Act with a similar program called Jobs, Energy, Technology, and Innovation program which continues to offer business location tax incentives. The new program does include some additional oversight requirements, and received bipartisan support.

Table 3.3 Policy intent and outcomes for tax cases

State	Year	Policy	Policy intent	Acknowledgment	Revision
TX	2001	Ch 313	The purpose of this chapter is to: (1) encourage large-scale capital investments in this state; (2) create new, high-paying jobs in this state; (3) attract to this state large-scale businesses that are exploring opportunities to locate in other states or other countries; (4) enable state and local government officials and economic development professionals to compete with other states by authorizing economic development incentives that are comparable to the incentives offered to prospective employers by other states and to provide local officials with an effective means to attract large-scale investment; (5) strengthen and improve the overall performance of the economy of the state; (6) expand and enlarge the ad valorem tax base of this state; and (7) enhance this state's economic development efforts by providing state and local officials with an effective economic development tool. (Texas Tax Code, Title 3, Subtitle B, Chapter 313)	Partial	Attempted revision in 2017

WA	1994	R&D tax credit	1. "Create "quality" employment opportunities in this state; and 2. Encourage expenditures in research and development supporting and sustaining the high technology sector as it develops new techniques and products."	Yes	Allowed to sunset in 2014
KS	2009	PEAK	It shall be the intent of this act to foster economic development and the creation of new jobs and opportunities for the citizens of Kansas through incentivizing the repatriation of business facilities, other operations, and jobs from foreign countries and to incentivize the relocation of business facilities, other operations and jobs from other states to Kansas. The primary objective of this legislation is economic development for Kansas. (Promoting Employment Across Kansas Act 2008)	No	No

Sources: The Texas Ch 313 language comes from the Texas Tax Code, Title 3, Subtitle B, Chapter 313 passed in HB 1200 in 2001 and can be found in the Texas legislative archives at https://lrl.texas.gov/LASDOCS/77R/HB1200/HB1200_77R.pdf#page=285. The R&D tax credit language comes from SB 6347 passed in 1994 and can be accessed at http://lawfilesext.leg.wa.gov/biennium/1993-94/Pdf/Bills/Session%20Laws/Senate/6347-S2.SL.pdf#page=1. The PEAK language comes from Senate Bill 97 from the 2009 legislative session in Kansas. The full document can be accessed at https://www.kansas.gov/government/legislative/bills/2010/97.pdf.

through either capping annual spending on the program or requiring regular evaluations of the success of the program. In 2017, Governor Abbott vetoed a further expansion of Ch 313, citing concerns about its oversight and contributions to economic growth, though he did not undo any existing legislation (Michels 2016). That same year, however, SB 600, which would have repealed Ch 313, failed to move past the House Finance Committee, leaving Ch 313 intact.

Washington: Research and Development Tax Credit

In 1994, the Washington State legislature passed the High Technology Research & Development Deferral/Waiver (Sales and Use Tax) and Credit (Business and Occupation tax, or the R&D tax credit) as part of the same tax law. The R&D tax credit allowed new or expanding high-tech companies to defer, and eventually waive, state and local sales taxes that resulted from investments in facilities, machinery, and research and development. The main goals of the original legislation were to create "quality" employment opportunities and encourage innovation (see Table 3.3). Like Texas, the Washington State legislature renewed the tax credit in 2004, shifting the sunset date back ten years to 2014. Unlike Texas, however, the legislature responded to increasingly negative reports about the policy's outcomes and allowed the R&D tax credit to expire on January 1, 2015. In a national assessment of tax incentive best practices, PEW Research Center heralded the move as one of a handful of instances in which a state successfully eliminated an existing tax credit (Huh 2017).

Kansas: Promoting Employment Across Kansas

The Kansas legislature passed the Promoting Employment Across Kansas (PEAK) program in 2009. This program allowed companies to retain 95 percent of the withholding tax for employees paid at or above the county's median salary. Businesses must create a minimum of five new jobs within two years and can claim the benefit for up to ten years. The legislation cited promoting economic development and the "creation of new jobs and opportunities," as well as attracting new businesses to locate in the state, as its key objectives (see Table 3.3). Several amendments followed PEAK's original passage, mostly expanding eligibility and rewards for the program. The program continues to exist today and, along with other tax incentives in the state, generates regular complaints from critics for perpetuating the costly and useless border war between Missouri and Kansas (Border War:

Kansas City 2012; Greenblat 2011; Morris 2015). While there are some vocal opponents of the PEAK program (mainly among the media), public officials have yet to successfully introduce or pass any meaningful revision of the program.

This chapter describes and justifies the use of comparative case studies to analyze when, how, and why elected officials recognize and revise policy failure. I described the details of how I chose the six case studies that inform this book's empirical findings, and briefly introduce each of the cases. I also briefly describe how I systematically collected and analyzed a range of archival, interview, and secondary sources to inform each case study. The next two chapters introduce the two concepts core to my theoretical contribution: data collection capacity and analytical capacity.

4

If You Aren't Counted, Your Problems Don't Count

Defining and Theorizing Collection Capacity

Indicators are not merely statistical tools. They also reflect a society's readiness to look seriously at difficult problems, to acknowledge trends, and, perhaps, to act. Though statistics cannot force policy changes, good data can enable a different level of discussion, permit more effective enforcement of rights, give awareness and tools to groups whose claims were dismissed before data were available. The absence, or refusal to collect, data on a basic social cleavage also conveys a very important message: The group that is not counted does not have the power to see that its problems are measured.

—Gary Orfield, *Why Data Collection Matters: The Role of Race & Poverty Indicators in American Education* (2001, 166)

In spring 2020, two crises shook the United States: the COVID-19 pandemic and a racial reckoning inspired by a series of highly publicized instances of police brutality. On April 1, 2020, a mere two weeks after the first stay-at-home orders to protect people from the COVID-19 virus began in the United States, Ibram Kendi, a renowned historian, author, and public intellectual who studies the history of race and racism, published an article in *The Atlantic* entitled "Why Don't We Know Who the Coronovirus Victims Are?" Indeed, the federal government had abdicated response to the pandemic to the states and the states, in turn, varied in how quickly they began collecting and disseminating data on the virus (James, Tervo, and Skocpol 2022). Over the next month, Kendi published three additional stories decrying widespread failures across the states to collect meaningful demographic data, particularly on race, of those afflicted by and dying of COVID-19. Kendi stressed that without data on the racial patterning of the virus's impact, public officials were missing vital information on how to

The Politics of Failed Policies. Sarah James, Oxford University Press. © Oxford University Press (2025).
DOI: 10.1093/9780197813645.003.0005

respond to the pandemic. More specifically, Kendi argued that experts could not possibly address the racial disparities in their states without knowing if, when, and how COVID-19 was affecting communities of color. In essence, Kendi echoed exactly what Orfield states in this chapter's epigraph on data collection in education: "the group that is not counted does not have the power to see that its problems are measured" (Orfield 2001, 166).

Kendi's articles kicked off a collaboration between *The Atlantic*, the Center for Anti-Racist Research at Boston University,[1] and a cadre of thousands of volunteers, journalists, and public health officials to collect and disseminate accurate information on COVID-19 cases, deaths, and demographic data for each case. The COVID Racial Data Tracker (CTP), rather than any state-created data source, became *the* foundation for analyses conducted by government officials, journalists, scholars, and citizens trying to assess the impact of the virus.

The information CTP collected subsequently appeared in more than 1,000 scholarly papers, dozens of federal and state reports about the pandemic, and more than 7,700 press statements (Glickhouse 2021). CTP's data collection efforts also facilitated data-driven government action. The Biden administration relied on the Tracker to inform its Day 1 COVID-19 response plan, and the CDC reported that the CTP's data was more accurate than their own (Glickhouse 2021). Knowing which states, counties, age groups, and comorbidities were most impacted by COVID—information that was not consistently available from state databases (e.g., Fowler and Fleming 2020)—allowed the vaccine advisory council to design a relevant rollout plan once Pfizer and Johnson & Johnson had developed a vaccine. A Bloomberg news headline even went as far as to say that "data heroes of COVID Tracking Project are filling the U.S. government void" (Armstrong 2020). The reliance on and enthusiasm for this grassroots effort to measure the impact of COVID-19 reflect how critical it is to have valid data to inform the calculations of public officials facing complex public policy challenges. Unfortunately, it also provides a contemporary and poignant example of how data availability can indeed be a question of life or death.

This chapter echoes the logic of Kendi and others involved with the CTP: collecting data is a choice, and it is a choice that reflects the priorities of

[1] This was a new interdisciplinary research center at Boston University, and in 2020, Kendi was tapped as its first director.

those in power. The failure to collect data has profound consequences for those whose experiences are recognized and legitimized in policy debates and political decisions. Only once data were gathered on the racial impacts of the pandemic could advocates for marginalized groups more credibly and powerfully demand resources commensurate with the realities they faced.

This chapter introduces a comprehensive theory for when and how elected officials recognize policy failure by integrating theories from political science with assumptions about data and policy evaluation from applied fields like education and public health. My theory advances existing political science scholarship by refining our definition and conceptualization of research capacity as the result of two distinct features of state functioning and policy evaluation: data collection capacity and analytical capacity. The first of these two concepts are introduced here; together they make up research capacity. By distinguishing the political will and institutional investments to collect data and from those required to analyze it, we can better model the resources needed at the state level to conduct robust policy evaluations.

Credible, valid, and relevant data are essential for creating the possibility of negative policy feedback loops for failed policies. The decisions about whether and how to invest in data collection early on in a policy's trajectory have substantial policy feedback effects on the political power of the policy's eventual beneficiaries and opponents. This argument connects the components of policy evaluation to the dynamics of politics—a connection that is not explicitly studied in the applied scholarship domains. The core assertion of this chapter is that collection capacity is necessary because it establishes the strength of the foundation on which future attempts to evaluate the policy can occur.

High collection capacity is necessary for an evidence-based response to policy failure because without high-quality data, there is no way for policymakers, policy entrepreneurs, interest groups, or the public—the actors that can turn a policy issue into a political one (Kingdon 1984)—to objectively know if a policy has failed to meet its intended outcomes. It is not always in the interest of public officials to seek out new information about policy effects (e.g., Weil et al. 2006). High collection capacity ensures that even in the absence of an incentive to study a policy's outcomes immediately upon implementation, there is groundwork to help future public officials learn about the policy's impacts, as compared with a policy for which no data is collected until its effectiveness is questioned. While insufficient, collection capacity is necessary for transitioning a policy failure into a political issue, particularly when those burdened by failure lack robust political power.

The rest of this chapter defines collection capacity and describes four key indicators of high collection capacity. Then it theorizes why collection capacity is necessary for recognizing policy failure using logic from the policy feedback literature. Collection capacity can be seen as a necessary foundation for catalyzing negative policy feedback cycles among elites for failed public policies. High collection capacity is more likely to generate credible data, which, in turn, creates the possibility that those burdened by policy failure can more easily shift the elite narrative to reflect their experiences and build support among elected officials to revise the policy. This discussion is followed by a comparison of the data collection capacity across my six case studies and shows how high capacity catalyzed (sometimes recalcitrant) elected officials to acknowledge policy failure and how low collection capacity perpetuated political support for failed policies.

From Reseach Capacity to Collection Capacity

The credibility of findings about policy outcomes is key to catalyzing failure recognition for two reasons. First, credible findings can corroborate anecdotal stories of policy failure. Politically powerful constituencies burdened by policy failure will not be shy about making their views heard, and, as many scholars have shown, elected officials are particularly responsive to the well-funded and tightly organized groups (Bawn et al. 2012; Hacker et al. 2021; Moe 2011, 2019). However, if the constituency burdened by the failure does not have substantial political clout, and those with political power *benefit* from the failed policy's existence, then generating enough political will to acknowledge and reform the policy will be challenging (Gilens and Page 2014; Kelly & Morgan 2022). Credible and compelling research suggesting that the narrative of the vested interests benefiting from failure is *inaccurate* can shift the power dynamics. By corroborating the narratives and anecdotal experiences of those burdened by policy failure, clear findings can shift the political calculus of elected officials.

Second, clear findings may mobilize those burdened by failure to ramp up their political pressure and incentivize additional participation and organization in calling for reform. As Béland and Cox (2010) argue in their book on the interplay between ideas, politics, and social science research, the concepts, relationships, and narratives we are exposed to shape how we define our political problems and goals and dictate what strategies we use in response. Information about policy effects is an important resource that activists and elected officials can use to motivate supporters, decide on strategic political alliances, and craft compelling narratives (Pierson 1993). Compelling research might also change the calculus of constituents not affected by policy failure to reassess the effectiveness of elected officials and their policies (Canes-Wrone 2015; Fiorina 1981; Jones 2011). High-quality policy evaluations create the foundation for research that will be harder for policy beneficiaries and elected officials to dismiss as inaccurate or politically motivated.

Research, and the ability to produce it, is the product of (at least) two distinct processes. Most importantly, systematic research requires data collection and analysis. As discussed in Chapter 1, scholars of policy learning and state capacity by and large refer to "research capacity" or "information capacity" as a key component of policy learning (Bennett & Howlett 1992; Brambor et al. 2020; Heclo 1977; Lee & Zhang 2017). More applied fields such as public health and education scholars have, at least implicitly, acknowledged the difference between the importance of data collection and analysis in their presentation of outcomes in their respective fields. For example, in a 2017 review of what they call evidence-based public health (EBPH) capacity, Brownson et al. (2018) define capacity as "the availability of resources, structures, and workforce to plan, deliver, and evaluate the preventive dose of an evidence-based intervention" (p. 27). Even in public health and education, however, scholars will also conflate data collection and analysis when they talk about policy evaluation broadly. As illustrated in Figure 4.1, convincing evidence is the product of at least two distinct components: the data used to make indicators about policy outcomes (collection capacity) and the subsequent analysis that generates information about trends in these indicators over time (analytical capacity). Together, collection and analysis produce evidence, which can then inform elected officials' preferences in and approach to policymaking. Importantly, each of these requires distinct resources, expertise, and timing. By failing to acknowledge

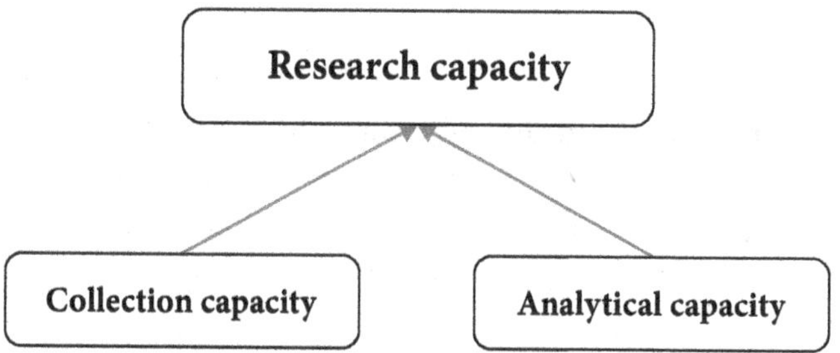

Figure 4.1 Components of "research capacity"

the unique resources needed to generate high collection capacity, scholars and practitioners are missing key levers for studying and evaluating the politics of policy failures.

Collection capacity can be defined as a state's available resources and motivation to *gather relevant and usable data* on a specific policy or policy area's outcomes. As is further illustrated in the next chapter, the resources, expertise, motivation, and sequencing needed to collect data differ from those needed to analyze it. Public health experts (Brownson, Fielding, and Green 2018) and historians (Kendi 2021) have emphasized that the collection of data is one of many important steps toward achieving a more accurate understanding of the impacts of policies. Education scholars have repeatedly shown that data collection is essential for addressing inequality in educational outcomes—a core challenge educators and policymakers are regularly trying to address (Orfield 2001; Skiba et al. 2011). We also know that biased data collection procedures can fuel justifications for discrimination, oppression, and inequality (Muhammad 2010; Stone 2020) and preclude appropriate responses to racial inequality (Cook and Fortunato 2023; Kendi 2021). One can expect to find these investments in state capacity happening through state bureaucratic personnel and procedures. The more insulated data collection processes are from electoral politics, the most credible it will likely be. State agencies can provide this insulation along with the reputations of authority and expertise (Carpenter 2001, 2014) that enhance the political power of the information they produce.

Clear definitions and state-orchestrated, centralized, and preemptive data collection plans characterize high collection capacity for a given state policy. These features can operate at different levels of observation. Some operate at the state level, while others operate at the broad policy area level, and still others are specific to the exact policy as it is designed and implemented. In what follows, I describe and justify each component of collection capacity and identify features of a state's institutional landscape that signal high collection capacity: state mandates and funding for data collection, clear and consistent definitions, centrally managed collection procedures and ongoing and overlapping collection efforts. Also discussed is the importance of the state's investment (as opposed to nonstate actors) in these features for enhancing their effectiveness.

State Mandates and Funding for Data Collection

Mandates for data collection both create a treasure trove of information for analyses and create a de facto first stop data source for those seeking policy evaluation. The first component of high collection capacity is establishing the expectations and resources needed to collect data. Scientists and policymakers have different "goals, attitudes toward information, languages, perception of time, career paths" and a "lack of mutual trust and different views on the production and use of evidence and different accountabilities" (Choi et al. 2005, 62). Furthermore, policymakers are rarely trained researchers, and their electoral incentives and lack of expertise make them particularly ill prepared to distinguish between "good and bad data and [are] therefore more prone to the influence of misused 'facts' often presented by interest groups" (Brownson, Chriqui, and Stamatakis 2009, 1577). The PEW Results First Initiative, which collaborated with states to implement evidence-based policymaking, specifically measures whether states incorporate clear legislative mandates to "help leaders creatively and routinely incorporate information on program effectiveness into funding and policy decisions" (Davies et al. 2017, 8). In other words, data collected in response to a mandate from the original policy itself creates an important and logical starting point for policy evaluation.

The availability of high-quality data, in turn, can lessen dependence on data from vested interests and other actors with a specific policy preference. This may be why elected officials can more credibly ignore or dismiss evidence that is national in scope or from a different state (which is the process involved in policy diffusion) as not being directly relevant to their unique context. State-collected data in response to a state's unique policy and political context may more strategically bridge the two worlds of evidence that policymakers and researchers inhabit. State-collected data is less easily dismissed as "not relevant to our state" when the research did in fact occur in the state using the exact policy in question.

Bureaucrats are rarely awash in extra time or money, and the legislature, at least at broad levels, influences what bureaucrats prioritize with these limited resources (Headrick, Serra, and Twombly 2002; McCubbins and Schwartz 1984). Mandating and funding data collection directs state bureaucratic resources to data collection and therefore indicates an investment in collection capacity. Requiring data collection at the outset of a policy informs the bureaucracy that they should consider evaluation when designing implementation. Being regularly informed about policy outcomes from the bureaucracy can also build habits among elected officials that systematic information can be a part of their decision-making process (Pierson 1993). The stylized policy feedback process (shown in Figure 4.2 reflects the importance of the timing of when and how data collection begins by intentionally showing collection capacity beginning *alongside*, or in some cases before, policy implementation. The earlier data is collected, the more compelling it will be. Policies subject to mandated data collection from the legislature will much more likely have early and consistent data availability. Both, in turn, will increase the likelihood that the data can inform more reliable and accurate analyses.

Finally, by simply stating that the legislature is interested in learning about policy outcomes, the legislature signals that it has some investment in understanding the policy outcomes that may influence the extent to which the affected constituencies feel they have an opportunity to voice their concerns about failure. The threat of review from the legislature that an explicit data collection mandate provides can also influence bureaucratic behavior (Brehm and Gates 1999; Carpenter 2001; Wilson 1989). Unlike nonstate entities, the legislature can bring bureaucrats in for hearings and initiate investigations if the data collection does not meet expectations.

Requiring data collection is important but does not in and of itself guarantee reliable and comparable data. Clear definitions and centrally managed collection plans, the next two features of high collection capacity, refine the process with which data is collected and enhance the data's validity.

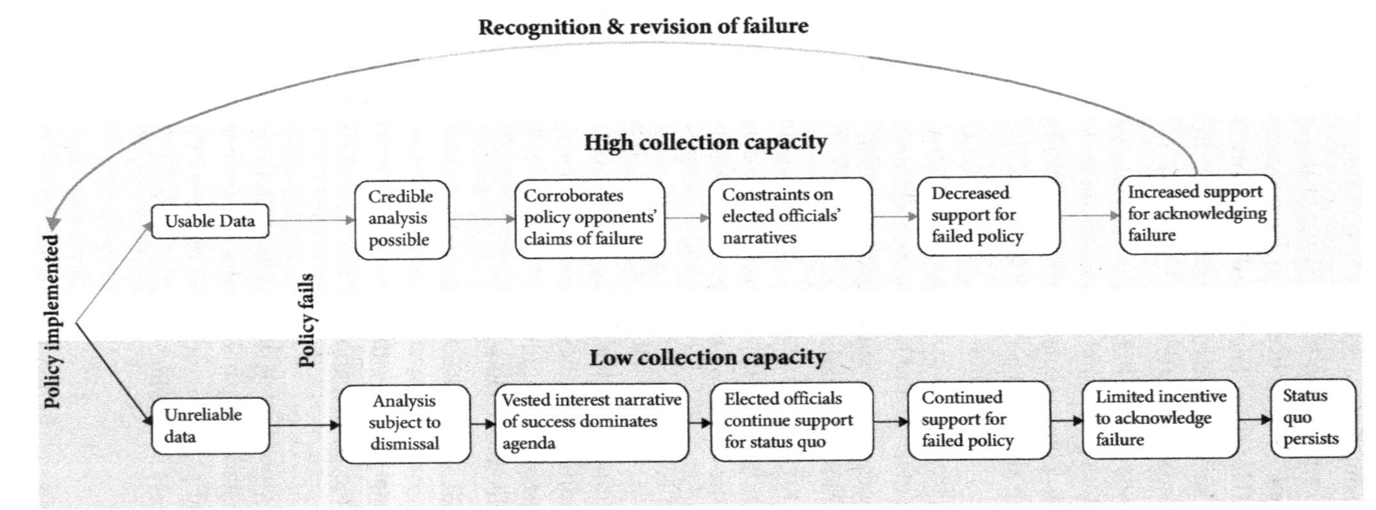

Figure 4.2 Collection capacity and negative policy feedback cycles

Clear Definitions

State-funded and -mandated data collection increases the chances that at least *some* information will be collected; however, it does not necessarily guarantee that the data collected is usable or relevant. Returning to the COVID-19 example that opened the chapter, note that one of the key findings from the CTP audits of state data collection found that "more than a year into the pandemic, definitions of basic data points—like what even counts as a COVID-19 case [were] still not standardized across states" (Simon 2021). One of the important value-adds of the CTP data was the clarity in methodology they shared which ensured consistent definitions and measurement strategies that permeated reporting across the states.

An important step in answering any research question is deciding how to define the variables and relevant indicators that offer more precise insight into the question at hand. This process of choosing and defining indicators is not usually straightforward and is often subject to the biases, experiences, and preferences of those making the decisions (Stone 2020). For example, defining exactly what the legislature means by "truancy" is an essential first step in knowing whether a new policy affects truancy rates. Does a student need to miss the whole day to be considered absent? How many absences over what period of time constitutes a pattern of truancy? How should excused absences be account for? The tax cases present a similar need for clear definitions. What counts as economic growth? Over what period of time do we expect to see evidence of growth? What sectors should be included? How should researchers account for various control variables that would help isolate the policy in question rather than state or national economic trends? There is also the further challenge that what experienced researchers or bureaucrats might think is a meaningful metric may not be politically relevant or of interest to elected officials or the public.

Without consistent, centrally defined parameters, data are incomparable in most useful analyses because changes in definitions do not show if outcomes are due to noisy, inconsistent data or to an actual change in outcomes. Establishing clear definitions of important terms and concepts related to policy implementation is critical to collection capacity for a given state policy. Important parameters may include definitions of critical variables and the frequency and reliability with which data is collected and recorded. Therefore, state policies that have developed clear and consistent definitions of concepts and measurement strategies demonstrate a greater capacity for data collection.

Ideally, the legislature establishes clear definitions in the original legislation or mandate for data collection, but they can also refine these definitions over time. Alternatively, researchers or street-level bureaucrats who are more familiar with the realities of policy implementation and data collection may request clarification as they gain experience with the policy.

Centrally Managed Collection

Centrally managed data collection efforts build on the foundation of consistency and comparability offered by clear definitions and stated mandated collection efforts. Very little in American government and politics is centralized. We live in a federal system that prioritizes the rights of states and localities to implement policies. While a decentralized approach may help subnational and substate units develop and implement policies in ways that meet their unique contexts, it can easily preclude the collection of usable data. Decentralized data collection procedures increase the chances that the software, variable definitions, frequency of data collection, and other data collection procedures will vary across jurisdictions. For example, if a state leaves data collection up to individual counties, it is not unreasonable to think that the counties and the public officials working in data collection in each county may have slightly (or substantially) different views on how to collect data on a given policy. While slight variations may be easily solved with statistical manipulation, there are many data collection decisions—say, for example, radically disparate collection frequencies or failure to collect information on important control variables or at different units of observation—that can render the data incomparable and therefore unusable.

Designating a specific agency or team as responsible for the collection and management of indicators increases collection capacity. In their report on the status of evidence-based policymaking across the fifty states, the PEW Research Center explicitly identifies the value of centralized versus federated data collection plans in the description of how the Utah Office of Management and Budget "requires each agency to answer a set of questions when making funding requests for new programs, including the need for the service, the expected outcomes, and whether it is an evidence-based practice or supported by research, data, evaluation, or professional industry standard" (Davies et al. 2017, 8). In fact, the quantity of data collected on a particular policy alone does not guarantee that researchers can develop useful findings about the policy's outcomes. Relying on different methods and using different measures, though related to the same outcomes, creates insurmountable barriers to inference.

Ongoing and Overlapping Collection Plans

States with high collection capacity also engage in high-quality, regular, broad, long-term data collection on major policy domains in the state. One might also think about this capacity as evidence of a state's broader culture of evidence-informed policymaking. The regular data collection generates information that can be used to supplement, corroborate, or even replace data gathered in response to a specific policy. This wider culture of and investment in data collection is critical because even the best trained researcher cannot envision the myriad ways in which a policy might impact its targets, nor can they always fully predict what will be important measures to future policymakers or the public. Thus, if a state has invested in accurately collecting information from individuals and organizations over time, then researchers can leverage this data to supplement the data they may have from the specific policy itself.

Creating overlapping data collection plans—where different collection efforts may share a handful of variables—also creates the possibility of testing the effects of a policy using different measures or operationalizations of variables. Just as in social science research, this in turn can help build credibility for a finding if it holds across multiple specifications of a model or outcome. Furthermore, overlapping collection plans ensure that if one dataset is unreliable for some reason, there are other sources of information that researchers can access to evaluate policy outcomes.

If public officials implement a new policy, and data collection for that given policy area is already ongoing, it is less likely that supporters of the new policy will feel threatened by the data collection as a targeted effort to advertise policy failure. Instead, the data collection efforts may draw less attention and so may be allowed to continue without stoking political fears of the findings. This echoes the logic of the resilience of universal social programs compared with targeted ones (Skocpol 1991), in which universal programs are more resilient to retrenchment than their targeted counterparts. Data collection efforts targeted at a single policy, on the other hand, may be more likely to raise the hackles of the policy's supporters, fearing that opposition groups are intentionally attempting to document failure. The agencies implementing a given policy may also prefer to avoid specific data collection efforts targeted at policies they implement for fear that the executive and legislative branches or the public may disapprove of their implementation strategies.

The Unique State Role

A common theme across each of the four features described above is the power of elites to choose whether to establish and continually invest in each feature. Counter to some popular narratives about the objectivity of data, whether, when, and how policymakers choose to invest in collection capacity is a *political choice about the distribution of resources.* They may make this decision based on the anticipated effects of the policy, in response to pressure from groups that anticipate harm or benefit, or to adhere to values about the importance of evidence-informed policymaking. Identifying and understanding the investment elected officials choose to make in mandating and funding data collection, defining important outcomes of interest, and designing centrally managed collection procedures offers insight into the foundation on which a compelling movement for the recognition and reform of failure can build. Each feature of high data collection capacity should be more useful the earlier they are implemented. The state is uniquely positioned to mandate, fund, and monitor ongoing data collection efforts.

The importance of timing and privacy concerns with data collection also make the state better suited to managing effective and informative data systems. In states with low data collection capacity, institutions like the media and think-tanks may participate in the policy research and discussion fray. This suggests the unique role the state plays in collection capacity. Unlike what we will see in the following chapter with regard to analytical capacity, the state is uniquely suited to the large-scale collection efforts needed for policy evaluation, especially when confidential data may be involved.

As the entity responsible for policy implementation, state governments and bureaucracies are also more aware of opportunities to collect data on their own policies. Outside organizations may develop an interest only to learn more about a policy after experiencing the impacts of its implementation. Even when nonstate actors are interested in a policy's impacts from the outset, they are inherently at a disadvantage compared to the state for collecting detailed data about individual experiences and important covariates. However, given privacy regulations and confidentiality agreements between the state and recipient companies, much of the most useful information about job growth and economic investment is not available to these outside organizations. Nonstate actors may have ideological reputations and a national policy scope, or they may be reliant on publicly available information, all of which may undermine the credibility of their findings. As the original designer and implementer of social policies, state government officials are best positioned to gather the most granular and accurate data on a policy's implementation and effects.

The following section presents findings from the policy feedback literature to theorize *why* data collection capacity—and its constituent components introduced in this section—are necessary, but not sufficient, to catalyzing evidence-informed recognition of policy failure.

Collection capacity as the Foundation of Negative Policy Feedback Cycles

In American politics, the best resourced and most well-organized actors tend to have their preferences win out. Terry Moe (2011, 2019) has written extensively about the power of teacher unions to stymie education reform; scholars of the American political economy have shown the immense power of corporations to dominate the policy agenda (Hacker et al. 2021). When a policy's failure burdens these political powerful groups, they have the resources, knowledge, and connections to make their preferences heard, and according to the aforementioned scholars, enact them into policies. Having more data documenting policy failure certainly won't hurt the efforts of the most organized and well-resourced interests from achieving their reform, but politics-as-usual likely will have instigated a response from elected officials *without* the systematic data and analysis. Elected officials are less responsive to the most marginalized groups (Erikson 2015; Zelizer 2018). Therefore, we should expect them to be less responsive to these groups' claims of failure and calls for revision.

A core tenet of policy feedback theory is that new policies make new politics. My theory of state capacity makes a specific argument about when and how this happens: If, when, and how states build in the capacity for data collection into their state institutions and policies has long-term impacts on the political resilience of failed policies.

Figure 4.2 shows the stylized way in which a robust data collection capacity influences the potential for elected officials to learn about, recognize, and revise policy failure. Policies will fail regardless of whether researchers have collected data on relevant outcomes. As the top set of arrows and boxes shows in Figure 4.2, whether usable data was collected immediately sets the trajectory for whether failure is likely to be recognized. Policy failure in a high-collection capacity context may not be recognized immediately, but conducting credible analyses using reliable data is at least a possibility.

A comparison with the low-capacity context highlights the importance of data collection capacity for facilitating this negative feedback cycle. First and foremost, as Orfield (2001) argues in the epigraph to this chapter, the mere collection of data reflects a willingness to recognize the experiences of those impacted by the policy. Without any attempt to collect data on a policy, "the group that is not counted does not have the power to see that its problems are measured" and elected officials will similarly be blind to the problems (Orfield 2001, 166). In other words, if you are not counted, then your problems don't count. Elected officials can easily rely on the narratives of the most powerful and can credibly turn a blind eye to policy failures when there is no evidence to suggest the need to think otherwise.

Note that the boxes representing collection capacity begin *before* a policy fails or gets flagged as potentially failing. Collecting data on policy outcomes is not costless. It requires financial resources, expertise, and bureaucratic commitment (Brambor et al. 2020; Lee and Zhang 2017). Furthermore, elected officials may be wary of investing in these resources, worried that, in the complex world of public policy, "the more you look for problems, the more you find" (Baumgartner and Jones 2015, 3). Alternatively, elected officials may not believe that collecting data on policy outcomes is even all that important. Scientists and policymakers live in different "hierarchies" of evidence, making it challenging to negotiate between the power of anecdotes and the validity of larger studies (Brownson, Chriqui, and Stamatakis 2009). If elected officials designing a new policy think that anecdotal experience from the policy's implementation will be sufficient to uncover any important failures, they are unlikely to invest in their state's broad data collection capacity or to institute procedures specific to the policy in question.

This is all to say that deciding to dedicate resources to these efforts is a political choice that elected officials can make at any point during a policy's trajectory. As I discuss below, however, the earlier in the trajectory data collection begins, the more usable it will be. This echoes the importance of sequencing for understanding the political power of data (see Pierson 2011 for more details on timing and sequencing in politics). In addition, while necessary, data collection is not *sufficient* for catalyzing evidence-informed recognition of policy failure. Accurate analysis is also important, a subject that is explored in the next chapter.

Relying on a weak foundation of unusable data diminishes the possibility of shifting the political narrative away from the one touted by a failing policy's beneficiaries. With unreliable data come questionable analyses. Proponents of a failed policy can dismiss failure labels and calls for revision by talking about the inaccuracies of analysis. They can offer compelling anecdotes of the value of a policy based on carefully chosen individual experiences (McDonough 2001). Without trend-level data (as occur in the hollow and status quo cases discussed later in this chapter), failed policy beneficiaries can also more credibly dismiss stories of failure from those burdened by the failed policy as anecdotal or one-off and not worth addressing with policy change. Some elected officials may recognize the likelihood of failure and seek more information or call for revision based on the subpar analyses, but they will face substantial political headwinds from those supporting the status quo. In turn, we should expect widespread acknowledgment of failure and revision to be unlikely in this case. This is important because according to Smith's (2014) study of the dissemination of health inequalities research and public policy, it is ideas, not evidence, that change policy debates.

The readiness of elected officials to consider a range of perspectives on problems at a policy's outset has long-term implications for when and how we will learn about how different groups experience a policy. The failure to collect data may perpetuate the relative political impotency of traditionally marginalized groups, as they will have to work harder to make their policy experience known and viewed as legitimate in the eyes of elected officials and policy beneficiaries.

The following discussion focuses on each of my six case studies, grouped by the degree of acknowledgment that the policy in question had failed. The juxtaposition of the cases establishes that there is indeed variation in collection capacity across states and in state policies. First, I describe data collection capacity in Washington's R&D tax credit and Texas's truancy policies, and show that both states had centralized data collection plans managed by the state. Next, the I discuss the two cases with partial acknowledgment of policy failure: Washington's Becca's Bill and Texas's Ch 313. While each state attempted to establish a policy evaluation schedule for each policy, uncoordinated and ill-defined collection practices undermined the usability of the collected information. Finally, the chapter concludes with evidence of the near-total lack of data collection capacity in Kansas's tax credit policy and Wyoming's truancy policy—the two cases in which there is no meaningful acknowledgment of policy failure among public officials. Throughout the cases, a comparison is made within and across states and cases to highlight the role that high-collection capacity can have in elected officials' recognition of policy failure.

High-Collection Capacity Catalyzes Acknowledgment of Failure

Public officials acknowledged the failure of both the R&D tax credits in Washington State and the Failure to Attend School (FTAS) policy in Texas within two decades of each policy's passage. Examining what these two cases have in common offers insight into the importance of investing in the features of data collection capacity for incentivizing elected officials to recognize failure. In both Texas and Washington State, state agencies *centrally managed data collection* on both of the specific policies. In both cases, multiple *overlapping and ongoing data collection efforts* were made in the broader policy areas. Additionally, both states quickly established *concrete and clear definitions* for the most important outcomes for their respective policy areas. The combination of specific collection strategies, universal and ongoing collection plans, and consensus on important definitions associated with the policies facilitated meaningful measurement of each policy's impact.

The Clear-Cut Case: Washington's R&D Tax Credit

The R&D tax credit in Washington represents the most centrally planned policy evaluation among the six cases. Unlike the policies in Wyoming, Kansas, and Texas, the original legislation for the R&D tax credit in Washington lays out an explicit timeline for evaluating the success of the program. In addition to this clear mandate, the legislation also identifies the agency responsible for conducting the research and the goals against which the agency should assess the program. Passed in 1994, the R&D tax credit called for evaluations every three years beginning in 1997. According to the original legislation:

> assessments will measure the effect of the program on job creation, the number of jobs created for Washington residents, company growth, the introduction of new products, the diversification of the state's economy, growth in research and development investment, the movement of firms or the consolidation of firms' operations into the state, and such other factors as the department selects.
>
> (Engrossed Second Substitute Senate Bill 6347 1994, 4)

Benefiting companies in Washington were required to submit an annual survey to the Department of Revenue by April 30th of each year, reporting on the number of jobs created[2] and documenting the company's continued adherence to the requirements of the research and development component of the tax program.

Initially, undefined key terms characterized the R&D tax credit's evaluation instructions; however, the legislature quickly expanded and refined the definitions of success (see Figure 4.3) within a year of the policy's passage. These clarifications provided public officials and researchers with clearer guidelines for evaluating the policy's outcomes. The original guidelines, for example, offer an extremely broad definition for what could count as environmental technology, describing it as anything from "prevention of threats or damage to human health" to "development of alternative energy sources." It is not hard to imagine that both the companies seeking tax credits and

[2] Note that the survey for companies did not require that they distinguish between jobs created because of the tax credit and roles that would have been created anyway. This lack of distinction is what necessitated some of the more complex analysis that JLARC eventually conducted using additional employment data sources.

(8) "Environmental technology" means assessment and prevention of threats or damage to human health or the environment, environmental cleanup, and the development of alternative energy sources.

Original legislation (1994)

(v) **Environmental technology**. "Environmental technology" means assessment and prevention of threats or damage to human health or the environment, environmental cleanup, and the development of alternative energy sources.

(A) The assessment and prevention of threats or damage to human health or the environment concerns assessing and preventing potential or actual releases of pollutants into the environment that are damaging to human health or the environment. It also concerns assessing and preventing other physical alterations of the environment that are damaging to human health or the environment.

For example, a research project related to salmon habitat restoration involving assessment and prevention of threats or damages to the environment may qualify as environmental technology, if such project is concerned with assessing and preventing potential or actual releases of water pollutants and reducing human-made degradation of the environment.

(I) Pollutants include waste materials or by-products from manufacturing or other activities.

(II) Environmental technology includes technology to reduce emissions of harmful pollutants. Reducing emissions of harmful pollutants can be demonstrated by showing the technology is developed to meet governmental emission standards. Environmental technology also includes technology to increase fuel economy, only if the taxpayer can demonstrate that a significant purpose of the project is to increase fuel economy and that such increased fuel economy does in fact significantly reduce harmful emissions. If the project is intended to increase fuel economy only minimally or reduce emissions only minimally, the project does not qualify as environmental technology. A qualifying research project must focus on the individual components that increase fuel economy of the product, not the testing of the entire product when everything is combined, unless the taxpayer can separate out and identify the specific costs associated with such testing.

(III) Environmental technology does not include technology for preventive health measures for, or medical treatment of, human beings.

(IV) Environmental technology does not include technology aimed to reduce impact of natural disasters such as floods and earthquakes.

(V) Environmental technology does not include technology for improving safety of a product.

(B) Environmental cleanup is corrective or remedial action to protect human health or the environment from releases of pollutants into the environment.

(C) Alternative energy sources are those other than traditional energy sources such as fossil fuels, nuclear power, and hydroelectricity. However, when traditional energy sources are used in conjunction with the development of alternative energy sources, all the development will be considered the development of alternative energy sources.

Updated administrative rule (1998)

Figure 4.3 Example definition change in R&D tax legislation

Sources: Original legislation is ESSB 6347; updated administrative rules is WAC 458–20–24003.

public officials eager to label the policy a success might interpret these guidelines liberally. Furthermore, this broad description makes it difficult to know what exactly *does not* count as environmental technology.

Including specific directions for what, when, and how to measure policy effectiveness is one important component of collection capacity. Washington also collected other economic data that could inform the evaluation of the tax incentives. Although the Washington Department of Revenue relied on tax credit recipients' self-reports (a common practice), which tended to be glowingly positive, state-employed researchers had other sources of data they could leverage to corroborate company statements and evaluate the policy's impacts. Initially, different agencies portrayed strikingly different pictures of the effectiveness of the R&D tax credit. While the Department of Revenue consistently argued that the policy was effectively meeting its objectives, Judicial Legislative Audit and Research Committee (JLARC) and the Washington Institute for Public Policy's (WSIPP) studies relied on state-collected employment data and more complex statistical techniques. They uniformly found that the policy was, at best, not producing the additional economic growth promised, and, at worst, was costing the state extra money.

The Economic Security Department, which was a central clearinghouse for employment data across the state, had longitudinal data that researchers could use to double check companies' self-reported employment numbers. When JLARC was struggling to draw inferences with Department of Revenue's data, its researchers turned to the Economic Security Department's data. JLARC's 2013 report describes how researchers were able to use the two agencies' data to better assess the creation of quality jobs:

> We used confidential tax return data from DOR [Department of Revenue] and employment and wage data from the Employment Security Department (ESD) to overcome the problems we identified with the self-reported taxpayer survey data. However, the survey is the only source of information on the "quality" of jobs provided by beneficiaries.
>
> (2012 Tax Preference Performance Reviews 2013)

While this solution did not solve the challenge of delineating the "quality" jobs created, it did provide clear information on the number of jobs created and the number of tax credits provided (2012 Tax Preference Performance Reviews 2013, 103) beyond the rosy picture offered by benefiting companies' self-reports.

Prior to the 2004 renewal, the Department of Revenue was the only source of information on the policy's outcomes, and the legislature supported the first renewal with widespread bipartisan support. By the time the policy came up for a second renewal in 2014, JLARC and WSIPP had mined additional data sources to paint a more accurate picture of the policy's impacts. The legislature failed to renew the policy a second time in 2014. Greater data availability yielded a more accurate picture of the effects of the policy, suggesting that new information may have played a role in shifting policy preferences among public officials.

The Treasure Trove Case: Texas's Failure to Attend School

The Texas FTAS case echoes the critical role data collection plays in the politics of policy failure. It also more clearly highlights the latent power of state-mandated collection capacity. Unlike the situation associated with the recognition and revision of the Washington R&D tax credits, the FTAS legislation did not require any specific data collection to assess its effectiveness, nor did it establish any schedule for evaluating FTAS specifically.[3] However, the broader Education Code, in which FTAS was embedded, required data collection on student outcomes. In the throes of establishing accountability through standardized testing in the state, the Texas Education Agency (TEA) and the Texas Juvenile Justice Department happened to be collecting a significant amount of data relevant to FTAS. Statewide agencies used consistent definitions, data formats, and storage procedures. Given that the goals of FTAS were to decrease truancy and increase graduation rates and its implementation involved courts, jails, and the juvenile justice system, data from both the educational system and the criminal justice system offered the most accurate insight into the effectiveness of the policy. Texas's habit of extensive data collection resulted in the documentation of information that researchers could use to evaluate the effects of FTAS. In this case, there was no intentional data collection on FTAS specifically, but the tendency and capacity to collect longitudinal data in the state created a treasure trove of data that researchers could mine.

[3] An amendment to the original legislation in 2011 did require schools to begin reporting their truancy charges to the Texas Education Agency. While TEA could downgrade a school for failing to report their charges, researchers suggest this rarely happened (Fowler et al. 2015).

Between 2000 and 2006, the Texas Education Agency collected longitudinal data on the educational experiences and outcomes on the universe of students that entered seventh grade in the state between 2000 and 2002 (Carmichael et al. 2011). This data was uniquely suited to evaluating the long-term outcomes of various education policies, as it was centrally mandated. The study was designed and executed within a single agency, making definitional consistency and collection procedures more uniform. Importantly, the dataset also gathered information on every Texas middle school student and followed them for several subsequent years into college and career. Longitudinal data on the universe of the study population is a treasure trove for researchers. The first report that evaluated the impacts of school-based discipline openly lauded the invaluable asset these data provided:

> Although no state can provide a perfect case study of school disciplinary policies to which officials in any state can relate, Texas does offer a particularly useful laboratory to examine these issues. It is highly unusual in its maintenance of individual electronic records, rich with information about each public-school student. This system facilitates tracking of students over their school careers, even as they move from one school (or district) to the next. Individual electronic records are also maintained for youth who come into contact with the juvenile justice system. What further distinguished Texas from every other state at the start of this study in 2009 was the opportunity to study at least six years' worth of state student level education and juvenile justice electronic records and to benefit from broad bipartisan support for this research.
>
> (Carmichael et al. 2011, 11–12)

Interviews with researchers involved in this analysis confirmed the rarity of such a complete dataset on student educational experiences and outcomes. They also pointed to its completeness as critical to the evaluations' effectiveness in catching elite attention. The state's investment in collecting high-quality data created an opportunity for policymakers to learn about the outcomes for youth subjected to punitive consequences for their behavior.

Breaking Schools' Rules, the first report to be issued using this dataset to evaluate disciplinary policies, demonstrated that the rise of "zero-tolerance" school discipline policies had dramatically increased the rates of expulsion and suspensions, and these consequences, in turn dramatically decreased a students' likelihood of graduating from high school (Carmichael et al. 2011, 4). Furthermore, students of color were disproportionately more likely to experience this consequence than white students (Carmichael et al. 2011, x).

Another notable feature of the longitudinal Texas dataset is that it was centrally managed and not collected in response to a single policy outcome. The data collection had broad bipartisan support and was not targeted at evaluating any single policy. The more general nature of the data collection (i.e., not targeted at a single policy) may have provided some political cover such that schools and districts may not have been aware of exactly how the information was going to be used and therefore had fewer clear incentives to shirk reporting responsibilities.

Like the Washington legislature, the Texas legislature eventually refined its truancy-specific outcomes to better understand the impacts of FTAS. In 2011, after the publication of *Breaking Schools' Rules*, the legislature required schools to document the number of truancy charges submitted each year. While schools, in theory, would receive a lowered state rating for failing to report their truancy charges, public records requests for the data revealed that significant data was missing from the FTAS-specific reporting. Texas Appleseed's *Class Not Court* report describes the missing data as follows:

> Texas Appleseed requested from TEA the PEIMS data that school districts reported on the number of truancy/FTAS cases filed for the 2010-11, 2011-12, and 2012-13 school years. Upon reviewing the data, it was apparent that there are major problems with the data. The information received from TEA included data from less than half of all Texas school districts. According to TEA's 2012-13 report, there are 1,026 school districts in Texas, but the information that TEA provided to Texas Appleseed only included data from 446 districts. Many of these 446 districts reported filings for only one or two of the three school years that we reviewed, so for each individual school year, there were actually fewer than 446 districts reporting data. For example, only 323 school districts reported any truancy court referrals to TEA for the 2012-13 school year.
>
> (Fowler et al. 2015, 50)

Although compliance with reporting did vary, refining definitions and mandating additional data collection did provide additional evidence for researchers to incorporate into their studies of FTAS, which Texas Appleseed did in 2015. This suggests that state collection capacity creates the possibility of high-quality data, providing that the incentives of the agencies or individuals tasked with collecting and reporting data can influence the quality of the final information.

Building specific definitions into the original policy can help guide data collection, but institutionalizing statewide collection patterns can play a critical role in creating a strong foundation for high-quality analysis to reveal policy failure to public officials. In both the R&D tax credit and FTAS, a willingness to refine definitions and establish ongoing and overlapping collection efforts that the state's education and juvenile justice agencies managed centrally created valuable datasets for researchers to study the impact of each policy. Furthermore, both states refined definitions and data collection practices as public officials learned more about the policies and effectiveness of the original data collection plans. When existing data did not satisfactorily measure important outcomes, the legislature clarified the definitions of key terms and refined data collection mandates. Finally, these features were the direct result of political choices made long before the legislature agreed that the policies were failing.

Given the power dynamics between state and local governments, centrally mandating policy implementation and data collection does not always occur. The next two cases—tax credits in Texas and truancy policy in Washington—offer insight into the impact of uncoordinated and decentralized data collection efforts on state collection capacity.

Uncoordinated Data Collection Precludes Meaningful Analysis

The response of Washington and Texas to tax credits and truancy policy, respectively, suggests that each state's agencies are capable of collecting data and its public officials are capable of acknowledging failure. The other policy areas that I examine in each state—Texas's tax incentives and Washington's truancy policy—suggest that collection capacity varies not only across states, but also across policies within a state. For both the Ch 313 tax credits in Texas and Becca's Bill in Washington, a handful of public officials did argue that the policy failed to produce the intended results. And, in each case, legislators introduced legislation to revise the policies. However, in both cases, unlike the first pair examined, a consensus on failure fails to develop.

The vignettes that follow show that missing mandates, ambiguous definitions, and decentralized data collection more credibly allow public officials to dismiss suggestions of failure when doing so does not align with their preexisting or ideological preferences.

The Hollow Case: Washington's Becca's Bill

In keeping with Washington's decentralized judicial system, the original Becca's Bill legislation allowed counties to decide which local officials would take the lead in implementing the policy (Webster 1996, 12). This varied approach to implementation combined with vague or, in some cases, nonexistent definitions critical to policy implementation precluded accurate and useful data collection on its outcomes, making it emblematic of the hollow case. According to the first Washington State Institute of Public Policy (WSIPP) report on the policy, "In each county, different actors took the lead. Common leaders were presiding judges, deputy prosecutors, and school district superintendents" (Webster 1996, 12). The report goes on to show that many officials were initially confused about many aspects of implementing the policy and collecting data on its outcomes, including exactly what ages of students were subject to the policy and what type of legal representation students were entitled to for their first truancy hearing.

Further complicating efforts to collect data on the policy's impact, the original legislation did not explicitly define "truancy" or "unexcused absence," leaving it to the counties to determine the threshold for each condition (Becca's Bill 1995). The lack of a consistent definition for these key concepts precluded gathering reliable and interpretable data from all thirty-nine counties. In the inaugural report on Becca's Bill, published in 1996, WSIPP acknowledges that that varied definitions of unexcused absences and varied practices among school districts make it difficult to actually know what unexcused absence rates were pre-Becca's Bill, which in turn made it difficult to know exactly how the policy impacted truancy rates.

Similar to suggestions made early on in the R&D tax credit case, in 1996 WSIPP recommended clarifying the key definitions associated with policy implementation, such as "truancy" and "unexcused absence" (Webster 1996). WSIPP offered suggestions on possible definitions for each term in their first report on the policy, including an overview of how other states defined such terms. Although the two original sponsors attempted to refine the definitions in 1995, the legislation failed to make it out of committee after the House offered its amendments (SB 6646 1995). Thus, data collection remained challenging, given the decentralized system. This stands in stark contrast to the list of definitions the legislature provided for the R&D tax credit. Furthermore, unlike the situation in the R&D tax credit case, the legislature did not update definitions in Becca's Bill after the evaluating agencies identified vague definitions as a barrier to evaluation. Defining and operationalizing terms and concepts essential to accurately evaluate Becca's Bill, in turn, remained up to the court collecting data.

Without explicit direction, districts and courts varied in how they defined key variables and how accurately they recorded information. The 1998 report on Becca's Bill outlined several flaws in the data collection systems that influence the validity of the policy evaluation. The 1998 WSIPP report explained:

> Many school administrators assisting with this study emphasized that attendance problems are not solely restricted to unexcused absences; students who miss school with extended excused absences are also in danger of falling behind, losing credits, or dropping out of school. Schools in this study also provided information on the number of students with excessive absences (defined as missing 20 or more days of school, either excused or unexcused). Of students enrolled the entire school year, *15 percent* were absent 20 or more school days. Approximately two-thirds (*64 percent*) of the students with excessive absences were *not* marked as "truant" by their schools.
>
> (Burley and Harding 1998, 17)

Though state research agencies were explicitly *tasked* with examining the outcomes of the policy, the quality of data available to researchers constrained the researchers' ability to produce interpretable and reliable findings on the policy's impacts statewide.

Without analyzable statewide data, WSIPP initially relied on case studies of counties that were able and willing to provide data on their truancy outcomes. In 1998, WSIPP conducted a ten-county study in which they examined truancy outcomes. The case studies suggested that the truancy petitions may have been "changing behavior patterns," but they also pointed out that these effects seemed to apply only to students "experimenting" with truancy, as opposed to those who had established patterns of truancy (Burley and Harding 1998, ii). However, across these case studies, the authors were quick to acknowledge that the findings are not generalizable to the remainder of the state. A second case study from WSIPP in 2008 most explicitly identified the data challenges researchers faced, stating, "Most programs are not evaluated and those that are evaluated generally use research designs and methodologies that do not permit us to draw conclusions about causality" (Kilma, Miller, and Nunlist 2009, 5). In other words, the state's analytical capacity was impotent without reliable data.

Two years later, and fifteen years after the policy was first implemented, WSIPP's policy evaluations continued to lament the challenges their researchers faced trying to analyze, at best, incomparable, and, at worst, nonexistent, data on truancy. The researchers point out that without information on attendance before Becca's Bill's implementation and consistently defined data collected after it took effect, it was impossible for them to make meaningful claims about the policy's impact:

> Unfortunately, despite our best attempt to analyze this question with rigorous statistical methods, we cannot provide a scientific answer as to whether the law is having a positive, negative, or no effect on student outcomes. Sometimes research can provide answers to central questions, and sometimes it cannot; this is a question of the latter. The 1995 Becca Laws were implemented statewide and a random assignment study—the type of study offering the best scientific evidence—was never possible or envisioned. In addition, the historical data available for our study do not allow us to measure a vital aspect of the Becca laws: the number of unexcused absences from school. Without this information, it is impossible to employ appropriate statistical methods to study the question of Becca's Bill's effectiveness.
> (Miller, Kilma, and Nunlist 2010, 1)

Knowledgeable and willing researchers with a deep understanding of statistical inference evaluated the truancy policy's impacts (a feature explored more in depth in the following chapter). But a paucity of data renders even the best trained researchers helpless to generate meaningful conclusions. Notably, the Washington State researchers articulated that there are no clear findings, and while this may preclude the acknowledgment of policy failure, it also opens the possibility for ideologically or preference-driven narratives during policy debates, since the official state research organization has declared that, for better or for worse, they could not be sure about the impacts of the policy.

Social policies impact people in complex ways, influencing outcomes that may not be under the jurisdiction of any single state agency. In the case of truancy in Texas, it took the cooperation of the Texas Education Agency and the Juvenile Justice system to evaluate the impact of detention and court involvement on long-term educational and criminal justice involvement outcomes to convince public officials that the policy was not creating a solution. Rather, it was exacerbating undesired outcomes (i.e., more criminal justice involvement and lower graduation rates). Washington State Center for Court Research (WSCCR) did eventually manage to integrate data from multiple agencies regarding long-term outcomes for youth in 2015 and was able to provide a more precise and accurate picture of the impact of the policy. In their discussion of their findings that truancy rates had not dropped in the face of more stringent sanctions from Becca's Bill, WSCCR articulated the value-add of integrated agency data:

> Recent developments in cross-agency data sharing in Washington State have only recently made it possible to track the educational and career progress of court-involved youth prior to their court contact and afterwards, through college and entry into the workforce. These findings demonstrate the power of integrated data to answer questions that were previously out-of- reach, while providing a glimpse into the myriad educational challenges facing truant youth in Washington State.
>
> (Coker & McCurley 2015, 17).

Recognizing the power of longitudinal and clearly defined data collection, the Washington State legislature did pass HB 2449 in 2016, which, among other changes, required the state to develop an annual report on juvenile detention in the state. The legislation also changed the collection and reporting requirements for all juvenile courts, mandating participation in a centrally managed database for juvenile court involvement. While this legislation did make reporting more consistent, it did not immediately address the differences in how the courts defined relevant variables and collected data across courts, and so the original policy remained intact.

The Status Quo Case: Texas's Ch 313

Texas has state agencies with the capacity to collect meaningful and analyzable data, as the FTAS case suggests, but this does not guarantee that it will occur in all cases, as the story of Ch 313 tax incentives demonstrates.

Ch 313 represents the status quo case. The outsourcing of compliance management for Ch 313 to the states over 1,000 school districts—entities not trained in collecting, analyzing, or reporting on the economics of corporate earnings and employment statistics—and the reliance on self-reporting for Ch 313 data collection undermined the integrity of the findings on policy outcomes. This in turn allowed public officials to double down on their preexisting ideological narratives about the tax credit.

The original Ch 313 legislation did establish some semblance of collection capacity by requiring the collection of data on participating projects. Ch 313 stipulates that the State Comptroller should count the number of projects, the estimated value-add, and the estimated costs of the projects benefiting from the tax credit (Brimer 2001). However, the legislation established the school districts and the recipient companies themselves as those responsible for collecting data and reporting it to the State Comptroller. A 2014 report from the State Auditor's Office on the policy described how much the data collection process depended on schools and recipient companies:

> Oversight [of Chapter 313 agreements] relies primarily on self-reported information that businesses certify. . . . To determine whether businesses with agreements complied with . . . Chapter 313, the four school districts audited relied primarily on the certification of the annual eligibility forms and biennial progress reports that businesses submitted to confirm the businesses' capital investment and the number of jobs they committed to create or had created. . . Chapter 313 does not require school districts to verify that information, and the school districts audited did not perform verifications.
>
> (Keel 2014, 2)

Farther on in the report, the auditors explain how this information travels from school districts to the Texas Education Agency and the State Comptroller's Office, both of which accept the reported numbers at face value because the school districts vouched for the information:

> School districts provide the information that businesses submit to the Comptroller's Office and the Texas Education Agency (TEA) as the basis for additional state aid paid to the school districts for (1) property tax revenue losses associated with agreements and (2) tax credits associated with agreements. Because school districts certify that information provided

> is true and correct, neither the Comptroller's Office nor TEA verifies the information.
>
> (Keel 2014, 2)

Aside from their inexperience in evaluating corporate financial data, school districts are also notoriously limited in resources, further precluding the likelihood that a district will question the information passed along to them. Furthermore, most schools face an intense conflict of interest as the compilers of data on Ch 313's effects. Through Ch 313, Texas empowered school districts to dispense tax credits to businesses locating within their boundaries. The state, in turn, reimburses the school districts for any tax revenue lost to tax credits through Ch 313. Thus, as long as schools are receiving reimbursements, there is little incentive to spend the money or time to dig deeply into the data provided by the companies. This self-reported data leaves the usually optimistic outcomes open to criticism from the program's skeptics (Michels 2016). Furthermore, reliance on self-reported data precludes any other interested parties from conducting more credible evaluations unless additional data collection occurs.

Unlike the case for Washington's R&D tax credits, there were no other major statewide efforts at collection data on employment opportunities, tax incentives, and business relocation decisions. This meant that no other state agency was able to step in and provide any alternative information about the employment opportunities or economic growth associated with the Ch 313 projects, leaving the analysis reliant on the self-reported (and therefore likely positively biased) data on the impact of Ch 313. Both Democrats and Republicans have proposed bills to end the program over the last two decades, but no bills have ever made it out of committee. Hearings on these bills reflect substantial support for the tax credits, with legislators arguing that Ch 313 brings in important business to their districts. As of 2017, Ch 313 remained an active benefit available to companies looking to relocate or open a business in Texas, despite the attempts to limit its scope.

The decentralized and unstructured nature of data collection in both Washington's Becca's Bill and Texas's Ch 313 yielded information lauded by the policies' supporters and reasonably dismissed by skeptics. Furthermore, unlike in the R&D tax credit and FTAS cases, there were no supplemental datasets that could provide meaningful information on the policies in question. Uncoordinated data collection offered data integrity as a key point of debate, rather than the effectiveness of the policy, making limited acknowledgment, often along ideological lines, the most likely outcome. Uncoordinated collection strategies—a laissez-faire collection strategy for truancy data in Washington and a reliance on self-reporting from benefiting corporations of Ch 313 in Texas—precluded a credible and politically powerful analysis of these policy outcomes. Instead, supporters and opponents remain engaged in a tit-for-tat competition of research findings, with no meaningful political movement among those harmed by the policy dedicated to effectively demand reform.

Low-Collection Capacity Paralyzes Researchers

The four cases presented thus far have some semblance of collection capacity, either at the state or the policy level, though effective implementation varied. This section describes how the two cases in which there has been no meaningful acknowledgment of policy failure—truancy in Wyoming and tax credits in Kansas—compare with the cases of full and partial acknowledgment in Texas and Washington. The comparison highlights the finding that in Kansas and Wyoming, data collection was, at best, ad hoc and, at worst, nonexistent. Kansas and Wyoming show how failure to invest in data collection enhances the opportunity for those in power to dominate the narrative about failed policies and, subsequently, stymie revision attempts.

In Kansas, attempts have been made to collect data to analyze the Promoting Employment Across Kansas (PEAK) outcomes. However, they are idiosyncratic and specific to particular gubernatorial administrations, resulting in no consistent, longitudinal information on the policy's impact. Wyoming represents a case in which no attempt has been made to require data collection on juvenile justice and truancy-related outcomes. The data that do exist in the state resulted from national juvenile justice organization efforts. The lack of systematic data collection—be it from ad hoc collection strategies or the complete absence of any systematic data collection attempts—precluded generating information on a policy's outcomes, a basic condition for evidence-informed policymaking. The final two cases demonstrate the obstacles that arise when no data collection processes are created through which elected officials can acknowledge policy failure.

Kansas Taxes

The legislation establishing the PEAK program (SB 97) suggests a review of the policy as a useful practice, but it does not establish any specific schedule or allocate any resources for doing so. Without any data collection, there is no reliable evidence to inform policymakers about the outcomes of the program, nor is there any incentive to reevaluate the policy on the basis of evidence.

The first attempts to evaluate PEAK's impact occurred four years after it was first implemented. The Legislative Post Audit Committee (LPA) conducted three audits of the program between 2013 and 2017 and in each audit identified the lack of credible data as a substantial roadblock for assessing the program's outcomes. In the 2013 audit, the researchers plainly stated the challenges they faced in examining the effects of the policy, "Assessing the benefits of the PEAK program is difficult because the Department of Commerce has not compiled meaningful information on the program" (Economic Development: Determining Which Economic Development Tools Are Most Important and Effective in Promoting Job Creation and Economic Growth in Kansas, Part 1 2013, 11). In their third audit of PEAK, the LPA report further highlighted how Kansas relied on self-reporting from companies, which have a substantial vested interest in portraying the PEAK program as an effective promoter of job growth and economic gains. The report states:

> Job and capital investment data from the Department of Commerce and Department of Revenue are based on company-reported information that is largely unaudited. Most projects do not have records for the entire time period we included in our analysis, therefore jobs, capital investments, and incentives are based, at least in part, on estimates. Although we took steps to ensure our estimates were reasonable, we do not know how far the estimated jobs, investments, and incentives shown in this report may vary from the actual jobs and investments that will ultimately be created and incentives that will be provided.
>
> (Economic Development: Determining Which Development Tools Are Most Important and Promoting Job Creation and Economic Growth in Kansas, Part 3 2014, 2)

The state's low capacity for collecting data meant they had limited investment both in the personnel and in expertise for conducting audits and data collection, and it at least partially explains the anemic datasets. The LPA directly states, "Officials told us they had not been able to keep up with these reviews because of staff shortages, several legislative changes to the program, and a growing number of participating companies collection capacity" (Economic Development: Determining Which Development Tools Are Most Important and Promoting Job Creation and Economic Growth in Kansas, Part 3 2014, 2). Like Texas, Kansas relied on companies benefiting from tax credits to self-report employment numbers and other key metrics about economic growth. However, companies regularly fail to comply even with these basic reporting standards. Moreover, according to the LPA, the state agencies charged with collecting the data explicitly identify lack of funding and manpower as the reason they cannot enforce data reporting more consistently. This suggests even lower collection capacity than that available in the Texas tax credit case.

The 2013 LPA Audit continued this trend of identifying limits of data availability and focusing on whether or not the Department of Commerce was doing its job properly rather than actually analyzing outcomes of the program given the data limitations. Highlighting major challenges to reliable data collection from the Department of Commerce's operating procedures, the audit notes:

> By contrast, PEAK is new, and results are based on potentially verifiable information, but the Department of Commerce has failed to compile that information which severely limits the ability of the department, the Legislature, or anyone else to properly evaluate the effectiveness of the program. Further, the department has done a very poor job of staffing and managing the PEAK program. It has failed to enforce reporting requirements, compromising its ability to ensure that companies are meeting their obligations under the program. Equally disturbing are the delays in processing reports, which has prevented some companies from receiving the program's benefits in a timely fashion.
>
> (Economic Development: Determining Which Economic Development Tools Are Most Important and Effective in Promoting Job Creation and Economic Growth in Kansas, Part 1 2013, 28)

The fourth finding, entitled "Including More Detailed Information in the Annual PEAK Reports Provided to the Legislature Would Help Assess Compliance with Statutory Benefit Limits" in the 2017 LPA Audit, suggested that the Department of Commerce did little to change its reporting procedures, relying on unenforced and unverified self-reporting from benefiting companies (Kansas Department of Commerce Department Overview and Special Initiatives 2017, 6).

These observations about data collection in Kansas further highlight how a vicious feedback cycle that reinforces, rather than undermines, a failed policy's resilience can unfold when there is no expectation that the state will thoroughly and accurately document policy outcomes. The policy beneficiaries—in this case, the companies—self-report outcomes that are universally in line with their interests, thereby providing evidence to supportive policymakers that the program is producing the intended outcomes. Armed with this evidence, policymakers can expand the program based on its "success," offering new companies the opportunity to benefit from the policy and, presumably, advocate for its continued existence.

Critics of the policy, on the other hand, must rely on anecdotal evidence and limited, publicly available records to build a case against the policy's effectiveness. Critics are also left to argue from the position of the unknowable counterfactual. In Kansas, this left critics to argue that any economic growth *would have happened anyway* even without PEAK, but without systematically collected data to support this claim, the evidence (and narrative) that tax incentives were driving economic growth dominated the policy conversation and the public's attention (e.g., Bishop 2012).

Wyoming: Juvenile Justice Act

Wyoming's experience with its truancy policy represents the lowest capacity for data collection in the set of case studies. There has been limited discussion, let alone acknowledgment, of the policy's failure among public officials.

In 2011, the Education Commission of States identified Wyoming as one of the two remaining states that has not yet established a longitudinal data system to track its K–12 students (Frey 2011). A 2004 report on youth case processing in Wyoming identified the "lack of a unified juvenile justice system and lack of centralized data makes it difficult to both implement and evaluate the impact of policies" (Freng et al. 2004, 9).

Wyoming's Juvenile Justice Act itself did not include any provisions requiring the state to collect information on implementation of the specific policy. Without a clear mandate to collect data and without direction on when and how to do so, individual courts, school districts, and public officials were left to decide how their jurisdiction approaches data collection, if they do so at all. While this "no one-size fits all approach" can be helpful in policy implementation, it causes substantial challenges for assembling a coherent dataset that can be analyzed to produce meaningful insights into the realities of policy outcomes. Wyoming relied almost exclusively on data from national organizations[4] to shed light on the outcomes of their juvenile justice system, and even then it opted out of participating in the National Incident-Based Reporting System (Wyoming State Advisory Council on Juvenile Justice: Annual Report 2008 2008, 9). Wyoming's Survey and Analysis Center (WYSAC), in its 2008 report on criminal justice, stated that "Criminal justice data for the state of Wyoming is in a relatively early stage of development." In a speech to the Joint Judiciary Interim Committee in 2011, the Governor's Juvenile Justice policy advisor, Gary Hartman, explicitly identified the need for a better data collection system before it could discuss reforms to state prosecutions of juveniles. In his comments, he specifically pointed to the disorganization and paucity of data as the obstacle to reform, "I've known for some time that we have a deficiency in collecting data. . . . We have something like 27 agencies (or counties) collecting data on juveniles, and we haven't been able to collate or integrate that at all" (Brown 2011).

National data collection efforts, however, even when successful, did not generate confidence among state public officials. Several public officials and nonprofit leaders reported that the disparities between nationally reported data and perceptions of local outcomes generated fears about agenda pushing from outside of Wyoming (Brown 2011; PBS roundtable discussion). This furthered distrust of state-level findings, encouraging some to wonder if the state findings were the result of biased research (Brown 2011). In response to a particular disagreement between ACLU-collected data and state-collected data, Representative Kermit Brown (R-Laramie) pointed to the challenge of accepting information from an organization with a clear agenda, like the ACLU. He argued that the state needed to have its own information to best understand the challenges it faced and the best options for reform (Brown 2011).

[4] Namely, the Statewide Automatic Child Welfare Information System (SACWIS) administered by the Office of Administration for Children and Families and the Census of Juveniles in Residential Placement conducted by the Office of Juvenile Justice and Delinquency Prevention.

When either presented with national data suggesting juvenile detention is counterproductive or when asked about the effectiveness of juvenile detention in Wyoming, public officials acknowledged the need for more data rather than the failure of existing programs. For example, in 2008 the *Wyoming Tribune Eagle* described the response from one juvenile justice coordinator for the Wyoming County Commissioners' Association with the following:

> The research is less clear, however, in regard to whether transfer laws deter potential offenders. Beth Evans, Juvenile Justice Project coordinator for the Wyoming County Commissioners Association, said data is not collected to assess juvenile recidivism throughout the state. "As I said to (the Wyoming Legislature's) Joint Judiciary (Interim Committee) last week, Don't ask me about recidivism, because I don't know," she said.
>
> (Van Cassell 2008)

Echoing a similar sentiment earlier that year, Hartman did acknowledge that the "numbers need to go down," but also commented that the "state needs a better data collection system if it is going to move forward with any plans to reform how the state prosecutes juveniles" (Wolfson 2008). A Republican state representative pointed out that there was "information overload and better data collection is needed" (Brown 2011). Notably, these public officials skirted a clear statement on whether the policy itself is effective and instead focused their comments on the limits of data collection practices. In turn, reforming Wyoming's truancy practices remained off the legislative agenda, and the policy remains intact.

In 2013, Wyoming considered adding $500,000 to the budget to enhance data collection for its Department of Family Services, which could, in part, have helped provide more information on truants' outcomes. However, the state legislature voted the measure down, citing concerns about the price and potential data security issues (Brown 2013).

In Wyoming, there was little to no coherent structure for collecting data on policy outcomes in juvenile justice. As a result, the policy discussion on truancy, when there is any, focuses on decrying the merits of existing national data and debating the cost-benefit analysis of collecting data specific to Wyoming. Instead of discussing the failures of existing policy and innovating potential solutions, public officials could throw up their hands with a *je ne sais pas* and avoid taking a stand.

Conclusion

This chapter makes two arguments. First, I introduce data collection capacity as a distinct and necessary, but not sufficient, feature of a state's institutional landscape for the evidence-informed recognition of policy failure. The six state policies in this chapter show that states vary in their willingness, available resources, and knowledge of how to collect usable data that can provide evidence of a policy's success or failure. I present state policies in pairs, according to how widespread the acknowledgment of failure was among public officials. These comparisons suggest that states' policies with high collection capacity share three key features: a mandate for data collection in the original policy, clearly defined terms and measurements, and centrally managed collection plans. The third feature—ongoing and overlapping collection efforts—is a feature of the broader state policy landscape. but it influences the possibility of evidence-informed acknowledgment failure for specific policies. Table 4.1 summarizes these findings. The juxtaposition of cases across and within Texas and Washington suggests that collecting data, in and of itself, does not promise any insight into policy outcomes. The quality and exhaustiveness of the data influence its ability to be useful in subsequent analyses that evaluate policy outcomes.

Second, credible data creates the potential for negative feedback effects that can disrupt stakeholder dynamics and alter elected officials' incentives to put a policy failure on the political agenda. Without the investments of the four features of collection capacity, partisan, ideologically motivated,

Table 4.1 Collection capacity components and acknowledgment outcome, 1994–2017

Case	Collection requested?	Collection Capacity			Failure Ack?
		Centralization	Definitions	Overlapping	
WA R&D tax credit	Yes	Yes	Yes	Yes	Yes
TX Truancy	No	Yes	Yes	Yes	Yes
WA Becca's Bill	Yes	No	Yes	No	Partial
TX Ch313	Yes	No	No	No	Partial
KS PEAK	No	No	No	No	No
WY Truancy	No	No	No	No	No

and vested interests that dominate state politics for a given policy will most likely control the narrative about policy outcomes. The decision to collect data about a policy is a political one. Policymakers can choose to require it or not, fund it or not, or update definitions and collection mandates or not. And it is a decision that has long-term policy feedback effects among elites. By creating a foundation for analysis that can credibly corroborate or undermine the narratives of vested interests, data collection can catalyze a negative feedback cycle for a failed policy. Without the willingness and interest at the outset to understand policy outcomes, little data is collected, and whatever data does get scavenged may not be especially relevant or convincing to those skeptical of policy failure. Without compelling evidence, there is no reason to expect that a negative feedback cycle will begin: if the failed policy's beneficiaries are politically powerful, then the failure will continue.

5

Moving beyond Counting: Defining and Theorizing Analytical Capacity

> *One cannot repair a weak research design with strong data analysis. Almost inevitably what seems too good to be true is, and one is simply substituting untestable assumptions for the information one does not have.*
>
> —Richard Berk, *Towards a Methodology for Mere Mortals* (1991, 316)

In a *Future Trends in State Courts* magazine article published in 2012, the chief justice of the Texas Supreme Court, Wallace Jefferson, decried the criminalization of school-based behavior for young people. He began by offering extreme examples of students who had been ticketed for silly or childish behaviors, like sporting baggy pants or wearing excessive perfume. Jefferson then referenced *Breaking Schools' Rules,* a 2011 study from the Texas Public Policy Research Institute at Texas A&M University, which found that disciplinary referrals in school were *the* leading predictor of future involvement with the juvenile justice system. Wallace dedicates well over half of the four pages of his article to a section entitled "The Studies' Findings Are Troubling." This section includes the following description of the most up-to-date findings regarding ticketing in schools:

> Ticketing is also common, used most often to punish students for low-level, nonviolent offenses like disruption of class, disorderly conduct, and truancy. Texas Appleseed conservatively estimates that more than 275,000 nontraffic tickets are issued to juveniles as young as six in Texas each year, 120,000 of those for truancy (2010c: 1, 18, 76). One municipal court judge in Houston estimates that he sees approximately 150 juvenile ticketing cases per day during the school year (St. George 2011). Texas Appleseed conservatively estimates that more than 275,000 nontraffic tickets are

The Politics of Failed Policies. Sarah James, Oxford University Press. © Oxford University Press (2025).
DOI: 10.1093/9780197813645.003.0006

> issued to juveniles as young as six in Texas each year, 120,000 of those for truancy (2010c: 1, 18, 76). One municipal court judge in Houston estimates that he sees approximately 150 juvenile ticketing cases per day during the school year (St. George 2011).
>
> (Jefferson 2012)

Jefferson's post, in its entirety, contains over forty references to investigative journalism, academic studies, and national and state reports on juvenile justice.

Unsurprisingly, Jefferson had not conducted any of the data analysis himself; instead he relied on analysis and summaries provided by expert researchers. As the Chief Justice of the Texas Supreme Court, Jefferson had neither the time nor, presumably, the statistical and computational skills to develop, test, and interpret models showing the effects of ticketing on student outcomes. Indeed, even before he introduces the data that informed his new understanding, Jefferson credits two organizations—Texas A&M University's Texas Public Policy Research Institute and Texas Appleseed—for their "extensive studies" that drew attention to the state's failing approach to disciplining young people. Notably, none of Jefferson's sources were state-run research organizations; even the Texas A&M study was the result of a research group at the university that serves public and private clients, not just the state's government. He also emphasized the data source that informed two of the studies—the longitudinal study of the universe of Texas middle schoolers described in the last chapter.

It probably is safe to say that Jefferson would not have personally known of this dataset prior to reading these reports. Even if he had, he is not likely to have been able to personally derive meaning from the nearly one million observations. Researchers with expertise in quantitative data analysis played a vital role in generating meaning from the data and then communicating the meaning to elected officials (Greenberg and Robins 1985). Jefferson himself acknowledges the important role of the researchers who conducted these analyses, saying that "two extensive studies of Texas public school students shed light on the relationship between school discipline, dropout rates, and involvement in the juvenile justice system" (Jefferson 2012). Jefferson's reflections on how he came to learn about the failure of his state's truancy policy suggests that research-oriented institutions—both those formally within the state bureaucracy and those that may informally collaborate with them—can play an important role in analyzing and disseminating findings about policy outcomes, assuming data was collected.

Texas is not often cited as a leader in evidence-based policymaking (Davies et al. 2017). Yet, when confronted with compelling findings about FTAS, elected officials did change their minds about the effectiveness of ticketing and jailing students for truancy. Investing in obvious forms of analytical capacity—like state research agencies—or calling for policy evaluations is important for assessing policy outcomes. However, it is far from sufficient, and, as FTAS in Texas shows, state investment in this capacity may not even be necessary. In this chapter, I build on the distinction made in Chapter 4 between collection and analytical capacity by describing the role of analytical capacity in catalyzing elected officials to acknowledge policy failure. Unlike collection capacity, analytical capacity can, in some circumstances, be successfully supplemented by nonstate actors. I leverage comparisons among my case studies to show that, while necessary, analytical capacity is not sufficient to generate consistent and compelling policy evaluations that can catalyze negative policy feedback cycles among elites for failing policies.

Defining Analytical Capacity

While data collection capacity is a necessary condition for public officials to engage in evidence-based acknowledgment of failure, analytical capacity also plays a critical role. The existence of high-quality data does not guarantee its analysis. A state's *analytical capacity* refers to a state's investment in the human capital, procedures, and organizations that enable drawing scientifically valid and reliable inferences and conclusions from data. This includes having the human capital, technological, and financial resources to conduct accurate statistical tests and develop meaningful models using data. However, this does not mean that all states with analytical capacity always produce valid, reliable, and convincing research. *A key contribution of this book is to suggest that collection and analytical capacity are separate institutional features of the state. They are differentially dependent on state involvement for successfully producing convincing information that can alert elected officials to policy failure.*

Analytical capacity influences the acknowledgment of and response to policy failure because low capacity is more likely to result in nonsystematic and unreliable research, and "when the results are undisputed, the process likely doesn't matter much, but process matters much more if people are not willing to accept the numbers or the premise upon which they were collected" (Lindblom and Cohen 1979, 66). Analytical capacity on its own, however, should have little impact on catalyzing the acknowledgment of policy failure. In what follows I describe three indicators of analytical capacity—state-sponsored research bureaucracies, legislation mandating policy evaluation, and regularly published policy reports—and explain how each contributes to a state's ability to draw convincing information from data they have collected.

Research Organizations

An array of organizations that prioritize policy evaluation enhances a state's analytical capacity. Organizations formalize processes and can make them more efficient (Gibbons 1998). While ad hoc research teams and task forces can—and no doubt have—generated impactful analyses of policy outcomes, relying on this approach can reduce the reliability of the data analysis in two ways. First, identifying and convening relevant experts for analyzing data is costly, and in turn, there will be limited incentive for elected officials to do so regularly. In a world where every policy evaluation entails requests for funding, recruitment and training of experts and time to orient to a state's data systems, culture, and political system, we might expect only the most politically salient policies to get evaluated. The most politically salient policies, however, are not always the ones that are most likely to fail.

Second, when the investment in the analytical capacity is reactive, the results of the research—regardless of how credibly it was conducted—can much more easily be dismissed as politically motivated. To consider this phenomenon from the other direction, established organizations staffed with career researchers are much more likely to be insulated both from the political shifts within a state and from accusations of political motivations, as their work can be more credibly portrayed as ongoing regardless of the perspectives of those in office. Researchers trained in the nuances and latest methods of their respective fields are also likely to have incentives to conduct analyses in line with these norms to maintain respect and authority within their field, which again provides some credible motivation for fair analyses regardless of the public or elite opinion *du jour*.

The status of these organizations as independent evaluation and research agencies is an important aspect of constraining the ability of public officials to reframe a policy's failures. These research organizations are not directly involved in implementing any specific policy; instead their goal is to analyze data and identify the most accurate measure of policy outcomes. Thus, they should experience fewer incentives or political pressure, at least compared with the agency tasked with policy implementation, to produce positive or negative evaluations or to shirk or sabotage their analytical responsibilities.

State-sponsored Research Agencies

Sunshine laws make an array of government-collected datasets available to the public. Advances in computational science—such as web scraping and text analysis—have further increased the ability of interested parties to gather and analyze data relevant to evaluating policies. Thus, I expect to find that state-sponsored research agencies are *not* necessary for a state to have analytical capacity. However, it can be expected that, on average, their state involvement—whether that be through cooperation or direct ownership of research agencies—will facilitate the analysis of policy outcomes, at least compared to reliance on nonstate-sponsored research agencies.

While organizations, not-for-profits, or ad hoc working groups can theoretically collect longitudinal data that relies on clear and consistent definitions and measurements and can hire professional researchers to analyze it, these data best practices are more likely to produce reliable data when developed and managed by a permanent agency whose mission—or at least partial mission—is to evaluate policy outcomes. A state agency dedicated to research is more likely to be involved in the collection *and* analysis of data, which should result in more coherent and consistent data analysis. Furthermore, these research organizations can pressure[1] individual agencies to release data that they may not be eager to share publicly. These organizations may serve specific branches of government or the state more broadly. Unlike universities, which house professional researchers who might also conduct policy evaluations, state-sponsored research bureaucracies increase a state's analytical capacity specifically because their very existence depends on their evaluation of policy outcomes, while researchers from universities or, especially, think-tanks, can pick and choose when to evaluate local policy outcomes.

[1] This may involve direct efforts to enforce legislative oversight or explicit requests from the governor or merely the threat of legislative or gubernatorial involvement.

Researchers in state bureaucracy are likely to have much more time to design, implement, and communicate their research compared with their university-based counterparts. Career bureaucrats care deeply about their reputation and authority (Carpenter 2001, 2014). Career researchers within the state bureaucracy not only have the incentives of their training and professional reputation among scholars to uphold; they also may feel the pressures of protecting their autonomy and reputation within their government job. Practically, career researchers in state bureaucracies generally focus on research as their full-time job, without the opportunity (or obligation, depending on your perspective) to teach. Bureacrats' access to legislators can also facilitate increased policy innovation (Amenta et al. 1987; Bornstein 2012). Others have shown that policymakers tend to rely on their networks to learn during times of uncertainty and crisis (Wichowsky and Moynihan 2008).

Universities as Sources of Analytical Capacity

State-sponsored research agencies can be a source of influence over policymaking given their ties to elected officials through the legislative oversight process and their service at the discretion of the executive. However, they are far from the only place this analytical capacity can exist. Universities are traditionally the site of much of the systematic research conducted by trained scholars. Universities are also major players in a state's political economy—they are recipients of state aid (Bound et al. 2019), targets of state policies (Lowry 2007), and participants in state politics (Lowry 2007). Universities recruit experts in research, and, through their tenure and promotion system, they incentivize scholars to seek new data sources to generate a healthy stream of publications. Many higher education institutions—particularly those that are part of a state system—have explicit missions or mandates to benefit their home state. Certainly, as many social scientists can attest, the ease of access to data that comes with geographical proximity can focus scholars' attention on their own state as an important source of data and study. Some states, Idaho, for instance, even have a formal relationship with research groups in their state universities to conduct public policy research (Idaho Policy Institute 2023). The formal and informal incentives among scholars in higher education institutions to study local policy outcomes adds to a state's resources and potential for analyzing data. Thus, institutes of higher education—especially those that have policy schools or established public policy research groups—will likely enhance a state's analytical capacity.

While universities enhance a state's analytical capacity, they likely do not improve it as much as state-sponsored research agencies might. Scholars have several professional roles—including teaching and administrating—which takes time away from research. Furthermore, in general, scholars working in higher education have the flexibility to choose the projects and research questions on which to focus their limited resources, and they may not always be interested or motivated to study the same policy outcomes consistently—particularly if the policy in question is not in vogue in their respective disciplines or if the scholar doesn't expect to find something novel that would be likely to get published.[2] Relying on universities, then, will provide less consistency in the breadth and frequency of policy evaluations.

Finally, in an era of politicized science, the ideological reputations of institutes of higher education might also complicate how convincing elected officials (and the public) find the research that professors produce.[3] Certainly, the right has increasingly attacked higher education for being too liberal (Pinsker 2019), though there are also institutions with conservative reputations (e.g., George Mason University, University of Notre Dame, and Brigham Young University) that liberals may look upon skeptically. While many elected officials might also be skeptical of state agencies, the principal–agent relationship and oversight between bureaucracies and the state legislature is much clearer and could reasonably inspire elected officials to feel more trust toward career researchers in the bureaucracy versus academia. The ability to focus on and access state data can make these officials, on average, more impactful. In sum, universities can supplement analytical capacity, though not always as effectively as institutionalized efforts with the state can do.

Legislation Mandating Policy Evaluation

As formal institutions, agencies and universities represent long-term investments in the capacity to analyze policy outcomes, but the circumstances in which their capacity is leveraged can vary. We should expect this variation

[2] See Franco et al. (2014) on the effects of publication bias.
[3] See Smith et al. (2010) for evidence that suggests universities are not, in fact, politicized.

to be more likely when there are explicit mandates for evaluating policy. States that establish expectations for a regular cadence of policy evaluation demonstrate a higher capacity for data analysis because this sets a mandate for building institutional capacity to analyze data. Furthermore, a preestablished schedule for policy analysis lends the findings an air of credibility, as it was the original legislature to pass the policy that required an examination of of its effects, undermining the ability of public officials to assert that the findings of a policy evaluation are the result of a partisan agenda.

Mandates also increase a state's internal capacity for evaluation, which is valuable for incentivizing studies on policy outcomes among researchers within the state. Analysis conducted by state organizations on data collected from the state itself may be more compelling than information collected from elsewhere for motivating elected officials to recognize and address policy failure. The literature on policy diffusion shows that state-elected officials do look to states that are ideologically and geographically proximate or to similar states to adopt policies (Butler et al. 2017). However, when it comes to taking the political risk of acknowledging failure, elected officials will likely be more hesitant to act based on information gathered in a different jurisdiction. Just because a policy failed in New Hampshire doesn't mean it can't work in Vermont. States have different political economies, histories, cultures, and institutions (Elazar 1972; Patterson 1968), and these differences in turn influence contemporary policymaking (Miller 1991; Morgan & Watson 1991). Evidence based on data collected and analyzed in other states can be easily—and sometimes even rightfully—dismissed as not representative of how a policy is functioning in a different state. Thus, having mandates within a state for policy evaluation increases the likelihood of internal policy evaluations, which we should expect to be more compelling than external ones.

Regularly Published Reports

Once conducted, analyses can easily be put in a drawer, hidden from media, elected officials, and activists. Research informs practice insofar as the right people know about its findings and these same people trust that the findings are accurate (see Greenberg & Robbins 1985 for a discussion of the importance of communication as part of the policy evaluation process).

A clearly established regular cadence of reporting on the findings of policy evaluation thus represents another important marker of analytical capacity for a given state policy. The regular publication of reports establishes an expectation for research dissemination and can create a culture in which it is acceptable to regularly revise one's position based on the most up-to-date findings. Furthermore, a research organization with a regular publication schedule, report format, and dissemination plan likely inspires more confidence in their findings compared with an organization that sporadically releases its findings. Callen et al. (2017), in their study of policymaker decision making, find that the quality of policy reports can influence how policymakers interpret information. Specifically, the authors argue that accurately analyzed reports can constrain policymakers' ability to interpret and process evidence and can encourage them to update their policy preferences. Zelizer (2018) finds similar effects, suggesting that processed policy information can help legislators take new positions by reducing uncertainty, particularly if the source of the analysis is a trusted entity. He goes on to argue that the most trusted experts are those with "heterogenous ideologies and partisan affiliations," suggesting that state bureaucracies, with career bureaucrats should generate more trusted reports than self-declared "nonpartisan" think-tanks (Zelizer 2018, 596). Regular publication of high-quality reports also changes the information available to policy entrepreneurs, who may be looking for opportunities to frame new policies as the solutions to existing problems (Boswell 2009; Jones & Baumgartner 2005; Kingdon 1984; Mintrom & Vergari 1998).

The Role of Analytical Capacity in Negative Policy Feedback Cycles

Chapter 4 established the importance of the data collection. Without it, credible analysis is impossible (see the lower path in Figure 5.1). Having defined analytical capacity and described potential sources, I now return to the stylized depiction of the negative policy feedback cycles that can generate the recognition and revision of failed policies. Collecting data does not automatically mean it will be analyzed, nor does it mean that the subsequent findings will be disseminated. There is yet another fork in the road on the path from policy failure to the recognition and revision of the failure: whether the data is credibly analyzed. If, as Figure 5.1 shows, no credible analysis occurs, then

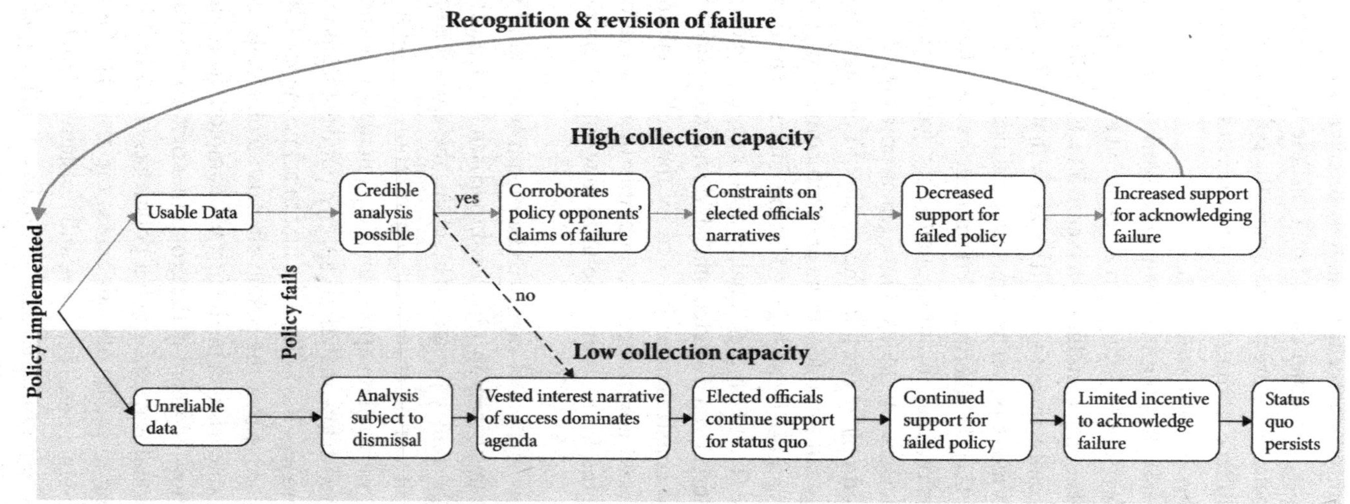

Figure 5.1 Analytical Capacity and Negative Policy Feedback Cycles

the policy trajectory of a failed policy merges with that of low-collection capacity states. Without compelling analysis to catch the attention of the legislators, governors, and other elected officials, the narratives from those benefiting from a policy's failure can dominate the political agenda. In turn, elected officials will face minimal pressure to reassess or revise the status quo, and the failed policy will continue.

It is worth emphasizing the mechanism at work here: the constraints elected officials face in constructing narratives about a failing policy (shown in the shaded boxes in both conditions in Figure 5.1). Elected officials should be responsive to electoral incentives, and we know that well-resourced organizations have enormous power in American politics (Hacker et al. 2021; Kelly & Morgan 2022). Furthermore, constituencies are often more motivated by loss aversion than by the potential for gain (Arceneaux 2012; Druckman and McDermott 2008). Thus, when powerful vested interests benefit from a failed policy, elected officials should not have much incentive to acknowledge failure unless there are both compelling evidence *and* mobilization among those being harmed by the failures. The dissemination of credible analysis (based on high-quality data) can draw elected officials' attention to the failure. Even if elected officials do not take notice of the analysis independently, constituencies harmed by the policy failures or news media looking to hold government accountable then have a new opportunity to advertise the findings and mobilize new supporters of reform in response.

In states with low analytical capacity, the organizations and individuals performing the analysis may inspire less bipartisan trust, as they are not a regular part of the policy debates. Therefore, the entrance of any given think-tank, university, or other research organization may be seen as being more issue-driven, rather than approximating a neutral reporter of results. Therefore, in states with low analytical capacity, public officials with an ideological opposition to a policy will be the first to acknowledge failure. In this scenario, it makes sense that the public officials ideologically aligned with the findings of the analysis will be the first to champion the results. We *may* see bipartisan acknowledgment *if* the group that first acknowledges failure can identify additional ways in which a policy has failed that is more ideologically appealing to public officials across the aisle. Depending on the partisan breakdown in a state's executive and legislative branches, this coalition building may be required to reform a policy. When a policy contains some sort of sunset provision, low analytical capacity states may be able to achieve reform through sunset provisions by *not* acting and by preventing the minority from acting.

In what follows, I present evidence from the six state policy trajectories to show the role analytical capacity plays in generating the clear and consistent findings that can catalyze negative policy feedback cycles. I show that analytical capacity is necessary for converting data into meaningful and interpretable findings to catch policymakers' attention. Furthermore, on its own, analytical capacity is not sufficient to instigate reconsideration of failed policies. I leverage within-state comparisons in Washington to show that analytical capacity alone is not sufficient to generate the conditions for acknowledging policy failure. A comparison of Texas tax credit and truancy policies shows that nonstate actors can supplement analytical capacity when state bureaucracies are not fully equipped or willing to do so themselves. However, they too are limited by the availability of data. The Kansas and Wyoming cases, which exhibit low analytical capacity, show how ad hoc evaluation efforts called for by those ideologically opposed to the policies undermine the credibility of policy evaluation attempts.

Analytical Capacity Relies on Data Duality: the Washington Cases

States vary in how many of their agencies they have dedicated to conducting research relevant to their state affairs. Figure 5.2 shows the percentage of each state's total agencies, as of 2017, that reference policy research or analysis as at least one of their main goals. While agency-level mission statements certainly undercount the resources that states spend on these efforts—and do not account for the budget and personal investments across the different agencies, this does suggest that states have differing approaches to enshrining research processes in their state agencies. Organizations that encourage evidence-based policymaking also emphasize the presence of established research-oriented agencies as a sign of commitment to evidence-based policymaking (Davies et al. 2017; Lester 2018). This approach assumes that states with more agencies explicitly advertised as conducting policy research both reflect and encourage ongoing investment in data-driven policymaking.

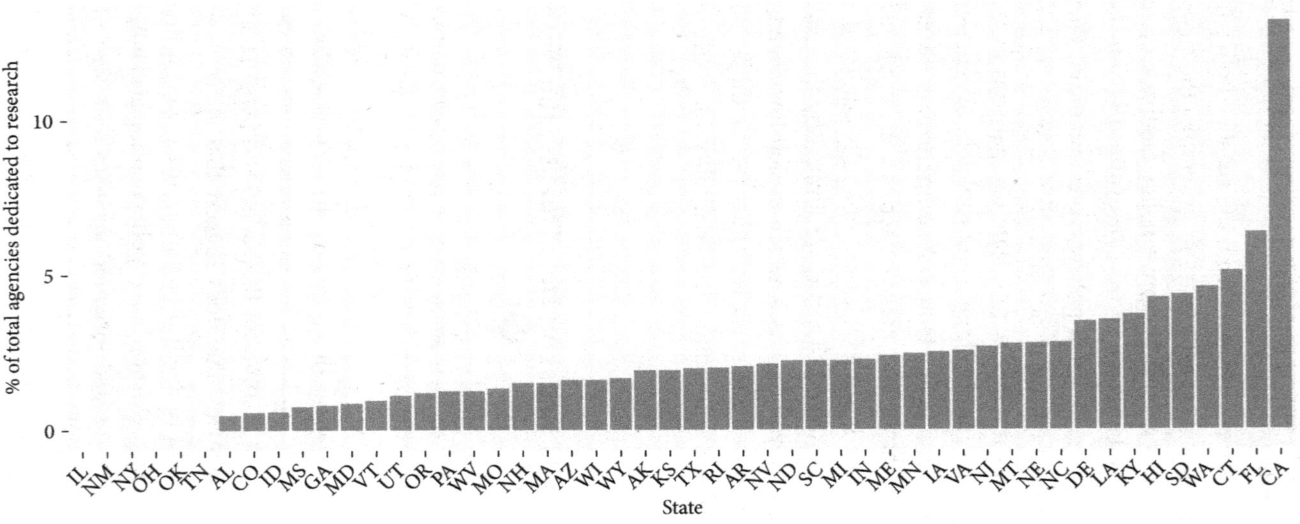

Figure 5.2 State agencies focused on policy analysis

Sources: Author's calculations based on keyword searches on state agency directories.

Table 5.1 Washington State research agencies

Research Agency	Year Founded
Office of the Washington State Auditor	1889
Joint Legislative Audit and Review Committee	1951
Washington Tree Fruit Research Commission	1969
Social and Health Services: Research and Data Analysis Division	1970[a]
Red Raspberry Commission	1976
Washington State Institute for Public Policy	1983
Washington State Transportation Center	1983
Washington State Center for Court Research	2004
Education Research and Data Center	2007

[a]Their first publicly available report is from 1970, suggesting it had to be up and running, by the latest, in 1970.
Source: Author's compilation from searches for agencies with titles or mission statements including the terms research, statistics, and data. Searches were conducted on the Washington State Agency Directory, which can be accessed at https://access.wa.gov/agency.html.

Overall, Washington State has the most robust analytical capacity of the four states in this study. Each branch of government[4] has at least one, if not multiple, research agencies charged with evaluating policy and generating data and analyses for their respective clients to better understand public policy challenges at hand (see Table 5.1). The mere existence of permanent state agencies demonstrates a far higher base level of analytical capacity than Texas, Kansas, or Wyoming possessed.

These organizations are also carefully constructed and overseen to maintain, if not outright bipartisanship, at least the appearance of it, and they are empowered by the legislature to evaluate policies and possible policy changes considered in each branch of government. The statement of audit authority from the Joint Legislative Audit and Review Committee (JLARC) offers a representative example of the statement of purpose these state bureaucracies tend to have:

> The Joint Legislative Audit and Review Committee (JLARC) works to make state government operations more efficient and effective. The Committee is comprised of an equal number of House members and

[4] This includes the judiciary, which established the Washington State Center for Court Research in 2004 as the research arm of the Administrative Office of the Courts (Washington State Center for Court Research n.d.).

> Senators, Democrats and Republicans. JLARC's non-partisan staff auditors, under the direction of the Legislative Auditor, conduct performance audits, program evaluations, sunset reviews, and other analyses assigned by the Legislature and the Committee. . . . Those standards require auditors to plan and perform audits to *obtain sufficient, appropriate evidence to provide a reasonable basis for findings and conclusions based on the audit objectives.* The evidence obtained for this JLARC report provides a reasonable basis for the enclosed findings and conclusions, and any *exceptions to the application of audit standards have been explicitly disclosed in the body of this report.*
>
> ("2007 Full Tax Preference Performance Reviews" 2007, emphasis added)

While these organizations exist, their efforts can be stymied by the lack of usable data and politically powerful individuals who may be invested in achieving certain findings or outcomes. The comparison of tax and truancy policies in Washington State shows the power of state agencies and their reliance on effective data collection to bolster narratives of failure and incentivize elected officials to acknowledge policy failure.

R&D Tax Incentives: The Power of High Collection and Analytical Capacity

In the case of Washington State's Research and Development (R&D) tax incentives, the fabric of overlapping agencies reporting on policy outcomes paired with varying credibility of the findings suggest the importance of high analytical capacity for documenting and advertising policy failure. Three agencies analyzed the impact of the R&D tax credit: the Joint Legislative Audit and Research Committee (JLARC), the Washington Institute for Public Policy (WSIPP), and the Washington State Department of Revenue. The analysis of tax credits in Washington leaned most heavily on JLARC and the Department of Revenue.

As early as 1997, the Department of Revenue acknowledged the limitations of their analysis, given the data that recipient companies were required to submit to the state. The 2000 Department of Revenue report on the R&D tax credits offers a typical example of how the Department explicitly names the challenges they faced in conducting meaningful analysis:

> In conclusion, a major difficulty in analysis of these programs is that the information that is the basis of the analysis is not always provided by the firm and is not readily available from other sources. The taxpayer is required to report proprietary information in some circumstances, but may exclude proprietary information in other circumstances.
>
> (Tax Incentives for Investment in Research and Development: Sales Tax Exemption & B&O Tax Credit 2000, Ch. 4, p. 5)

The 2000 report goes on to recommend conducting a survey to collect more useful information, and it argues that matching data with information from other agencies might be "necessary for analysis of these programs" (Tax Incentives for Investment in Research and Development: Sales Tax Exemption & B&O Tax Credit 2000, Ch. 4, p. 5).

Even when the Department of Revenue's reports do include statistics about the programs, they are grounded in the self-reported information provided by the companies benefiting from the R&D tax credit without additional corroboration from other sources, and they are rarely contextualized. For example, the main finding reported for the 2003 study states that the main purpose of the programs is to generate job creation, company growth, and geographic diversification. Yet the analysis presented only provides raw counts of the number of firms and approved projects, with no contextualization for whether this indicates the program is meeting its goals:

> To date, 1,311 firms have utilized the B&O tax credit resulting in tax savings of $204 million. There have been 393 approved projects eligible for the sales tax deferral/exemption program and the total tax exempted amounts to $324 million.
>
> (Rice 2003, 1)

The report concludes that the study provides "evidence that high tech firms are increasing their investments in R&D in response to Washington's tax incentive programs," despite any over time comparison or assessment of the role of the incentives in change over time (Rice 2003, 1).

This basic reporting style stands in stark contrast to the information that JLARC and WSIPP provide on their research methodologies and relevant counterfactuals. When reporting on the number of new jobs, JLARC carefully caveats their conclusions:

> Beneficiaries of the high technology R&D incentives have invested an estimated $2.9 billion in facilities and equipment and spent $93.8 billion on R&D operating expenses over the lifetime of the tax preferences (from 1995 through 2010). It is not clear how much of this R&D spending may have occurred because of the tax credit. (2012 Tax Preference Performance Reviews 2013, 104)

The JLARC report also argues that a mere 454 new jobs (~0.5% of overall job growth) would not have occurred without the tax credit, and it recommends that the legislature "clarify this tax preference to determine toward its high technology R&D objectives is sufficient. . ." (2012 Tax Preference Performance Reviews 2013, 108).

Not only does JLARC report different outcomes than does the Department of Revenue, but it also questions the Department of Revenue's more optimistic findings. In describing what evidence exists showing how the tax credit contributes to achieving public policy objectives, JLARC notes that

> there are problems with DOR's collecting and reporting of information on the annual survey. . . . It is not clear how much the tax incentive has been claimed and how many new jobs have been added. It is also not clear from the survey whether an increase in jobs and how much of an increase in R&D spending has occurred as a result of the tax preferences.
>
> (2012 Tax Preference Performance Reviews 2013, 103)

The Department of Revenue relied on surveys and self-reporting from the companies benefiting from the tax credit, while JLARC and WSIPP depended on additional data sources to examine the veracity of companies' self-reporting. This divergence in findings is not particularly surprising when we consider the incentives and expertise of each organization. The Department of Revenue's expertise is in implementing economic policy, and therefore they have an incentive to portray their efforts as effective. JLARC and WSIPP's main purpose on the other hand is to accurately evaluate policy outcomes, and their reputation relies on the accuracy of their findings rather than on the success of any given policy.

The sequencing of each agency's reports suggests that the state's evaluation of the policy's impact mattered for elected officials' support. The directness and honesty with which JLARC reports results offer clear signposts for public officials to understand the meaning of the data that the organization analyzed, compared with the Department of Revenue's reports, which leave interpretation open to the reader's baseline assumptions. The original R&D tax credit was set to expire after ten years, in 2004; however, the legislature renewed the policy for an additional ten years, through 2014. Notably, prior to this first renewal vote—which suggests legislative confidence in the policy's outcomes or at least a calculation that the political costs did not outweigh the benefits of supporting its continuation—the Department of Revenue published four of the five reports on the policy's outcomes. WSIPP had published a report with unclear findings about the policy's outcomes in 2004, but it summarized the weak findings in the broader economic literature on the positive outcomes of tax credits more generally. The report made the following conclusion:

> Despite these technical improvements, the relationship between state taxes and economic activity remains unclear. A substantial number of studies find a statistically significant and negative impact of state taxes on employment or other statewide measures of economic activity.
>
> (Lerch 2004, 8)

Between 2004 and 2015, when the policy failed to garner sufficient votes for a second renewal, JLARC published two additional reports that confirmed the, at best mixed, at worst, negative, findings about the R&D tax credits (see Table 5.2). The combination of extensive, high-quality data and high analytical capacity—which stemmed from multiple agencies conducting evaluations using different datasets and statistical techniques—resulted in clearer findings that created a politically tenable environment for public officials to acknowledge the policy's failure, despite continued support for the policy from some local businesses and other powerbrokers.

The original R&D legislation required the Department of Revenue to examine the program's effect on "job creation, company growth, the introduction of new products, the diversification of the state's economy, growth in research and development investment, the movement of firms or the consolidation of firms' operations into the state, and such other factors as the department selections" by January 1, 1996 (Engrossed Second Substitute Senate Bill 6347 1994, Sec. 10). Over a decade later, after the tax credit's first and only renewal, HB 1069 established the Citizen Commission for Performance Measurement of Tax Preferences and directed it to create a

Table 5.2 Washington research agency reports on R&D tax credits

Year	Agency	Evaluation
1997	Department. of Revenue	+[a]
2000	Department of Revenue	+
2003	Department of Revenue	+
2004	Washington State Institute for Public Policy	-
2004	Legislature *renews* policy through 2015	
2009	Department. of Revenue	-
2012	Judicial Legislative Audit and Research Committee	Mixed
2013	Department of Revenue	+
2013	Judicial Legislative Audit and Research Committee	-
2014	Legislature *fails to renew* policy past 2015	

[a]Of the six metrics, the Department of Revenue reports positive findings for two categories and positive trends for the four remaining ones, while also acknowledging that the limited time of implementation for the policy significantly limits their ability to evaluate its impacts in these categories (Kiga 1997).
Source : Author's summary of reports from state agencies.

regular schedule for evaluating tax preferences, with JLARC being responsible for conducting the reviews (2007 Full Tax Preference Performance Reviews 2007, 97). Following up on the clear direction provided in the 1994 legislation, HB 1069 provides a clear set of ten questions to be answered for every audit. In their 2012 report, JLARC also included taxpayer savings per job, finding that the tax credit claimed for each job was ~$45,000 but the direct and indirect earnings for each new job was around $25,000, suggesting the policy is not in fact paying for itself (2012 Tax Preference Performance Reviews 2013, 104). These more sophisticated reports also consistently offered fewer positive evaluations of the program. Perhaps the best evidence of the high analytical capacity in the R&D tax credit case is the fact that JLARC researchers innovated on measures for the policy's success, in addition to tracking and reporting on the measures outlined in the original legislation.

JLARC also commented on ways that changes in data collection could improve the analyses it conducts. In 2012, JLARC published a review of the policy and recommended that the legislature "review and clarify: to determine if progress towards its high technology R&D objectives is sufficient and to consider identifying targets for investment and employment" (2012 Tax Preference Performance Reviews 2013, 97). The following year, in 2013, the Senate established new requirements to improve the clarity of tax preferences and performance expectations for any credits created in the future. In particular, it required that all future tax preference bills include a specific statement of the "legislative purpose" of the new tax, and then it outlines the possible purposes the legislature could choose from (Engrossed Substitute Senate Bill 5882, 2013).

In 2014, after four reports appeared outlining the failure of the policy from its own state agencies, the Washington legislature allowed the R&D tax credits to expire. This analytical capacity exists in Washington State, but, as the next case shows, research agencies rely on the availability of usable data to influence the policy agenda.

Washington's Becca Bill: Analytical Capacity Produces Hollow Findings Without Reliable Data

A comparison between the policy trajectory of Becca's Bill and the R&D tax incentives in Washington State demonstrates the critical importance of the data collection capacity for drawing attention to policy failure. In Washington State, four organizations were tasked with examining the effects of Becca's Bill: the Washington State Institute for Public Policy (WSIPP), the Administrative Office of the Courts (AOC), the Washington State Center for Court Research (WSCCR), and the Washington School Information Processing Cooperative (WSIPC) (George 2011). In turn, these agencies relied on data from the Superior Court Management Information System (SCOMIS) and the Juvenile Court Information System (JUVIS), along with the Office of the Administrator for the Courts (OAC) and the Office of Superintendent Public Instruction.

Regardless of their expertise, training, or experience, researchers cannot draw firm conclusions from inconsistent or incomparable data. As described in the last chapter, the decentralized data collection procedures established for Becca's Bill yielded incomparable and unusable data. Thus, even though the legislature tasked WSIPP with evaluating and reporting the success of Becca's Bill every two years, the robust analytical capacity did not produce clear findings on the impact of detaining truant students.

The first two reports suggested that the policy was potentially helping truancy, but these reports were followed by several others that stated the researchers could not draw meaningful conclusions from their findings (see Table 5.3). Despite robust state investments in analytical capacity, researchers were unable to generate usable findings based on the limited data. With a range of contradictory findings to choose from, public officials could cherry-pick findings that supported their perspective on the policy. This in turn resulted in limited acknowledgment of the policy's failure.

While assigning responsibility and establishing a schedule for policy evaluation signals high analytical capacity, the findings are impotent without

Table 5.3 Reports on Becca's Bill from Washington State bureaucracies with findings, 1996–2017

Date	Agency	Title	Findings
Jan 1996	WSIPP	Truancy: Preliminary Findings on Washington's 1995 Law	Mixed
Jan 1998	WSIPP	Truant Students: Evaluating the Impact of the	Mixed
Sept. 2000	WSIPP	Assessing the Impact of Washington's Truancy Petition Process	+
Oct. 2002	WSIPP	Keeping Kids in School: The Impact of The Truancy Provisions in Washington's 1995 "Becca Bill"	+
May 2004	WSCCR	Truancy Case Processing Practices	-
Jun 2009	WSIPP	What Works? Targeted Truancy and Dropout Programs in Middle and High School	Descriptive
Jun 2009	WSIPP	Truancy and Dropout Programs: Interventions by Washington's School Districts and Community Collaborations	Descriptive
Oct 2009	WSIPP	Washington's Truancy Laws in the Juvenile Courts: Wide Variation in Implementation and Costs	Descriptive
Feb 2010	WSIPP	Washington's Truancy Laws: Does the Petition Process Influence School and Crime Outcomes	No conclusion
2011	WSCCR	Truancy in Washington State: Trends, Student Characteristics, and the Impact of Receiving a Truancy Petition	-
Sept 2015	WSCCR	Truancy in Washington State: Filing Trends, Juvenile Court Responses, and the Educational Outcomes of Petitioned Truant Youth	-

Key: + outcomes in line with policy intent;—outcomes not in line with policy intent
Source : Author's summary based on state reports.

effective data collection to support valid findings. Forced to produce reports in accordance with the timeline established by the legislature, Washington research agencies studied what they could using the best available information, but this resulted in flip-flopping findings on the policy's impact (see Table 5.3). In several cases with Becca's Bill, WSIPP and JLARC acknowledged contradictory findings and flaws in prior statistical methods, and, eventually, revised their findings and recommendations. For example, in their 2002 report, WSIPP made the following observation:

> We found that the truancy provisions of the Becca Bill appear to result in a statistically significant increase in high school enrollment. Thus, the bill seems to be achieving one of its intended outcomes: helping to keep youth enrolled (this is the number of enrolled 15–17 year olds/total 15–17 year olds) in high school . . . [there is] indicative but not causal evidence that truancy petitions are associated with lower juvenile arrest rates.
>
> (Aos 2002, 20)

However, the 2010 WSIPP report backtracked and retracted their statement about the effects of the policy:

> Earlier Institute reports found that the increase in petitions following enactment of the Becca Bill appeared to increase high school enrollment in Washington. However, an update of that analysis, using a longer time period and an improved statistical method, no longer shows a statistically significant relationship between petition filling and enrollment.
>
> (M. Miller, Kilma, and Nunlist 2010)

Though accurately reflecting the best available findings on the policy's outcomes at the time of their publication, this back and forth provided evidence to both the policy's opponents and supporters. (The way each side employs the research to their benefit is presented in Part II.)

Consistent with the practices of the JLARC and WSIPP in the R&D tax credit case, WSIPP openly acknowledged the limits of its findings in its public reports. For example, the reports published based solely on case studies included a statement that inference beyond these localities was questionable, but that the study did establish a base for continuing to study the policy's impacts. Furthermore, the state agency's reports often explicitly admitted their inability to draw firm conclusions given the incomparable data collected by the courts. For example, the 2008 WSIPP report directly stated its inability to draw concrete conclusions about the impact of the policy in question:

> Overall, the state of knowledge about the effectiveness of truancy and dropout programs is lacking. Most programs are not evaluated and those that are evaluated generally use research designs and methodologies that do not permit us to draw conclusions about causality.
>
> (Kilma, Miller, and Nunlist 2009, 5)

Several reports explicitly identified the challenges with the data and inference that researchers faced when evaluating the policy. For example, a 2011 Washington State Center for Court Research (WSCCR) report outlined its empirical strategy and then delineated its findings:

> To evaluate the impact of receiving a truancy petition on youth outcomes, a sample of several thousand non-petitioned truants were matched with court- petitioned truants using a method called propensity score matching. The two groups were then examined across time with respect to attendance, grade point average, graduation, and juvenile crime. *This study did not find any evidence that court-petitioned truants fared differently than non-petitioned truants on any of the assessed variables.*
>
> (George 2011, 3, emphasis added)

The way in which JLARC researchers acknowledge the limitations of their findings further highlights the experience of the researchers working for the state. Unlike reports from Texas, Kansas, or Wyoming, Washington State reports often described, albeit in layperson terms, the statistical reasons behind their failure to reach a clear conclusion. This both reflects the sophistication of the analytical expertise available in Washington State and the impotence of this expertise without usable data. Rather than offer the politically popular interpretation of the findings or imply more certainty than actually exists, the Washington State agency reports examined for this project acknowledged the limits of statistical analysis, given available data (e.g., Webster 1996, 6).

In 2007, a task force examining Becca's Bill enlisted the financial support and analytical capacity of the MacArthur Foundation to better understand the impacts of juvenile justice policy in the state, including use of the valid court order exemption and detention for truant students. One core recommendation made by the MacArthur Foundation was that the state needed to invest in carefully defined and centrally managed data collection to take better advantage of the capacity of its research agencies. Given the paucity of usable data, the resources of the MacArthur grant went toward creating not one but *two* new databases—the Court Contact and Recidivism Database and the Educational Research Database—to facilitate research on truancy and other outcomes related to juvenile justice. Given that the researchers could not turn back time and collect new or better data, these databases relied on whatever state and local authorities had already collected. The final result accounted for just over half of Washington public school students between 2003 and 2004. This statistic stands in stark contrast to the near 100 percent coverage Texas was able to achieve with its longitudinal dataset (which will be discussed in greater detail below).

The final report using the data collected with MacArthur Foundation money did generally show that court-petitioned truant students fared worse on graduation and other life outcomes compared with their nonpetitioned peers. In addition to limited coverage in their dataset, the researchers had to rely on propensity score matching—a statistical technique that identifies similar observations and compares their outcomes of interest—among this subset of the population. While this technique is certainly a reasonable one, it is much more easily dismissed (and frankly, misunderstood) than a direct comparison of the universe of students and their outcomes.

The MacArthur Foundation's injection of resources and expertise in evaluating juvenile justice programs was certainly a major step forward for understanding the impact of Becca's Bill on Washington's youth. However, as a nonstate actor entering the policy discussion almost a decade after the policy's implementation, their support was limited to collecting new data going forward and reorganizing the limited data that was already available. The MacArthur Foundation could not successfully supplement analytical capacity because no effective data collection plans were in place to give them the information they needed for analysis. While their work did provide new insight into truancy trends, it was far from convincing to Becca's Bill's most ardent supporters.

In 2105, four years after the WSCCR report was published, Democratic Senator Jeannie Darnielle introduced legislation to eliminate detention as an option for juveniles, but it failed to advance in the legislature. Thus, while some slight amendments were made to Becca's Bill—most notably requiring counties to establish Community Truancy Boards to implement preventive measures in 2016—none removed the key policy failure of allowing detention for young people.

Although Becca's Bill benefited from established state-backed research organizations and trained researchers examining the policy's outcomes, the paucity of reliable data resulted in conflicting findings regarding the efficacy of the policy, with earlier reports advertising its success and later reports suggesting its failure. Efforts to generate support for its revision were limited and ultimately unsuccessful. This shows that high analytical capacity alone is not sufficient to create an environment in which public officials are likely to acknowledge policy failure. High analytical capacity must be paired with high collection capacity; otherwise, elected officials and vested interests can frame findings to meet their political needs.

Supplement Potential: Nonstate Actors and Available Data

Comparing the two cases within Washington highlighted the critical importance of the data collection capacity, even in the face of high analytical capacity. Although the MacArthur Foundation stepped in to help address collection and evaluation needs for Becca's Bill, researchers were limited by the original data collection plans that had been put into place. Juxtaposing the two cases in Washington with the two cases in Texas—Ch 313 tax credits and Failure to Attend School (FTAS)—reveals the conditions under which nonstate actors can successfully supplement the state analytical capacity conditional on the availability of data. Texas has lower state analytical capacity. Compared with the policies in Washington state, neither FTAS nor Ch 313 identified a specific agency responsible for conducting an evaluation of the policy's outcomes. However, both Texas cases have nonstate research organizations conducting analysis and advertising findings and policy preferences. In the case of FTAS, a combination of excellent data and partnerships between state organizations and reputable, nonpartisan research organizations lent their findings the credibility necessary to gain the attention of both liberal and conservative interests. For the case of Ch 313, limited data availability yielded contested evaluations. This, in turn, kept much of the policy debates focused on the quality of the data and the analysis rather than on the actual policy itself.

Texas Truancy: Data Availability and Nonstate Analytical Capacity

Nonstate actors researching the impacts of FTAS played a pivotal role in providing convincing analyses that eventually resulted in bipartisan support for decriminalizing truancy. With the gold standard of an observational dataset—a longitudinal study on the universe of Texas middle schoolers—a treasure trove of data existed, if only researchers could access it. Elected officials helped nonstate researchers access reliable state data. These research organizations then produced compelling analysis that caught the attention of both liberals *and* conservatives, albeit for different reasons. The increasing national awareness of the adverse financial and equity consequences of mass incarceration combined with clear data connecting FTAS to this trend likely connected the policy to national policy sentiment. Clear findings also demonstrated that the concerns about government spending (for conservatives) and equity (for liberals) in the national dialogue were also happening in Texas.

In Texas's case, the capacity for data analysis resided not with the state agencies but, in large part, with the higher education research system. According to interviews with the researchers who worked with politicians to get access to the data, the Texas Education Agency was both understaffed and ill-informed on how to leverage the treasure trove of data it collected (Interview with policy analyst at the Texas Public Policy Research Institute at Texas A&M 2017). Although there were no agencies explicitly charged with analyzing data, as there are in both Washington cases, there were a plethora of trained researchers in and around Texas.

Just because an agency has information on policy outcomes does not guarantee that it will want the information analyzed. The Texas Education Agency had implemented a longitudinal study of the educational experiences and life outcomes for the universe of Texas middle schoolers in 2000. However, the data was not easily accessible for analysis. According to several researchers at Texas Public Policy Research Institute (TPPRI)—the research organization at Texas A&M that first analyzed the Texas Education Agency data for *Breaking Schools' Rules*—getting access to the information from the agency was extremely challenging. According to one of the researchers involved in the *Breaking Schools' Rules* study, the Texas Education Agency was reluctant to share its data and make it difficult for researchers to be able to access the data. It therefore converted the data to a usable form that would comport with the information coming from the Juvenile Justice system. In fact, the legislature even set up the possibility of research hotspots where researchers could download data, but TEA made the requirements for both establishing a research hotspot and then later getting access to the data incredibly onerous.

The *Breaking Schools' Rules* report describes how a bipartisan team of four committee chairs, and leaders from the executive and judicial branches exerted political pressure required to get the data from the Texas Education Agency to the expert researchers for analysis:

> [R]epresentatives of the state's juvenile justice system, both from the executive and judicial branches of government, expressed strong support for the project at the outset. These legislative leaders, from both political parties, plus court officials and representatives of the executive branch informed the CSG Justice Center that they were interested in learning more about school discipline issues in Texas. The Justice Center partnered with the Public Policy Research Institute (TPPRI) of Texas A&M University (TAMU) to conduct this investigation.
>
> (Carmichael et al. 2011, 4–5)

Getting access to the data required strongarming by the governor and the Council on State Governments, the leader of which had some relationship with the state. In other words, state public officials partnered with a handful of nonstate actors, namely, the Council on State Governments and the Texas Public Policy Research Institute, to gain access to and analyze data on relevant policy outcomes.

These findings in turn, caught the attention of several public officials and additional policy organizations. Led by its Chief Justice, Wallace Jefferson, the Texas Supreme Court's policy arm took on FTAS and related criminalization policies as a key policy priority in 2013. According to leading policy experts in the Texas Judicial Council, it was the reliability and completeness of the research published by TPPRI (Interview with Policy Expert on the Texas Judicial Council 2017), Texas Appleseed, and other researchers in the Texas university system that caught their attention. The policy experts in the Texas Judicial Council also suggested that, while the research coming out of the think-tanks was compelling, the university-driven research was most helpful in that policymakers viewed it as more objective than information put out by more partisan think-tanks. Senator John Whitmire (D-Houston) and chair of the Criminal Justice Committee led the legislative effort to amend FTAS. According to his office, a combination of the data and anecdotes from constituents led to his intense support for decriminalizing status offenses generally and truancy in particular (Legislative assistant 2017). By 2013, there was bipartisan support for decriminalizing status offenses, including FTAS and reform passed in the subsequent legislative session.

Texas Ch 313: No Clear Data Collection and Limited Analytical Capacity

FTAS shows the latent potential created by robust data collection efforts and the power of nonstate actors to supplement the state's analytical capacity. Reliance on self-reported, nonaudited data and anemic analytical capacity for studying tax programs left Ch 313 vulnerable to the whims of Texas's politics-as-usual, unlike the dynamics that played out with FTAS. While nonstate actors convincingly supplemented the state's analytical capacity for evaluating Texas's truancy policy, the actors that stepped in to evaluate Ch 313 had clear partisan ties. The organizations conducting analysis in the Ch 313 case had established reputations for being pro- or anti-business in a state that is deeply attached to supporting economic growth through limited regulation and small government. The more blatant role of ideological missions of the organizations conducting analyses combined with inconsistent data collection yielded conflicting information that seemingly offered confirmation to both supporters and opponents of the policy.

There were some state-led attempts at evaluation, but they were conducted by agencies and organizations without expertise in or capacity for policy evaluation. The Texas State Auditors, the Comptroller, and the Legislative Budget Board conducted their own audits and evaluations of the program, but they did so using data that was self-reported by the businesses themselves. The Texas State Auditors and the Comptroller generally conducted case studies, which precluded any robust evaluation of the program's actual impacts. Yet, their findings tended to suggest that Ch 313 had produced the positive economic impacts intended by the legislature. In one report, the Comptroller estimated that "businesses that have already been granted Chapter 313 agreements will derive approximately $7.1 billion in tax savings through the lives of their existing agreements, even if the program were to end today and no new agreements were added" (Senate Committee on Natural Resources and Economic Development: Interim Report to the 85th Legislature 2016, 63).

In 2011, the Legislative Budget Board identified several concerns with Ch 313, however, stating that though the program was cost neutral for local government and districts, its cost to the state was potentially "limitless" (Legislative Budget Board Staff 2011, 1). The Board went on to explicitly identify the lack of accurate analysis of the program's impact by stating that existing reports constituted "a reporting of information, rather than an analysis of the economic impacts of the proposed projects" (Legislative Budget Board Staff 2011, 1). Further emphasizing the Comptroller's inability to evaluate the program, the Legislative Budget Board's report went on to recommend that the legislature amend the Texas Tax Code to explicitly require the Comptroller to evaluate the economic impact of proposed projects (Legislative Budget Board Staff 2011, 1). The Texas House Committee on Economic Incentives released a report on the program in 2015 that relied exclusively on hearings conducted in six cities across the state. The report refrained from making a clear statement on the effectiveness of the program and instead called for more transparency and evaluation (Interim Report to the 84th Legislature: House Select Committee on Economic Development Incentives 2015).

According to the original legislation, school districts are required to maintain an "inventory of all Ch 313 agreements, including states to which the benefitting companies considered moving to, but chose not to, along with their rationale for choosing Texas instead," along with an assessment of the "effectiveness of the incentives provided by Chapter 313, Tax Code," including descriptions of the projects and agreements (Brimer 2001, 481.0044). Section F then states that "the comptroller should assist the governing board and the department in complying with Subsection (e)." Three notable features of this evaluation plan explain the limited analysis available on the policy. First, unlike the case in Washington State, the legislation does not describe *how* or *how often* to evaluate the "effectiveness of the incentives," leaving this open to interpretation. Second, while the legislation does require an inventory of existing agreements, it places the school district's governing board in charge of collecting information and evaluating program effectiveness, with assistance from the Texas Comptroller. Evaluating policy effectiveness is incredibly difficult, and it is unlikely that a school governing board, particularly one with an interest in maintaining their Ch 313 agreements, will be equipped or motivated to rigorously analyze each agreement's effectiveness. Third, while Ch 313 recipients are required to submit annual reports describing job creation, benefits provided, or estimated value-added to the community, the legislation does not require school districts to independently verify any of this information (Keel 2014, 1). Thus, any analysis that may occur relies on a foundation of data susceptible to exaggeration and bias in favor of program effectiveness. In their 2011 examination of the program, the Legislative Budget Board explicitly identifies this conflict of interest as a concern about the current structure of the program (Legislative Budget Board Staff 2011, 1).

Unlike the situation with FTAS, nonstate actors did not credibly supplement state capacity. A handful of researchers at Texas universities, relying on more sophisticated statistical methods, tended to find that the program fails to produce the intended benefits. A 2006 article co-authored by a researcher from the University of Texas-El Paso and a member of the El Paso Metropolitan Planning Organization, uses time-series data to get causal leverage on the impacts of tax abatements in El Paso and finds no improvement in the economic performance of the surrounding communities. This finding echoed those from a similar 2002 study by one of the report's authors (Fullerton 2002). A 2016 master's thesis from a student at the University of Texas at Austin used propensity score matching to evaluate the impact of program participation and growth in property values. After explaining which types of districts are more likely to enter into Ch 313 agreements, she stated:

> Lastly, I find no evidence of a relationship between abatement participation and growth in industrial property values. Findings suggest that some features of the Ch. 313 program may exacerbate inequality and confer disproportionate share of benefits, such as payments-in-lieu of taxes and state aid subsidies, to property wealthy districts. Moreover, the state is currently investing billions of dollars into the program without evidence that these investments produce the intended industrial property investment in Texas communities.
>
> (Randall 2016, vi–vii)

Despite several attempts made since the inception of the program, including a bipartisan-sponsored attempt in 2011, to increase the reporting requirements, add staff to verify companies' reporting, and study the program's outcomes, the program expanded, rather than contracted. In 2017, Senator Konni Burton (R) even proposed ending the program entirely, but the bill failed to leave the House Ways and Means Committee. The narrative that Texas cannot compete without these tax abatements ruled the day.

The nonstate organizations that released evaluations had less cross-partisan credibility, *and* they produced contradictory findings. While evaluation and reporting responsibilities remained opaque among state actors, nonstate actors took it upon themselves to analyze the program's outcomes, usually producing findings that were in line with the organization's ideological leanings. That most of the existing data on the effectiveness of the program comes from the program recipients themselves further exacerbates accusations of biased and ideologically driven findings.

Supporters of the program (generally conservative, free-market-leaning organizations) found that the program works, and they point to the data from the state to support their arguments, while opponents of tax credits were left to find ways to gather more plausibly objective data. For example, the conservative Texas Taxpayers and Research Association (TTARA) argued that Ch 313 created jobs and saved $134 million in school spending during the 2015 school year alone, and Dale Craymer, the president of TTARA, argued extensively that Texas cannot compete with other states without these tax incentives (Copelin 2012).

Liberal-leaning organizations also tended to label the program a failure. Local media reports, particularly from the liberal-leaning *Texas Observer*, the *San Antonio Express News*, and the *Austin American-Statesman* regularly reported on the policy's failure. A 2012 *San Antonio Express News* article, which described the Comptroller's own admission that the program was often benefiting companies that were not producing the promised number of new jobs, called for the Legislature to deal with the problems with the program before allowing the program to be renewed (Texas' tax abatement program too broad 2012). A 2015 watchdog report, tellingly titled "Big Dollars, Little Oversight?" by the *Austin American-Statesman* echoed similar findings. The Center for Public Policy Priorities,[5] a policy-focused social

[5] The Center for Public Policy Priorities rebranded as Every Texan in May 2020.

justice organization, argued that the state gave away abatements to companies that would have located in Texas regardless of the tax breaks. Notably, Dick Levine, a senior fiscal analyst on the Center's Invest in Texas team, often discussed the fundamental problem of causal inference by arguing that its officials never know whether or not the company would have stayed without the tax incentives. He also maintained that the company's existing infrastructure in the state and its access to natural resources made it likely that most companies would remain in the state regardless of the tax incentives available (Copelin 2012).

Texas Ch 313 faced anemic analytical capacity, *and* it relied on irregular and inconsistent data collection strategies, yielding unconvincing reports that could be framed politically by supporters and opponents. However, a comparison between the Texas cases highlights the role that nonstate research organizations *can* play in setting the stage for public officials to acknowledge failure. In both FTAS and Ch 313, there were nonstate actors—mostly university researchers, university-based research organizations and think-tanks—eager to evaluate policy outcomes. But similar to Becca's Bill in Washington State, the paucity of reliable and objective data on Ch 313 both yielded conflicting reports about the policy's outcomes and offered critics and supporters alike a credible opportunity to claim that undesirable outcomes were the result of politically driven data mining rather than a reflection of reality.

Insufficiency of Nonlocal Studies

In Chapter 4, I showed that both Wyoming and Kansas lagged in their capacity to collect data on juvenile justice and tax incentives, respectively. Given that both states had anemic collection capacities—a necessary condition for acknowledgment of failure—we should not expect any acknowledgment. Below, I provide additional evidence that both states also lagged in their analytical capacity, and I provide evidence that this results in public officials debating the issues of collection and analysis, rather than the merits of the policy at hand and more effective alternatives. In particular, these cases highlight the value of locally collected and analyzed data. When the data and analysis are not local to the state in question, then it is easier for public officials to dismiss them as being the result of meddling outsiders rather than useful insight into potential policy changes.

Wyoming Juvenile Justice Act

Wyoming has an inconsistent and weak history of supporting analytical capacity. The main research organization that supports state government, the Wyoming Survey and Analysis Center (WYSAC), is part of the University of Wyoming system rather than the state bureaucracy. However, unlike Texas, the organization is the *only* major research center[6] in the state. WYSAC had come in and out of existence in several forms since 1984, suggesting that the state and the University of Wyoming may not be fully invested in its usefulness or in maintaining its existence. The first iteration of some independent state-sponsored research agency occurred in 1972, with the Government Research Bureau, which conducted biennial statewide election surveys. In 1989, the University of Wyoming established the Survey Research Center to continue administering the election survey. In the 1980s Wyoming had a "federally recognized clearinghouse for research in criminal justice" (About WYSAC 2019) as part of their Department of Criminal Investigation, but this unit ended in 1994. Six years later, the Governor created WYSAC at the University of Wyoming through Executive Order, in order to continue research into criminal justice. This sequence of events suggests that Wyoming had some minimal analytical capacity, but it was unreliable, inconsistent, and not fully institutionalized within the state bureaucracy.

Furthermore, unlike the research organizations in Washington and Texas, WYSAC did not initially serve all of Wyoming and it was not solely focused on statewide issues. The history of the organization describes fielding a nationwide survey and analyses for "states in the region" as an initial part of the organization's work. Furthermore, the organization acknowledges that it did not work in all twenty-seven Wyoming counties until 2007, seven years after its founding, again demonstrating that while it supported some work in the state, its resources were not being fully deployed for Wyoming's benefit (About WYSAC 2019).

In 2004, WYSAC collaborated with the National Center for Juvenile Justice to collect data for a case study of youth processing in four Wyoming

[6] Some of the departments have directors of research and analysis (e.g., see the Director's Unit for Policy, Research, and Evaluation in the Department of Health), but my research shows that they serve at the discretion and direction of the departmental director, rather than the policymakers themselves. There is also a Department of Research in the Wyoming Department of Transportation, but it appears to be the result of federal legislation rather than a state-level initiative.

counties. According to the eventual report, the researchers faced enormous challenges in tracking down data and reconciling variable definitions of truancy by county. The report also notes that the researchers had to individually check all cases of youth processing in two of the four counties because the available data appeared to be so unreliable (Freng et al. 2004).

Several national organizations attempted to supplement Wyoming's analytical capacity, but lack of usable data and skepticism among state elected officials about outsider judgments stymied the effectiveness of these attempts. For example, Wyoming was an early participant in the Anne E. Casey Foundation's Juvenile Detention Alternatives Initiative (JDAI), which explicitly aims to bolster a state's analytical capacity. The JDAI "provides training and technical assistance to JDAI sites in participating jurisdictions" (Juvenile Detention Alternatives Initiative 2019). JDAI also supplements a state's analytical capacity by publishing and distributing "a wide range of analyses and tools with information on detention reform, including: practice guides, "Pathways to Detention Reform" reports, issue briefs, start-up materials, and assessment tools" (Juvenile Detention Alternatives Initiative 2019). The ACLU had also been involved in examining the juvenile justice outcomes in the state. These organizations attempted to combine the anemic state data with indicators collected by national agencies but were unable to generate any meaningful findings about the impacts of the program.

These various efforts resulted in conflicting accounts of the extent of the problem and policy failure. In a 2011 Joint Judiciary Interim Committee meeting, three different sources presented different estimates of the number of youths who had experienced detention (Brown 2011). In response to these conflicting reports, the governor's juvenile justice policy advisor acknowledged that "I've known for sometime that we have a deficiency in collecting data. . . . We have something like 27 agencies (or counties) collecting data on juveniles, and we haven't been able to collate or integrate that all" (Brown 2011). Echoing the poor data collection for Becca's Bill in Washington, this statement points out both the futility of poor collection and the analytical capacity that Wyoming faced.

Elected officials were defensive in the face of these mismatched estimates of Wyoming's juvenile justice outcomes in national and local data. In an interview with the *Tribune Eagle* after learning of these different estimates, "Representative Kermit Brown (R-Laramie) who co-chairs the interim committee, added it is important to get the data from someone who is not pushing an agenda. 'It's troublesome, and I know we are going to have to (create the data system),' he said. 'But how much money do we have to spend to tell the ACLU that it is wrong?'" (Brown 2011).

Several of the other legislators on the committee also commented on the barriers posed by the state's low analytical capacity: they complained of "information overload because of all of the different data that various groups support" (Brown 2011). In particular, one representative went on to explicitly request "easy to understand information so that lawmakers can make an informed choice" (Brown 2011). Notably, Gary Hartman, the governor's juvenile justice policy advisor, suggested implementing uniform statewide reporting methods modeled after the Wyoming Criminal Justice Information System, which had been implemented for adults several years earlier (Brown 2011).

As a small state with limited resources for professionalizing its state government, it is perhaps unsurprising that Wyoming did not have several state organizations focused on policy research. Even when outside organizations came in, they were hamstrung by limited and poorly collected data. This problem, combined with nonlocal origins of reports on its juvenile justice practices, kept it off the political agenda. When Wyoming did attempt to evaluate its juvenile detention program, researchers faced insurmountable challenges from poorly collected data. Juvenile detention in turn remained off the political agenda.

Kansas: Local Analysis Diminishes Credibility

With erratic data collection and no institutionalized research organizations or consistent evaluations of the Promoting Employment Across Kansas (PEAK) program, Kansas's elected officials could easily dismiss evidence of PEAK's failings. The original PEAK legislation did require reporting on the PEAK program, but the reporting was focused on compliance, not the outcomes of the policy. Furthermore, the evaluation efforts were housed within the agencies implementing the policy, and so there was a possible conflict of interest in the outcomes.

The Kansas Legislature's audit team—the Legislative Post Audit Committee (LPA)—is tasked with "conducting research on the efficacy and efficiency of agencies and programs." The LPA was founded in 1971 and takes on projects at the direction of a bipartisan Legislative Post Audit Committee. Importantly, the PEAK legislation explicitly mandates reporting to monitor compliance with the program's expectations and puts the secretary of the Department of Commerce in charge of both approving PEAK deals and evaluating their success and adherence to legislative guidelines. Section 3, part C states the following:

> The agreement [between the benefiting company and the secretary of the Department of Commerce] shall commit the secretary to certify to the secretary of revenue: (1) That the qualified company is eligible to receive benefits under this act; (2) the number of new employees hired by the qualified company; and (3) the amount of gross wages being paid to each new employee.
>
> (Promoting Employment Across Kansas Act 2008)

The legislation goes on to state that a company not meeting the state requirements will lose its PEAK benefits. Sections 5 and 6 of the legislation state that the Secretary of Revenue should develop "rules and regulations necessary to implement and administer" the act, including "conduct[ing] an annual review of the activities undertaken by a qualified company" to ensure that companies comply with the act's provisions.

In addition to putting the secretary of the Department of Commerce in charge of the agreements and monitoring compliance, the PEAK legislation lays out a series of reporting requirements that the secretary of the Department of Commerce must comply with, but all the reports focus on company compliance, rather than assessing the actual outcomes of the policies. For example, (as shown in Figure 5.3), Section 7 of the legislation states that the secretary of the Department of Commerce must provide a report to various committees in the legislature detailing various components of each PEAK deal. Notably, unlike the situation in Washington State, the legislation does not require any analysis of the *effectiveness* of the program.

To evaluate the program's effectiveness, the LPA Committee had to vote an evaluation into effect. They did so in 2009, and the first audit occurred in 2013 and 2014, four years after the program began. Notably, during these four years, the legislature *expanded* the program, broadening the types of businesses that could qualify (Department of Commerce: Evaluating the Department's Compliance with Statutory Caps for the PEAK Program 2017).

The first 2013 LPA report found major gaps in the data the state had been collecting. Thus, while Kansas had slightly stronger analytical capacity than Wyoming, with its LPA, its analysis was neither automatic nor frequent.

New Sec. 7 The secretary shall transmit annually to the governor, the standing committees on taxation and assessment and commerce of the senate, the standing committees on taxation and economic development and tourism of the house of representatives and the joint committee or economic development, or any successor commitee, a report, based on information received from each qualified company receiving benefits under the act, describing the following:

(a) The names of the qualified companies;

(b) The types of qualified companies utilizing the act;

(c) The location of such companies and the location of such companies' business operations in Kansas;

(d) The number of new employees hired;

(e) The wages paid for such new employees;

(f) The annual amount of benefits provided under this act;

(g) The estimated net state fiscal impact, including the direct and indirect new state taxes derived from the new employees hired; and

(h) an estimate of the multiplier effect on the Kansas economy of the benefits received under this act.

Figure 5.3 Description of policy evaluation for PEAK program

Thus, the audit team was not empowered to study the program until several years into implementation of the program and only when explicitly ordered to do so by the legislature.

Once the legislature directed the LPA to examine PEAK, the subpar data collection relegated much of LPA's analysis to describing the lack of conclusions they could draw and to criticizing the Department of Commerce for failing to enforce expectations about reporting from the participating companies. The 2013 report directly stated that "assessing the benefits of the PEAK program is difficult because the Department of Commerce has not compiled meaningful information on the program" (Economic Development: Determining Which Economic Development Tools Are Most Important and Effective in Promoting Job Creation and Economic Growth in Kansas, Part 1 2013, 11). It then went on to describe interviews with officials who, theoretically, were responsible for overseeing PEAK and their inability to keep up with the demands of monitoring participating companies:

> Officials told us they had not been able to keep up with these reviews because of staff shortages, several legislative changes to the program, and a growing number of participating companies.

(Economic Development: Determining Which Economic Development Tools Are Most Important and Effective in Promoting Job Creation and Economic Growth in Kansas, Part 1 2013, 12)

Essentially, even though LPA *does* eventually attempt to analyze the program, it is hindered by both the limited data collection and staff attention from the Department of Commerce (DoC).

Without more objective measures of value-add, the LPA relied on surveys of participant companies and compared the outcomes of the program against the opinions of existing stakeholders versus the stated intentions of the policy. The LPA 2014 audit suggested that Kansas had the right programs in place because the five surrounding states also had similar programs, and the stakeholders (i.e., companies and lawmakers) identified the programs as useful. Notably, this evaluation does *not* consist of comparing a policy's outcome with the stated intention, but rather it assesses opinions among stakeholders who were likely benefiting from the policy (see Figure 5.4). Not surprisingly, PEAK's recipient reaction to the findings was that the policies should do *more* to help existing businesses (Economic Development: Determining Which Economic Development Tools Are Most Important and Effective in Promoting Job Creation and Economic Growth in Kansas, Part 2. 2014).

While the LPA argued that it could not draw clear conclusions about the effects of PEAK, nonstate actors offered their own, more evaluative analyses of the outcomes, in line with the political leanings of their donors or the philosophy of their foundation. In response to a request from the Kansas Department of Commerce, the Docking Institute for Public Affairs, for example, found positive outcomes for the program, stating that "for each $1 of revenue used by the PEAK Program, the Kansas economy grew $960" (Promoting Employment Across Kansas Program Evaluation and Economic Impact Analysis 2013, 5). They acknowledged some limitations of their analysis but emphasized the overall positive contributions of the program to the Kansas, "Although not every new job created by PEAK firms can be directly attributed to the PEAK Program, our analysis suggests that 60% of the economic benefits cited in the previous bullets can be directly attributed to the PEAK Program" (Promoting Employment across Kansas Program Evaluation and Economic Impact Analysis 2013, 5).

Interestingly, the Docking Institute nods to skeptics by acknowledging the challenges of taking companies' self-reporting at face value regarding

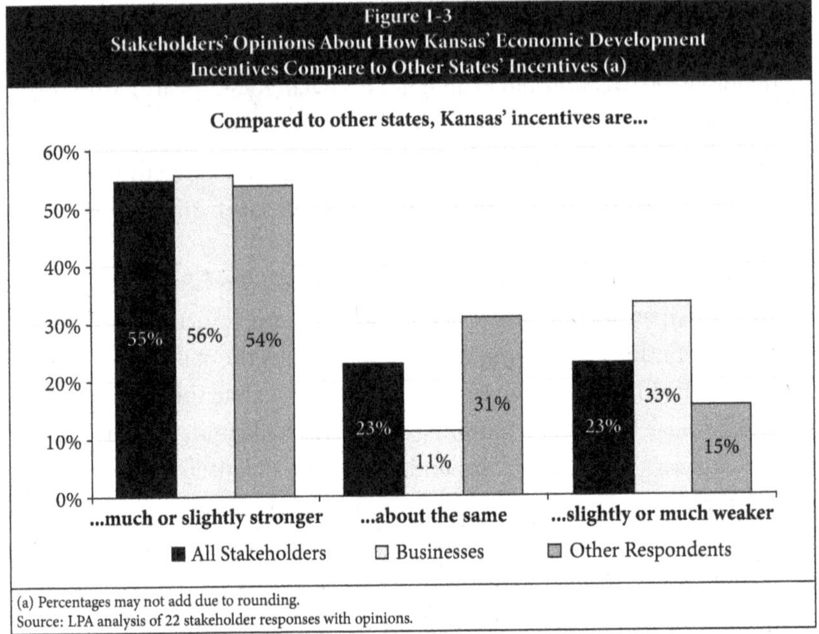

Figure 5.4 Survey results from LPA 2014 PEAK Audit
Sources: Author's calculations based on keyword searches on state agency directories.

the number of jobs they created. This suggests that regardless of this self-reporting, these companies are creating new job opportunities surrounding the companies in question:

> Respondents indicated that 75% of the new employees hired under the PEAK Program would have been hired even if the PEAK Program never existed. However, all of the new employees hired by PEAK firms relocating to Kansas represent additional jobs for the State, regardless of whether they would have been hired without the PEAK Program. These employees, plus most of the PEAK employees of firms starting or already located in Kansas which respondents indicated would not have hired had it not been for the PEAK Program, represent 60% of the employees hired under the PEAK Program.
>
> (Promoting Employment across Kansas Program Evaluation and Economic Impact Analysis 2013, 5)

In a literature review at the end of the report, the Docking Institute report also argued that existing research on tax incentives falls into three categories:

supportive, skeptical/hostile, and objective. The report concludes that, at worst, PEAK deserves more careful study and that, at best, the tax incentives are an important and effective economic development tool.

More progressive learning organizations, on the other hand, tend to find that the tax incentives are wasting public resources. For example, the Hall Family Foundation, which emphasizes equity, poverty alleviation, and a holistic approach to helping "all people" in their mission statement, is a staunch opponent of business location tax incentives, arguing that most of the incentives go to companies that only "shuffle" jobs back and forth across the state border dividing Kansas City between Kansas and Missouri. In one hearing held in 2014 for a Missouri bill that would have restricted tax incentives, Hall argued in support of eliminating tax incentives in the region:

> We are waging a wasteful economic development border war—and both states are losing. We do not oppose the use of incentives such as Missouri Works [or PEAK] when they create new economic activity. We do oppose the wasteful use of incentives when they shuffle existing jobs and produce little or no economic development.
>
> (Hall Family Foundation study shows Missouri has lost $217 million in taxes in border war 2014)

Hall cited a study that his own foundation conducted on the tax incentive programs in Kansas and Missouri, and found that the programs had reduced state revenue by $217 million while companies "shuffled" jobs back and forth across the state border dividing Kansas City.

While at least a handful of local power players questioned the effectiveness of PEAK, the program remained state policy in Kansas. Its opponents pointed to the program's exorbitant cost and unclear benefits but failed to convince state officials to end the program or even to radically change the reporting requirements. Without clear reporting requirements or the capacity to enforce even minimal compliance reporting among program recipients, those calling for PEAK's reform were left to conduct their own studies. State officials appear to write off or endorse these studies, depending on the alignment of the findings with the public official's views, dismissing undesirable outcomes as the result of politicized studies coming from outsiders that don't know the Kansas context.

Conclusion

Without a consensus on the path forward for a policy, public officials can explain away ideologically undesirable findings by blaming a faulty process. The comparison between FTAS and Becca's Bill demonstrated the impotence of robust analytical capacity to make up for anemic data collection practices. Comparing the three tax credit cases demonstrates the flaws of relying on self-reported data from policy beneficiaries. No amount of analytical capacity in any of the three states could address concerns about the biased results of self-reported data. In Washington's R&D tax case, however, there were trained researchers who could leverage data collected by other agencies to provide a clearer picture on the policy's outcomes.

Digestible information is essential for gaining the attention of elected officials. They cannot process data, and, without clear evidence suggesting otherwise, they are incentivized to support the status quo. Unlike the case with data collection capacity, analytical capacity can be supplemented when a constituency or elected official wants to question the policy. However, the utility of analytical capacity is limited by the quality of data that the state has collected since the inception of the policy.

In the case of the R&D tax credits, Washington State agencies were able to combine a range of high-quality evidence from multiple sources to convincingly demonstrate the failure of the tax credit, while similar data analysis efforts for Becca's Bill were stymied by the lack of quality data. A comparison of Texas's tax credit and truancy policies shows that nonstate actors can supplement analytical capacity when state bureaucracies are not fully equipped or willing to do so themselves. In FTAS, where university research groups led the charge on analysis, widespread acknowledgment followed. However, in the case of Ch 313, more partisan-driven think-tanks stepped in to conduct an analysis of limited and unreliable data, creating conflicting analyses of the policy's outcomes and stirring partisan-driven acknowledgment of policy failure. I provide evidence that both Kansas and Wyoming lacked the resources to make sense of any information they did happen to collect, subject to the whims of those in power.

Part I has argued that to better understand when public officials acknowledge policy failure, we must think about a state's capacity for policy evaluation along two separate dimensions: data collection capacity and analytical capacity. Part I was organized thematically to define, develop, and support the introduction of the data collection capacity as a separate institutional feature from a state's analytical capacity most logically. As I turn to explore the political dynamics of policy revision in Part II, I will shift to organizing chapters around each of the four main case studies. While I entered my study of the cases with some expectation about the role that collection and analytical capacity would play in acknowledgment, I approached understanding the impacts of these features on the politics of revision much more inductively. The case-centered organization allows me to reflect the research process most genuinely and to acknowledge the complexities of the politics of revision. Furthermore, sequencing becomes especially important for understanding the political dynamics in each of the cases, thus telling a more chronological (vs. thematic) story presents important developments most clearly.

Kansas and Wyoming, with their essentially nonexistent collection and analytical capacities, served as illuminating foils for the Texas and Washington cases in Part I. However, given that there was no evidence-informed acknowledgment of failure in these states, there is no need to probe the politics of revision and therefore do not appear in Part II. Readers may question why Ch 313 in Texas remains in Part II. While collection and analytical capacity were also limited in this policy, there was some expectation, however poorly executed, that the policy be evaluated and revisited. There was some evidence that it had failed, though few public officials acknowledged as much.

I arrange the chapters in Part II based on the likelihood of widespread acknowledgment and revision of policy failure. Within each case, I find that collection and analytical capacities interact with three features of each policy: the policy's origins, the policy's original design, and the groups mobilized in support and opposition to the policy. I begin with Washington R&D tax credits to highlight how collection and analytical capacity can coalesce to produce genuine policy learning and subsequent revision. Texas FTAS follows. FTAS demonstrates how the involvement of nonstate research organizations may influence the politics of revision and the conditions necessary for high collection capacity and low analytical capacity to result in policy revision. In chapter 8, Becca's Bill demonstrates the fatal pitfalls of limited collection capacity on encouraging public officials to risk policy change in the face of uncertainty. Chapter 9 on Texas's Ch 313 rounds out Part II, evincing the starring role ideology and partisan preferences will likely play in the absence of clear data and objective analysis.

Each case chapter follows a parallel structure. I first introduce the case and remind the reader which of the four types it represents. Then I describe the political, social, and economic context of the original legislation. The remainder of the chapter examines the interaction between the policy's original design and the data collection and analytical capacity available for the program. In the third section of each chapter, I show how the availability (or lack thereof) of compelling findings affected the power and resources of vested interests that had benefited by the failing policy and the more diffusely organized and less resourced groups harmed by the policy. The conclusion of each chapter makes comparisons across states, policies, and within states and policies over time to show that clear information can alter the inertia of the status quo for failed policies.

PART II
CASE STUDIES

6
The Clear-Cut Case (Washington Taxes)

The case of R&D tax credits in Washington represents the clear-cut case from the typology of state capacity. It showcases how high collection capacity and high analytical capacity can incentivize elected officials to acknowledge and address policy failure. The politics of the clear-cut case and the learning that occurred highlight the power of early investments in the collection and analytical capacities to draw attention to the failing policy outcomes despite pressure from vested interests to continue supporting the policy.

This chapter describes and analyzes the conditions that led elected officials to recognize and respond to the failure of the R&D tax credits by refusing to renew the policy a second time. Establishing a strong data collection capacity from the outset combined with Washington State's high analytical capacity yields insight into how this case of clear-cut evidence and analysis on policy failure produced new information that corroborated the voices of students, families, and economic justice organizations over that of businesses in the fight to revise the policy. The original policy's features, combined with the changing power dynamics between vested interests (e.g., corporations and business associations) and diffusely organized groups (e.g., students, social welfare organizations, and educational institutions) that bore the burden of the policy's failure changed the incentives for elected officials' support for the R&D tax credits.

By 2014, two decades after its enactment, opponents of the R&D tax credits could point to state-provided research showing that the policy was not actually producing the intended outcomes: creating more jobs or economic growth. Furthermore, given the budget crisis the state faced, educators pointed to an explicit harm that the policies were causing, namely, limited funding for science education. They argued that without a workforce trained in STEM fields, no tax credits would help lure companies to locate within the state.

The R&D tax credits contained a sunset clause through which the program would automatically expire unless renewed by the legislature every ten

The Politics of Failed Policies. Sarah James, Oxford University Press. © Oxford University Press (2025).
DOI: 10.1093/9780197813645.003.0007

years. An over-time comparison between the 2003–2004 successful renewal and the 2013–2114 failed renewal attempt illustrates how robust collection and analytical capacity alters the narrative possibilities and the political power of the different constituencies harmed and benefited by the failing policy.

This chapter presents an overview of the political, economic, and social context of the origins of the R&D tax credit in Washington State. I next describe the original policy design features of the policy that affected the data collection and analytical capacity for the program. To identify the policy feedback effects of both the original context and design of the policies, each is connected to later political outcomes. The interest groups that supported and opposed the revision of the policy are identified, followed by a discussion of how the power dynamics among the groups changed over time as new data corroborated a narrative of policy failure.

Policy Origins: New Times Call for New Policies

A simple declaration, "The industrial revolution is over," opened the 1994 report *Incentives for High Technology: A Study of Ways to Encourage Growth and Diversification*. Facing over two decades of a rapidly declining timber industry, which was once a mainstay of the Washington State economy, Governor Mike Lowry (D) had commissioned Washington's Department of Revenue to study strategies to increase employment opportunities and diversify Washington State's economy. The report outlined the Department of Revenue's findings, including the suggestion that a new two-pronged tax relief program be established for high-technology (high-tech) companies.[1] The report offered extensive justification for the state's investment in tax relief for high-tech companies, arguing that Washington already had a strong reputation for incubating high-tech companies, with Microsoft, Boeing, and several aerospace companies located within its borders. The report also pointed out that high-tech jobs grew at almost twice the rate of other jobs statewide, and it credited the high-tech industry

[1] The legislation specifically identifies advanced computing, advanced materials, biotechnology, electronic device technology, and environmental technology as specific high-technology sectors eligible for the tax program.

with helping the state weather recent economic downturns relatively unscathed.

Elected officials responded to the changing economic contexts and took up the state's tax structure for technology-oriented companies in the next legislative session. The Department of Revenue released their report in early January of 1994, and by July of that year, the bulk of the report's suggestions, including the Research & Development (R&D) tax credit and the Business & Occupation (B&O) tax waiver, had been signed into law with a bipartisan supermajority in the Washington legislature (see Table 6.1). The R&D tax deferral allowed companies to defer the sales tax on purchases related to research and development, while the B&O tax waiver provided a tax credit against cost incurred "against state business and occupation tax for costs incurred in research and development activities" (Kiga 1997). Though the R&D tax credit and the B&O waiver technically passed as separate policies, they were often described as a single policy under the R&D label. Hence, they are so described here.

The new legislation explicitly acknowledges its purpose as that of responding to the changing economic context within the state. The original R&D tax credit outlined the purpose of the program as diversifying employment opportunities and increasing the availability of high-wage jobs in the state. According to the original enacted legislation:

> The legislature finds that high-wage, high-skilled jobs are vital to the economic health of the state's citizens, and that targeted tax incentives will encourage the formation of high-wage, high-skilled jobs. (Engrossed Second Substitute Senate Bill 6347 1994)

In addition to stating this purpose, the legislature also mandated that the tax incentives "should be subject to the same rigorous requirements for efficiency and accountability as other expenditure programs." The suggestion was that, from the beginning, the legislature and governor were aware of evaluating and revisiting the impacts of the program (Engrossed Second Substitute Senate Bill 6347, 1994). Notably, the legislation also established a sunset date for the program in 2004.

After implementing the policy, the legislature amended it several times, including passing a ten-year extension of the policy in 2004 (see Table 6.2). By 2012, however, there was mounting evidence that the program was not

Table 6.1 Yea votes to reform or renew R&D tax credit as a percentage of total party votes, Washington, 1995–2015

Year	Bill	Status	Impact	House	Senate
1994	SB 6347	Passed	• Established the R&D tax credit and the B&O tax exemption • Original sunset date: December 2004	**92%** D*-92% R-92%	**85%** D-78% R-90%
2004	HB 2546	Passed	• Extended benefits to universities • Changed the formula for calculating the amount, effectively reducing the size of the credit • Required beneficiaries to file annual surveys about jobs created, etc. • Extended the policy through December 2014	**88%** D-80% R-98%	**82%** D-69% R-95%
2011	SB 5044	Passed	• Directed JLARC to study tax incentives using the WA Input Output model	**58%** D-98% R-2%	**63%** D-100% R-18%
2012	HB 2532	Failed	• Would have removed survey requirement • Extended tax credit to 2022	Left pending in committee	
2013	SB 5882	Passed	• Clarified the performance expectations for policies	**88%** D-75% R-100%	**68%** D-51% R-87%
2013–2014	HB 1303	Failed	• Would have extended the tax breaks through 2035	Left pending in committee	

**Yeas calculated as the percentage of members voting yea from each party/total members voting yea*
Source: Summary of bills, which can be accessed using session year bill numbers at https://app.leg.wa.gov/billinfo/. Roll-call votes are noted in accompanying documentation for each bill.

producing the jobs and economic growth that supporters had promised. Concerned about the rising cost of the program in the context of a substantial state budget deficit, the legislature twice abstained from renewing the program a second time before its 2014 sunset date, effectively eliminating the failed policy by the start of 2015.

Table 6.2 Evaluation outcomes for R&D tax credit, 1997–2014

Year Month Organization	1997 Sept DOR	2000 Sept DOR	2003 Sept DOR	2004 Jan WSIPP	2009 Dec DOR	2012 Feb JLARC	2013 Dec DOR
Category							
Job creation	+	+	Mixed	–	Mixed	–	Mixed
Jobs created for WA residents	+	+	+	–	–	–	+
Company growth	+	Mixed	+	N/A	Mixed	N/A	–
Diversification of state economy	Mixed	–	Mixed	N/A	+	N/A	+
Growth in R&D investment	Mixed	–	+	N/A	Mixed	N/A	+
Introduction of new products	Mixed	+	+	N/A	Mixed	N/A	Mixed
Movement of firms or consolidation of firms into the state	+	Mixed	Mixed	N/A	–	N/A	Mixed
Other factors	N/A	N/A	+	+	N/A	N/A	N/A
Overall tone	Positive	Positive	+	Negative	Negative	Negative	Mixed

DOR-Department of Revenue, WSIPP: Washington State Institute for Public Policy and JLARC: Joint Legislative Audit Research Committee.
Source : Author's summary of Washington State agency reports.

Policy and Institutional Design: Refined Definitions and Evaluation Schedule

The clear delineation of data collection expectations, definitions, and procedures in the original legislation and the ongoing statewide investments in state research agencies make the R&D tax credit in Washington State representative of the clear-cut case. The choices elected officials made during the design of the original legislation and its early implementation bolstered the collection and analytical capacity available for the program. The increasingly negative and credible findings constrained the ability of supporters to frame the policy as being effective and beneficial to Washington State residents and elected officials.

Clear and concrete definitions are essential to establishing high-collection capacity. The original R&D tax credit legislation defined the terms critical to regularly evaluating the program's effects. This purposeful data collection, in turn, facilitated the effectiveness of Washington's robust research

NEW SECTION. **Sec. 10.** The department shall perform anassessment of the results of the tax credit and tax deferral programs authorized under chapters 82.60, 82.61, and 82.62 RCW and deliver a report on the assessment to the governor and the legislature by September 1, 1996. The assessments shall measure the effect of the programs on job creation, company growth, the introduction of new products, the diversification of the state's economy, growth in research and development investment, the movement of firms or the consolidation of firms' operations into the state, and such other factors as the department selects.

Figure 6.1 Assessment description and schedule in ESSB 6347

bureaucracy. The original legislation also delineated the metrics—" job creation, company growth, the introduction of new products, the diversification of the state's economy, growth in research and development investment, the movement of firms or the consolidation of the firm's operation into the state, and other such factors as the department selects"—along which the Department of Revenue should measure the impact of the tax credits (Engrossed Second Substitute Senate Bill 6347 1994).

In addition to explicitly identifying these metrics, the legislation defined each of these factors and required that companies receiving the tax credit report this information to the Department of Revenue each year. Notably, the R&D tax credit designated a single organization—the Department of Revenue—to be in charge of collecting the data in a single, comparable format from all qualifying companies statewide.

The original R&D tax credit legislation established high analytical capacity by outlining a regular evaluation schedule, requiring policy evaluations in 1997, 2000, and 2003 (see Figure 6.1). The first three reports published by the Department of Revenue ranged from cautiously optimistic to glowingly positive about the impacts of the tax credit. The three original reports offered conclusions on the seven categories for evaluation established by the legislature (see Table 6.2). While the report cited mixed or inconclusive results for some of the metrics of interest for evaluating the policy, the key metrics cited in the legislation's intent—job growth and creation—received overwhelmingly positive evaluations in all three reports.

The Washington State legislators not only established clear guidelines for collecting data and analyzing it in the original legislation, they also maintained robust collection capacity by refining the data collection procedures and updating administrative rules for the program's implementation.

After the first policy evaluation in 1997, the Department of Revenue and skeptical public officials requested more clarity for what types of projects could in fact benefit from the tax credit to better assess company compliance. The legislature responded to these calls for refined definitions and data collection immediately. In the 1997 report, the Department of Revenue shared that the legislature was already in the process of finalizing a new administrative rule to clarify the definitions of the categories included in the original legislation, thereby enhancing the state's ability to collect meaningful data (Kiga 1997). The administrative rule adds over two pages of clarifying details about what counts (and does not count) under each category, along with the acceptable definitions for related terms (see Figure 6.2 for an example of the added detail from the original legislation to the updated rule implemented three years later). Quick responses to definitional challenges allowed the state research organizations to study outcomes as accurately as possible, and as quickly as possible.

The enthusiastic political support for the R&D tax credits reflects the tenor of the early reports on its effects. By the time the program faced its first renewal in the 2003–2004 session, the Department of Revenue's three reports had generally positive reviews of the program. The legislature renewed the R&D tax credits with bipartisan support, though a handful of legislators did change their positions on the program. Of the fourteen state senators who remained in office from 1994, eight voted to support the program, just as they had done in 1994 (see Table 6.3). The remaining six senators switched their votes. The three Democrats switched their votes from supporting the program to opposing it, and the three Republicans that changed their votes switched from opposing the program to supporting it (see Table 6.3).

Reflecting a continued commitment to investing in the state's capacity to collect and analyze data from this policy, the bipartisan coalition that renewed the R&D tax credits also refined the reporting and analysis requirements. This refinement set the stage for the legislators to eventually recognize the failures of the program. Along with renewing the R&D tax credits in 2004, the legislature once again adjusted the required documentation and analysis of the program's outcomes. Strong support for continuing the program accompanied demands for more transparent reporting from companies receiving the tax credit. Legislators concerned about the cost of the program given the unproven results argued that more information was needed to study the policy. In a public hearing prior to the 2004 renewal,

(8) "Environmental technology" means assessment and prevention of threats or damage to human health or the environment, environmental cleanup, and the development of alternative energy sources.

Original legislation (1994)

(v) **Environmental technology.** "Environmental technology" means assessment and prevention of threats or damage to human health or the environment, environmental cleanup, and the development of alternative energy sources.

(A) The assessment and prevention of threats or damage to human health or the environment concerns assessing and preventing potential or actual releases of pollutants into the environment that are damaging to human health or the environment. It also concerns assessing and preventing other physical alterations of the environment that are damaging to human health or the environment.

For example, a research project related to salmon habitat restoration involving assessment and prevention of threats or damages to the environment may qualify as environmental technology, if such project is concerned with assessing and preventing potential or actual releases of water pollutants and reducing human-made degradation of the environment.

(I) Pollutants include waste materials or by-products from manufacturing or other activities.

(II) Environmental technology includes technology to reduce emissions of harmful pollutants. Reducing emissions of harmful pollutants can be demonstrated by showing the technology is developed to meet governmental emission standards. Environmental technology also includes technology to increase fuel economy, only if the taxpayer can demonstrate that a significant purpose of the project is to increase fuel economy and that such increased fuel economy does in fact significantly reduce harmful emissions. If the project is intended to increase fuel economy only minimally or reduce emissions only minimally, the project does not qualify as environmental technology. A qualifying research project must focus on the individual components that increase fuel economy of the product, not the testing of the entire product when everything is combined, unless the taxpayer can separate out and identify the specific costs associated with such testing.

(III) Environmental technology does not include technology for preventive health measures for, or medical treatment of, human beings.

(IV) Environmental technology does not include technology aimed to reduce impact of natural disasters such as floods and earthquakes.

(V) Environmental technology does not include technology for improving safety of a product.

(B) Environmental cleanup is corrective or remedial action to protect human health or the environment from releases of pollutants into the environment.

(C) Alternative energy sources are those other than traditional energy sources such as fossil fuels, nuclear power, and hydroelectricity. However, when traditional energy sources are used in conjunction with the development of alternative energy sources, all the development will be considered the development of alternative energy sources.

Updated administrative rule (1998)

Figure 6.2 Definitions for "environmental technology," 1994 vs. 1998

Table 6.3 Votes for R&D tax incentives from members in office in 1994 and 2004

State Senator	Party	1994 Vote (SB 6347)	2004 Vote (HB 1303)
Deccio	R	N	Y
Haugen	D	Y	Y
McAuliffe	D	Y	Y
McCaslin	R	Y	Y
Morton	R	N	Y
Oke	R	N	Y
Prentice	D	Y	Y
Rasmussen	D	Y	Y
Sheldon, B.	R	Y	Y
Winsley	R	Y	Y
Franklin	D	Y	N
Fraser	D	Y	N
Hargrove	D	Y	N

Source: Author's summary of roll-call votes in legislative archives.

Senator Steve Conway (D) argued insistently that he supported the program *if* it in fact created more jobs, but he pointed out that the evidence was still questionable, at best, that the costs of the program were worth it:

> When [the Chairman of the Department of Economics] came before us we asked him if he had the necessary data to evaluate the effectiveness of these incentives and he clearly said, "no." And that is one of the reasons we have upped the ante on the disclosure issues relative to what kind of jobs are being produced. I think it is wrong for the other side to argue that I am against job creation. I want jobs, we need jobs, but we also need to be able to evaluate whether these exemptions are creating jobs. Let's not just assume they are, let's study them. There is some kind of fear of information here. This bill the chair has put together is going to provide the data . . . to evaluate clearly whether we are achieving the objectives we hope to achieve. (*House Finance Committee Public Hearing on SB/HB 2546, 2004*)

Later in the hearing, the chair of the House Finance Committee made a similar argument for the importance of transparency, maintaining that "in a time of scarce resources, taxpayers have every right to expect to see what we are doing with their money" (*House Finance Committee Public Hearing on SB/HB 2546, 2004*).

Passed in 2004, HB 2546 revised the R&D tax credit and extended it through 2014, and it enhanced the data collection capacity for the policy. Responding to concerns about data collection and disclosure, the new legislation required each recipient firm to submit an annual survey detailing the total number of "employment positions" at the firm, including information on salary, benefits, and full-time status. Firms were also required to submit the number of new products along with the "number of trademarks, patents, and copyrights associated with the research and development activities for which the credit was taken" (High Technology Tax Incentives 2004). The legislation expanded eligible organizations to include universities and created a new formula—which effectively reduced the size of the tax credit—for calculating the amount of credit each organization received.

While a policy's origins and its original design have important implications for whether or not public officials can learn about its impacts, these are not the only features that influence a policy's susceptibility to revision. Through conferring benefits (or disadvantages) and altering the distribution of resources, policies change politics (see Mettler 2005a; Pierson 1993). The R&D tax credits offered a major financial benefit to the local high-tech industry, while they also burdened an already strained state budget. In turn, organizations that relied on state funding, like schools, police, and fire departments, and social justice organizations, in turn questioned the value of the tax credits. In other words, educators, health care providers, and social justice organizations had every incentive to believe the state data indicating that the policy was failing to produce the intended outcomes, while the high-tech industry had an interest in being highly skeptical of the state data suggesting the tax credits were failing. As the availability of compelling evidence changed, the narrative possibilities for supporters and opponents of the R&D tax credits changed too. I now turn to exploring how supporters and opponents of revising the R&D tax credits leveraged state policy evaluations to their advantage in framing the outcome of the policy.

Group Dynamics: Data, Interest Groups, and Framing Failure

This section examines the political dynamics between supporters and opponents of the tax credits. Over the two decades of the policy's trajectory, the groups' ability to sway legislators to adopt their perspective on the utility of the policy changed as the availability of data changed. During the 2004 renewal attempt, those calling for revision of the tax credits failed to garner enough support, resulting in a decade-long renewal of the policy. However, the renewal triggered increased data collection and reporting requirements. In the 2013 legislative session, faced with clearer evidence of the R&D tax credits' failures, opponents of revision, in view of the evidence the state had collected, struggled and failed to reframe the policy issue as a success. During each renewal attempt, labor unions, church organizations, and educational institutions opposed renewal of the R&D tax credit, citing evidence that the program was not producing a net benefit for their constituencies (see Table 6.4). However, these opponents only garnered enough support to stymie the second renewal attempt in 2014. The overtime change in the politics of renewal between 2004 and 2013 demonstrates how compelling, locally collected data in the hands of local, career researchers can undermine the power of vested interests to positively frame failed policies.

The 2004 Renewal: Big Business Gets Its Way

The 2004 renewal of the R&D tax credits reflects the politics typical of the American political economy. The firms and organizations with the most resources to lobby consistently across multiple venues of state government saw their preferences reflected in policy (Hacker et al. 2021; Hacker & Pierson 2011). By 2003, the program had provided more than $500 million in tax credits and exemptions (High Technology Tax Incentives 2004).[2] As shown in Table 6.4, a collection of disparate organizations and interest groups coalesced to oppose continuation of the R&D tax credit during both the 2004 and 2013 renewal attempts.

Backed by the positive findings from state-sponsored program evaluations, the most ardent supporters of the tax policies—the biotech and high-tech companies—wielded substantial political power and resources to achieve their policy preferences. Some of the largest technology companies in the world, such as Microsoft, Amazon, and Boeing, operate out of Washington State and invested in lobbying to ensure that the political and economic contexts remained amenable. In 2004, high-tech companies successfully framed the R&D tax credits as an essential tool for increasing

[2] According to the 2003 memo from the Department of Revenue to the Senate Ways and Means Committee and the House Finance Committee, 1,311 firms had saved $204 million from tax credits, and 393 projects qualified for $324 million in tax deferral and exemptions for research and development facilities. The $500 million cost of the program comes from adding these two amounts together (High Technology Tax Incentives 2004, 1).

Table 6.4 Groups testifying for and against renewal of the R&D tax credit, 2004 and 2013

	Supported revision	Opposed revision
2004	AFL-CIO Service Employees International Union Washington Center for Public Policy Washington Association of Churches Washington Tax Fairness Coalition Evans America Washington State Action Council Economic Opportunity Institute Washington Association of School Administrators (Alliance of Educational Associations) Coalition for Jewish Voice	Columbia River Development Council WA BSA Software Alliance Physics Lab Washington Biomedical and Technology Association Seattle Biomedical Research Institute
2013	Individual educators NARAL (a pro-choice organization) Service Employees International Union Economic Future Coalition Association of the Students of the University of Washington Council of Firefighters Jewish Federation Washington Education Association Now Leaving the Voters	Washington Biomedical and Technology Assn WA technology and industry association Washington Roundtable Washington Economic Development Organization BATEL Bristol Meyer Squib Association of Washington Business

Source : Author's summary of witness lists from legislative hearings for HB 2546 and HB 1303, accessed through the Washington State legislative archives https://app.leg.wa.gov/billinfo.

Washington's economic opportunities, despite the substantial cost to the state budget. High-tech and their supporters dismissed the state's inconclusive findings with anecdotes about how their companies would not have located in Washington without the tax breaks, and convinced Washington legislators and the governor to renew the policy for an additional ten years.

In the 2004 hearings, this corporate strategy worked well. Those supporting continuation of the tax credits argued that several studies had shown a "direct correlation between job growth and those who take tax incentives." They also maintained that requiring any further public disclosures of additional details would reveal proprietary information and violate the individual employee's privacy in the smaller companies (*House Finance Committee Public Hearing on SB/HB 2546, 2004*). Several senators supported their citation of this observational data with anecdotes from their own constituents. One representative, in particular, shared a story about a constituent who thanked him through tears for helping bring jobs to her community, allowing her to get off of the state Medicaid program and onto private health insurance (*House Finance Committee Public Hearing on SB/HB 2546, 2004*).

Faced with generally positive evaluations of the program, groups opposed to continuation of the tax credits were unable to generate enough political opposition to prevent its renewal. Various public service providers (e.g., firefighters and health care workers), educators, students, religious organizations, unions, and organizations fighting economic inequality vocally opposed continuation of the R&D tax credit in 2004. These disparate groups framed the R&D tax credits similarly: if the budget is limited (and it indeed was quite limited in Washington at the time), then corporations are not the ones who should be receiving tax breaks. Educators and students, in particular, argued that in the long run underfunding education was also undermining an important resource for the tech companies: employees with robust training in math, science, and technology.

Given that the findings from the Department of Revenue available in 2004 ranged from inconclusive to positive, those supporting revision were limited to pointing out the inconclusive evidence about the benefit for the policy and the several harms that were likely exacerbated by continuation of the tax credit. For example, during a 2004 House Finance Committee hearing, a representative of the Service Employees International Union argued that there was *not* in fact significant evidence suggesting that the tax credit was producing additional jobs, and that her members were facing critical shortages in available resources for children, senior citizens, and health care workers. She pointed out that it was irresponsible for the state to continue subsidizing tech companies without clear evidence of benefits for Washington residents. The AFL-CIO representative pursued a similar logic, arguing that his organization opposed renewal of the tax credits because

> [e]very study has shown so far . . . [the program] has failed the cost benefit analysis of this plan . . . we don't know any contribution that the tax breaks are making . . . we can't separate it from the noise . . . we don't know if it is skewed by several large companies. (*House Finance Committee Public Hearing on SB/HB 2546, 2004*)

The representative went on to say that even if the cost-benefit analysis was unclear, legislators should consider the macro implications of the program. Moreover, with a blooming financial crisis in the state, increasing class sizes, and underpaid state employees, tax breaks for companies should not be a priority for lawmakers.

Of the organizations opposed to extending the R&D tax credit, most cited findings from the Department of Revenue's reports in their testimony. However, given the overall positive tone of the reports, they were left having to simply point out the uncertainty around the causal relationship between the tax credits and the job growth, and characterizing continuing such an uncertain policy as a gamble, rather than as a sound policy decision: "Given the funding problem the state is facing and the structural deficit, should we be taking the gamble with this money instead of educating our workers?"(*House Finance Committee Public Hearing on SB/HB 2546, 2004*). With some positive evidence, the policy *may* be creating new jobs, and with the encouragement of industry executives and lobbyists, the legislature and governor decided it was a gamble worth taking. As a result, the 2004 renewal passed with broad bipartisan support, and with even more fervent support from the House and Senate Republicans than when it had originally passed ten years earlier (see Table 6.1).

Framing the R&D tax credit as an unfair corporate welfare program that robbed the education, service, and health care sectors of desperately needed resources failed to convince elected officials in the state legislature of the policy's failure. The legislator renewed the program for another ten years. However, skeptics of the program did successfully incorporate additional reporting requirements for the program moving forward. The expected power dynamics of big business and the appeal of the status quo continued. By 2013, however, something had shifted, and elected officials did not renew the policy for a third decade before the 2014 New Year's Eve sunset date.

The 2013–2014 Renewal: Data Disrupts Power Dynamics

In the decade following the 2004 renewal, the additional reporting requirements and continued attention from state research organizations produced more conclusive and consistent findings about the costs and benefits of the R&D tax credits. These new and more precise findings suggested the program was failing, corroborating narratives from opponents and depleting the political will to continue the program. As the evidence suggested that the program was costing the state money without the promised economic or job growth, the nature of the claims that supporters could credibly make also changed. The more consistently negative findings from a wider range of state agencies corroborated the claims of failure coming from the program's opponents.

With the next expiration looming on December 31, 2014, and the availability of additional data on the policy's outcomes, discussion of renewing the tax credit came up again in January 2013. By 2013, the Joint Legislative Audit Review Committee (JLARC) had published two reports on the policy, and the Department of Revenue had conducted two more of its own followup studies. The newer findings of both organizations suggested the policy was not actually producing the intended outcomes, especially in job creation, which was one of the foundational purposes of the policy (see Table 6.2). Now with three state agencies saying the evidence showed the policy outcomes was, at best, producing mixed results, and, at worst, producing counterproductive outcomes, the policy's opponents had state-created information to point to in supporting their claims about the failure of the R&D tax credit to produce the promised economic growth.

Companies adopted a strategy similar to one they had used in 2004 to attempt to protect the R&D tax credits. The most recent evaluations, however, contradicted this narrative, and undermined legislators' willingness to support the tax credits through a second renewal. Despite the increasing evidence of the tax credit's failure that had emerged since the 2004 renewal, representatives from various high-tech business associations and companies once again pointed to the invaluable role of the tax credits for continuing investment in Washington State. Those opposing any revision to the policy implied that without these tax credits the economic growth, employment increases, and investments the state had experienced in this sector would diminish. For example, during hearings for the 2014 renewal, Chris Rivera, the president of the Washington Biotech and Biomedical Association, whose mission is to grow the industry in the state, testified that the "tax incentive is critical to the future growth of life sciences" (*Hearing on Public: HB 1260, HB 1301, HB 1303*, 2013). He then attempted to ground the evaluation of the R&D tax credits in data other than those provided by the state, pointing to several measures that suggested the policy was in fact producing its intended outcomes:

> Life sciences is one of Washington's fastest and largest industries. Between 2007 and 2011, jobs grew by 12% statewide, compared to a decline of about 2% for the rest of the private sector in the state of Washington. Life sciences adds approximately $11 billion to the state's GDP and an additional $7 billion in personal income and employs more than 92,000 directly and indirectly statewide. Nearly 70 cities are home to our nearly 186 biopharma companies, our 242 MedTech companies, or our 72 not profit research institutes. (*Hearing on Public: HB 1260, HB 1301, HB 1303, 2013*)

Rivera continued his testimony, listing life-changing medical inventions (e.g., defibrillators, ultrasound machines, several cancer treatments) that originated in the Washington research and development initiatives, and then he credited tax incentives for facilitating such research. Without R&D tax incentives, he implied, both Washington and humanity would suffer. He then explained how risky research and development can be for companies and cited information with no clear source about the number of organizations that took advantage of the tax incentive:

> Yet, it is a tremendous economic engine for the region that can keep it and grow it, and utilization of the R&D tax incentive is a key tool for us. By looking at the 2000 data from the R&D tax incentive, looking at life science organizations that took advantage of it, there were approximately 15 not profit research institutes and 80 companies utilizing the credits for a total of about 67 million dollars. (*Hearing on Public: HB 1260, HB 1301, HB 1303, 2013*)

Rivera also included a reminder that other *countries* were luring tech workers with impressive incentives and that research and development, as an industry was uniquely deserving of the tax credits because it is an "extremely capital-intensive" business. Henrik Anderson, senior director of Biologics Process Development, a subsidiary of Bristol Meyer Squib, followed this testimony with a similar plea, arguing that the R&D tax credit was a key driver to his company's choice to locate in Seattle and their ability to invest in subsequent innovations.

The vice president of Government and External Affairs for the Washington Technology and Industry Association adopted a more muted tone in justifying his organization's support for the tax credits. Notably, he implicitly nodded to the mixed findings regarding whether or not the tax credits have in fact created new jobs. Instead he said that while he would not "claim they create jobs," the tax credits "certainly create *conditions* that create jobs" (*Hearing on Public: HB 1260, HB 1301, HB 1303, 2013*). He then went on to leverage a different tactic than the first two business representatives; he described all of the taxes that his member organizations *had* paid over the last several years:

> In the IT sector, we grew 25,000 jobs between 2005 and 2011 with increasing level of salaries, the taxes generated just by IT sector is $500 million a year, just employee taxes. WRC report attributes two-thirds of the job growth since 1990 to high-tech and over $900 million-2.29 billion in taxes paid since 1994. We clearly contribute. We are not against taxes, we do not oppose the increase, but need tools to help our companies maintain competitiveness. (*Hearing on Public: HB 1260, HB 1301, HB 1303, 2013*)

This reframing statement relied less on assuming that the tax credits themselves created "conditions that create jobs" than on suggesting that the company's hands were tied, and without competitive incentives, they would simply have to look elsewhere. While it is hard to know for sure what would have happened without these encouraging words from business representatives, what is certain is their strategy of emphasizing that the tax credits had in fact helped Washington's residents. However, unlike the situation in 2004, there was substantial statewide evidence to suggest otherwise. By the time these hearings took place, the state's research organizations had already published six reports, several of which suggested that the payoffs of the tax breaks were not generating the promised effects.

The additional data and evaluations issued between 2004 and 2014 generated locally relevant and credible new evidence to support the narratives of those harmed by the program's failures. In the 2013–2014 renewal attempt, those opposed to the tax credits could combine their anecdotes of the policy's failures with corroborating evidence *from the state itself*. Nick Federici, a representative of Our Economic Future Coalition—an umbrella group for progressive labor and education organizations—testified against HB 1303. This legislation would have renewed the R&D tax credits, both in 2013 and again in 2014 when the bill resurfaced during the special legislative session.

Federici's use of state-provided analysis to highlight the policy's failure offers insight into how high collection and analytical capacity alters the power dynamics of policy revision by lending empirical support to the otherwise politically weaker groups' claims.

During his January 2014 testimony against HB 1303, Federici described his organization's position as "similar to JLARC," one of the state's research agencies. Instead of outright opposing continuation of the tax credit, Federici testified that, like JLARC, his organization simply wanted more transparency and accountability. He maintained that "some organizations are receiving it as an incentive that don't need incentivizing. . . . [We are] concerned it will hurt the state's ability to do its paramount duty of helping people in Washington" (*Hearing on HB 1303, HB 2101, HB 2177, HB 2175, 2014*). Instead of making a novel argument or citing research from his own organization, Federici instead claimed he was simply reiterating the stance of the state's own agency.

Demonstrating increasing skepticism within the legislature compared to the 2004 renewal, HB 1303 did not leave the committee during the 2013 regular session. The renewal did come up again for discussion in 2014 during the special legislative session. Federici returned and was able to cite negative reports from both JLARC *and* the Department of Revenue to support his organization's opposition to renewing the tax credits. He acknowledged the almost universally amenable policy goals—to create new jobs and economic growth—but then argued that they did not know if the R&D tax credit was accomplishing these aims:

> The policy goals are mom and apple pie, right? Good paying jobs, generally clean industry. I don't think there is any dispute about creating, maintaining, perpetuating these jobs and the growth of the industry. The number one question is this 60 million [dollars] doing that? Is it incentivizing things that we want to do? We don't think we should give some of the richest corporations in the history of the world a couple of extra million dollars just to say thank you. We think that should be something that is incentivizing some sort of behavior that is desirable. If we think jobs would go away in the absence of this, if we think that jobs would be created with this, then ask those organizations to prove it, just as the mom on TANF has to prove her income eligibility and what she is spending her money on. So should these corporations be accountable to the public in the same way. (*Hearing on HB 1303, HB 2101, HB 2177, HB 2175, 2014*)

Immediately following Federici's testimony, Representative Larry W. Crouse (R) acknowledged that he had made a fair point, and he asked about the impacts of eliminating the tax credit.

Supporters of the R&D tax credits faced more constraints on the claims they could credibly make about the effects of the program, given the new state reports on the program's effects. For example, the vice president for External Affairs of the Washington Technology and Industry Association was only able to say that many complicated factors influence companies' (re)location decisions and that all he could say for sure was that *not* having an R&D tax credit wouldn't *help* the state (*Public: HB 1260, HB 1301, HB 1303 Executive: HB 1183 Work Session: Tax Preferences for Economic Development Purposes* 2013). Notably, he refrained from arguing that the tax credit would in fact increase the chances of job and economic growth.

Teachers and students also testified in support of ending the R&D tax credits. Broadly, they echoed the logic from the opposition to the 2004 renewal, arguing that the tax credits left schools, teachers, and students with few resources to adequately prepare a highly skilled workforce. One of the teachers who testified in opposition to HB 1303 exemplifies the arguments that her fellow educators and students made. Julianna Dobbel implored the committee to think about the bill from the perspective of her students and all of the resources they deserved (i.e., counseling, health care, attention, smaller class sizes). She then argued:

> We can only attain a world class education if we pay for it. We must first focus on our greatest asset: our students in every science class in every neighborhood. The McCleary Decision[3] is present in every discussion. It makes the argument that students have to be prepared to enter the tech sector, and students deserve the education system that can operate robustly, but always working from deficit. 1303 is an insult to us. We all have a responsibility to the students in our state. (*Hearing on Public: HB 1260, HB 1301, HB 1303, 2013*)

Echoing the argument of the many different public sector groups that opposed continuation of the tax credits, Dobbel concluded by pointing out

[3] The McCleary Decision refers to *Mathew and Stephanie McCleary et al. v. State of Washington* in which several families sued the state, arguing that the state legislature, through its budgeting process, was failing to fulfill its constitutional duty to provide a free and sufficient education for all Washington children. The judge ruled in favor of the plaintiffs, which in turn prompted fines on the legislature until they budgeted additional money to support Washington public schools.

that one solution to the state's current budget crisis was to tax its citizens more, and that it seemed unfair to her to tax people without also taxing companies more as well. In essence, by 2013–2014, the coalition of opponents could more credibly frame the policy as a failure using state-generated findings. With more compelling analysis, the likely outcomes of the policy in question shifted from plausibly beneficial to, at best, cost-ineffective and, at worst, counterproductive.

In January 2014 the committee chair scheduled HB 1303 for additional hearings in the special session, given the number of new members on the committee. Arguments like the ones offered the year before pervaded the discussion. Once again, those impacted by the limited public funding that resulted from tax credits testified against extending the tax credit, including over twenty additional educators who went on record as opposing the bill, as did several firefighters and members of other community organizations. Reformers testifying in this second hearing more explicitly leveraged existing data and analysis from the state to support their arguments against extending the tax cuts. A senior researcher from Bristol Meyer Squib and the president of the Washington Biomedical and Biotechnology Association were forced to simply acknowledge that while they may not have clear information confirming the positive value-add of the tax credits, *not* having tax credits didn't *help* Washington add jobs, once again employing the "well-maybe it doesn't work, but everyone else does it" logic. Originally retained in its present status through the 2013 regular session and three 2013 special sessions, the bill finally died in committee without a roll call vote in the 2014 regular session, leaving the R&D tax credits to expire on January 1, 2015.

Conclusion

Washington's R&D tax credit case demonstrates how collection capacity and analytical capacity can empower a policy's opponents to highlight policy failure for public officials. The original R&D tax credit legislation established high collection capacity through its careful delineation of key terms integral to meaningfully assessing the policy's impacts. Furthermore, the legislature quickly refined and expanded their definitions when researchers argued that the original definitions were not sufficiently clear to facilitate policy evaluation. As described in Chapter 2, there were also several overlapping data collection efforts that allowed researchers to corroborate data collected through the guidelines established by the original legislation. The original R&D tax credit legislation also took advantage of the state's high analytical capacity by mandating regular evaluation of the policy's impacts.

The cast of organizations opposing and supporting the policy did not change between its first successful renewal in 2004 and the second unsuccessful renewal attempt in 2014. What did change, however, was the information available to public officials and the policy's opponents documenting how the tax credit was draining the state's coffers and undermining the very educational system that the tech industry needed to train future workers. This dynamic suggests that clear knowledge about a policy's outcomes can shift the power dynamic, undermining claims of success from the policy's vested interests to those being harmed by the policy. Once there was widespread analysis documenting policy failure, the availability of data increased the likelihood of revision by shifting the burden of proof away from the politically less powerful unions, educators, and service providers, and onto the uber wealthy high-tech companies that benefited from the tax credits.

While the mobilization of supporters and opponents is an important signal to elected officials about the immediate effects of a policy, they may also be swayed by their understanding of the policy's original economic and political context. As the initial quote in this chapter about the decline of the industrial revolution reflects, state public officials took a particularly long view on evaluating the state of the Washington economy when considering implementing new tax incentives in 1994. The R&D tax credit resulted from a measured, proactive strategy to consider the economic future of Washington. The timber industry was declining—an urgent economic matter for a state once so reliant on harvesting and processing these natural resources—but not a single catalyzing crisis required immediate action. Instead, aware of the impending issue, Governor Lowry commissioned a report from his Department of Revenue, which in turn gathered data from within the state and from state peers, and then he developed a proposal for a tax program tailored to the needs of the state. While there was no consistent evidence to suggest otherwise, benefiting companies successfully lobbied elected officials to maintain the R&D tax credits. However, once the coalition of opponents had state-provided analysis to corroborate their narrative, support for the program dwindled.

Three aspects of the original design of R&D tax credit data collection are noteworthy for understanding the impacts of collection and analytical capacity on public officials learning about policy outcomes. First, the centralized collection and analysis plans built into the original policy ensured that state agencies collected relevant data and produced meaningful statistics on the R&D tax credits. Second, the legislature quickly responded to the calls from state evaluators for clarification regarding definitions, facilitating useful data collection. Third, the 2004 legislation did not just renew the policy; it also increased the data collection capacity for the policy, requiring additional reporting from recipient companies. This addressed concerns about the elected officials' uncertainty about the policy's outcomes and paved the way for more robust evaluations before the next sunset date. With greater attention to centralizing data collection and refining definitions, Washington's robust analytical capacity was able to operate to full effect.

During the first renewal attempt in the 2003–2004 legislative session, the cast of characters on either side of the debate surrounding continuation of the R&D tax credits was what one might expect: companies that stood to benefit from the tax credits generally supported their continuation, whereas organizations that relied on state funding argued that it was an unreasonable drain on already strained state coffers. During the 2003–2004 renewal attempt, opponents did not have the data to support their framing of the tax credits as a net drain on the state economy and workforce. By the time the 2013–2014 renewal conversations came around, updated data collection practices facilitated more precise studies. There were more reports from a wider range of state offices that offered a more negative picture of the impacts of the policy. In the 2013 and 2014 hearings, using data about the state's budget, education spending, and the costs of the R&D tax credit program, those calling for its demise pointed out how underfunding science education would harm the state's ability to attract businesses in the long run, regardless of the tax landscape. Few policies have clear-cut impacts. Often the debate about policy failure centers on whether the policies' costs (both literally and figuratively) outweigh their benefits. In this case, high collection and analytical capacity coalesced to provide clear information regarding the policy's high costs and limited benefits. In turn, these findings empowered those disadvantaged by the policy—namely, public service workers, students, families, and teachers—to draw a clear connection between the continued reliance on tax breaks and the degradation of Washington's public education (at both the K–12 and higher education levels).

The design of the R&D tax credits also suggests that sunset provisions may also be particularly important because they flip the value of the outcome of inaction. This flip, in turn, may impact public officials' political calculations about the costs and benefits of supporting a particular policy without clear data suggesting it is successful. The R&D tax credits had a built-in sunset clause and received one renewal in 2004. However, despite two attempts (in 2011 and 2013), the R&D credit did not receive any additional renewals before its 2015 expiration. Sunset provisions alone are not a panacea for bad policies, but when combined with high-collection and high-analytical capacity, they further shift the dynamics of revision to favor the opponents of a policy. With increasingly clear evidence from state research agencies that the R&D tax credit was not actually producing additional jobs, economic diversification, or growth, supporters shouldered the burden of proof when arguing for their continuation. The sunset clause furthered the burden of proof on the high-tech industry which supported continuation of the policy, as they had to spur lawmakers *into* action, which was usually a more trying task than asking them to do nothing.

7

The Treasure Trove Case (Texas Truancy)

Washington's journey with R&D tax credits demonstrated the potential of high collection and high analytical capacity to credibly corroborate the narratives from groups experiencing the harms of policy failure. But what happens when a state policy exhibits high capacity in only one component of state research capacity? This chapter and Chapter 8 explore the politics of revision when a state policy has high collection capacity *or* high analytical capacity, but not both. I first examine the treasure trove case—represented by Texas's truancy program, Failure to Attend School (FTAS)—in this chapter. In the treasure trove type, there is high collection capacity but low analytical capacity. This combination *may* lead to the acknowledgment and revision of policy failure if nonstate actors can successfully supplement the state's analytical capacity.

Failure to Attend School echoes the some of the findings from Washington's R&D tax credit case. Robust data collection capacity is necessary to catalyze elected officials' recognition of failure. Nonstate actors can successfully supplement a state policy's analytical capacity, given that high-quality data is available for analysis. I also show that compelling analysis from plausibly nonpartisan researchers can incentivize elected officials' reconsideration of a failing policy. Finally, I echo the findings from Washington's R&D tax credits regarding the power of data to generalize anecdotal harms shared by those harmed by a policy's failure. Students, families, and public officials opposed to continuation of FTAS leveraged analysis of its impacts to successfully frame the policy as an unmitigated failure and generate bi-partisan support for revising the failed policy.

Policy Origins: Anonymous Beginnings Create Opportunity for Revision

FTAS's relatively anonymous beginnings (like Washington's R&D tax credit), in which legislators passed the policy to preempt an anticipated

The Politics of Failed Policies. Sarah James, Oxford University Press. © Oxford University Press (2025).
DOI: 10.1093/9780197813645.003.0008

challenge with accountability, created a policy climate in which elected officials were more willing to acknowledge a failure and make adjustments. As described earlier, legislators and judges considered FTAS to be a response to a global trend in attendance issues across the state and more stringent accountability standards. However, there was no single, headline-grabbing crisis that instigated the policy. The almost nonexistent debate about FTAS and the bipartisan support for it meant that no single lawmaker had to invest their time and reputation in building much support for it. It just made sense. FTAS's origin story, in turn, is the first quality that rendered it open to reform once policymakers acknowledged its failure.

Educators in Texas in the early 1990s faced two relatively new challenges. First, then Governor George W. Bush pioneered a new accountability system that considered student achievement, dropout rates, and attendance when allocating school funding. This meant that schools would face financial and reputational consequences if they failed to meet state benchmarks for each of these metrics. Second, there was a meteoric rise in national fear of teenage "super-predators," theoretical (and, implicitly, black and brown) teenagers unmoored by their conscience and empathy and prone to catastrophically violent acts. Scholars and educators warned that such individuals were on the rise among student bodies across the nation (e.g., Haberman 2014).

In 1995, the Texas legislature took up revising the Texas Education Code to accommodate the demands of the new accountability system. Buried in the over 40 hours of public debate on changes to the education code that year—ranging from the impact of accountability on teachers, students, athletes, and students with special needs to timelines for testing—was a single judge who testified for mere minutes about his support of proposed adjustments to the Education Code to address declining attendance in Texas schools. Judge Keith Baker supported reclassifying truancy as a Class C misdemeanor, stating:

> When we have exhausted all of our normal remedies and we haven't been able to get our child back in school, to have the ability to transfer the case up to juvenile court, and it has real teeth to enforce truancy laws. . . . There was an attorney general's opinion that pointed out that one of the current weaknesses is that no peace officer can pick up a child not attending school. If a child is in a gang they can show up at school, but not go to class. The police officers have no power to take that child into custody.
>
> (*74th Senate Education Committee Tape 1 of 5* 1995)

Echoing the general fears about teenage violence, Baker's testimony follows the popular broken-windows approach to policing (Wilson & Kelling 1982) in which stringent consequences for minor transgressions help establish order and prevent more disruptive crimes from occurring.

In the era of the broken-windows approach to policing and the warnings of increasingly violent teenagers, enforcing stringent consequences for early signs of rule breaking seemed logical. This mindset, along with the increased urgency to keep students in school for accountability purposes, made treating truancy as an adult criminal misdemeanor (which could result in jail time, fines, and mandated reporting on job applications) seem like a reasonable decision. One legislator, who eventually supported revising FTAS, admitted that, even as someone who thought of themselves as particularly in tune with the interests of underserved children in Texas, the policy seemed an entirely reasonable solution to the state's truancy challenges (Democratic State Senator in office in 1995, personal communication, June 18, 2015). On May 30, 1995, the legislature passed the Texas Education Code with Section 25.094, which contained the Failure to Attend School (FTAS) policy. It passed with bipartisan support and with little fanfare.[1] The final FTAS policy allowed schools to charge students with more than ten unexcused absences with a Class C misdemeanor and to take students into custody for skipping school more than the allowed number of days. By all accounts, FTAS passed as a preventive measure to address foreseeable challenges with a new accountability system, a persistent attendance problem, and a fear of unsupervised teenagers wreaking havoc in Texas communities.

For the first several years of its implementation, FTAS continued in relative anonymity. The legislature adjusted the age limits, initially increasing the severity of the consequences for truancy by adding a $500 fine in addition to the Class C misdemeanor and possible jail time in 2001 (see Table 7.1). That same year, the legislature added consequences for parents of truant students. However, by 2011, signs of doubt about the policy's effectiveness appeared. The legislature first decreased FTAS's stringency by limiting its applicability to twelve- to eighteen-year-olds (compared with the original applicability to six- through eighteen-year-olds). Then, in 2013, legislators introduced legislation to specifically ban ticketing for

[1] Proving a full comparison of those who supported the original punitive policy and the repeal in 2015 is not possible because the first bill was passed without a roll-call vote in the House and Senate (*Senate Journal 1995 Regular Session* 1995, 3346).

Table 7.1 Failure to attend school legislation, 1995–2015

Date	Development
1995	• SB1 allows schools to charge truant students, ages 6–21, with Class C misdemeanors, which can result in an adult criminal conviction.
2001	• SB 1432 adds in the possibility of parental conviction for truancy, under parent contributing to nonattendance, which includes possible fines up to $500 and a misdemeanor charge.
2005	• HB 1575 substitutes "excused" for "involuntary" as the type of absence students must prove in order to avoid a truancy charge.
2011	• HB 734 allows FTAS to be tried outside of juvenile courts if the county population exceeds 1.75 million, which practically facilitates more adult criminal convictions and fewer intervention supports. • SB 1489 limits FTAS charges to 12- to 18-year-olds.
2013	• The Texas Judicial Council identifies school ticketing and truancy as policy priorities for the 2013 legislative session. • Senator John Whitmire and Representative Royce West introduce SB 1234, which bans school-based ticketing for disruptive behavior and decriminalizes truancy. • Governor Rick Perry accidentally vetoes the decriminalization of truancy but signs the bans on school-based ticketing.
2015	• Chief Justice Nathan Hecht takes up the cause of revising FTAS. • Senator Whitmire and Representative West push to broaden the FTAS revision. • HB 2398 (which included SB 106, the version that originated in the Senate) revises FTAS by decriminalizing truancy and requiring schools to demonstrate prevention and intervention before sending students to juvenile court.

Source : Author's summary of Texas legislation related to FTAS using "truancy" and FTAS as search terms in the Texas legislature's archive—found at https://lrl.texas.gov/legis/billSearch/advancedsearch.cfm.

school-based misbehaviors. While this legislation passed the legislature with bipartisan support and Governor Perry declared his intention to sign it, according to multiple sources he accidentally vetoed the decriminalization of FTAS in 2013. Demonstrating their commitment to reforming the failed policy, in 2015 the legislature passed a revision to FTAS with bipartisan support for the second time, at which point the bill received the governor's signature.

The public testimony and debate in the Texas legislature on revising FTAS focused entirely on the contemporary impacts of the policy and on how judges had learned to use it as part of their toolkit to help young people. Compared with the debate on reforming Washington's R&D tax credits, there was a notable absence of any discussion of the specific purpose for which the policy was originally enacted. Given that FTAS was just one of many changes implemented to address student achievement, there was little reason to revisit the original purpose for the policy. Instead the debate centered on FTAS's failure to accomplish its original goals: to keep students in school and to increase graduation rates.

An opportunity for policy revision, however, far from guarantees that policy revision will occur (e.g., Kingdon 1984). Just as problems must be politicized, opportunities for policy revision must also become politically salient for change to occur. FTAS's origins created the possibility that public officials would be open to reform, but it was the clear and compelling findings on the policy that brought its failure to public officials' attention. The coalitions that formed in response to data on the policy's outcomes encouraged lawmakers to take concrete steps toward revision.

Policy and Institutional Design: A Story of Supplements

The design of FTAS and the relevant Texas state institutions reflects a broad investment in data collection and an anemic investment in analytical capacity. Unlike the case with the R&D tax credits in Washington State, the original FTAS policy did not mandate any data collection, nor did it specify agencies, timelines, or metrics for evaluating the program. However, preexisting state-run data efforts created the potential for meaningful evaluation. Once a pair of nonstate research organizations successfully accessed the collected data, they could supplement the anemic state's analytical capacity and produce politically compelling results.

Ongoing and universal data collection efforts initiated independently of FTAS created high collection capacity for the policy. As described in Chapter 3, between 2000 and 2006 the Texas Education Agency began collecting longitudinal data on the educational experiences and outcomes on the universe of students that entered seventh grade in the state between 2000 and 2002 (Carmichael et al. 2011). This data was uniquely suited to evaluating the long-term outcomes of various education policies, as it was a state-sponsored, centrally managed effort to gather data on each individual middle school student. According to *Breaking Schools' Rules,* the first report that evaluated the impacts of school-based discipline using the data, what made their research possible was "the opportunity to study at least six years' worth of state student level education and juvenile justice electronic records and to benefit from broad bipartisan support for this research" (Carmichael et al. 2011, pp. 11–12). Interviews with researchers involved in this analysis confirmed the rarity of such a complete dataset on student educational experiences and outcomes (Lead Texas Education Researcher, personal communication, June 22, 2015).

The more general nature of the data collection may have provided some political cover such that schools may not have been aware of exactly how the information was going to be used and therefore had fewer clear incentives to shirk reporting responsibilities. Notably, the longitudinal Texas Education Agency dataset that the Texas Public Policy Research Institute (TPPRI) used was centrally managed and not collected in response to a single policy outcome. Eventually, in 2011, after the publication of *Breaking Schools' Rules* and after the longitudinal data collection on middle schoolers, the legislature required schools to document the number of FTAS truancy charges submitted each year. While schools, in theory, would receive a lowered state rating for failing to report their truancy charges, public records requests showed substantial missing data in the FTAS-specific reporting. Texas Appleseed's *Class Not Court* report shows that fewer than 450 of the more than 1,000 school districts were present in the Texas Education Agency's dataset. Furthermore, of the districts that did submit data, many only did so inconsistently (Fowler et al. 2015, 50). This suggests that state collection capacity creates the possibility of high-quality data. However, the preferences, missions, and specific incentives of the agencies and individuals tasked with collecting and reporting data can influence the quality of the final information—those uninterested in empirically analyzing a policy may find ways to influence the usability of the data to complicate policy evaluation. Centralized collection plans—evidence of high collection capacity—may produce more usable data that results in analysis that is more resilient to partisan reframing. Prior to 2011, data had been collected, but no one was analyzing it. By 2011, researchers at Texas universities and advocacy organizations accessed the data and had begun disseminating their findings on the impacts of the program.

The lack of a specific policy target for evaluation may have facilitated the comprehensive data collection that the Texas Education Agency had conducted. The agency had no single policy that it intended to evaluate, and it expected to control access to this information. In fact, the data sat unanalyzed until 2010 when the governor and several legislatures demanded that

TEA release the data to TPPRI for analysis.[2] The general nature of the data collection may have avoided raising concerns about the data possibly highlighting agency failures. In addition to this more general nature of the data collection effort, its universal coverage ensured that it could be retroactively used to study a range of phenomena, given that it avoided the challenges to inference posed by studying only a sample of the population.

High-quality data existed, but no agencies or researchers had been charged with analyzing it. However, more than a decade into the policy, two local research organizations supplemented the state's analytical capacity and catalyzed the negative policy feedback effects for FTAS. The TPPRI at Texas A&M did release *Breaking Schools' Rules* in 2011 after collaborating with the Texas Education Agency and the Texas Juvenile Justice system to gain access to relevant data. While this document did not directly assess FTAS, it offered compelling insight into the awesome power of school-based discipline and the severe long-term impacts of adolescent exposure to the criminal justice system. This report showed conclusively that increasing the consequences (e.g., suspension and expulsion) for school-based misbehavior did *not* change adolescent behavior and in fact resulted in highly undesirable and costly long-term life outcomes (e.g., greater involvement in the criminal justice system and joblessness,).

The fruits of high collection capacity enabled a second organization, Texas Appleseed, to affect the policy process four years later when they released a damning report using state-collected data. Entitled *Class Not Court*, this report specifically measured the prevalence of FTAS across Texas schools. *Class Not Court* relied on Freedom of Information Act requests to gain access to data gathered by the Office of Court Administration on the rates at which students across the state were being charged with Class C misdemeanors for truancy. Furthermore, Appleseed was also able to highlight the extreme disparities with which this supposedly universally implemented policy was being enforced more regularly for students of color, students from low-socioeconomic-status families, and students with disabilities. Figure 7.1 shows an example of how *Class Not Court* presented these findings.

[2] At the time, the Office of Juvenile Justice and Delinquency Prevention was changing its grant-making guidelines to reward states that were meeting certain benchmarks for juvenile justice and juvenile detention. The Texas governor and legislature were eager to get more information about where the state fell according to these metrics and supported analyzing already collected data to better evaluate state trends.

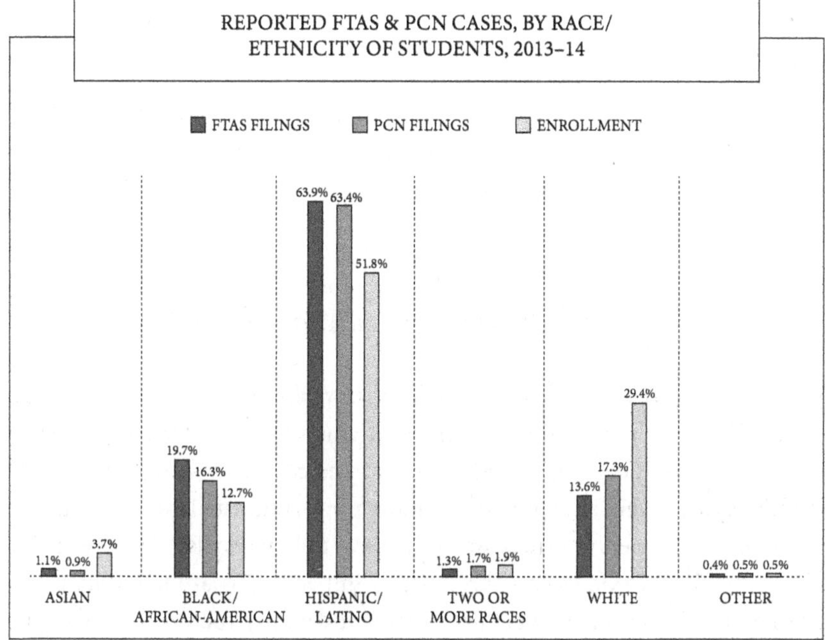

Figure 7.1 Infographic from Texas Appleseed's Report Class Not Court depicting racial disparities of FTAS filings
Source: *Class Not Court*, Fowler et al. (2015, 4).

The policy trajectory of FTAS shows that data collection capacity alone is insufficient to generate the political will to acknowledge failed policies. Not until nonstate researchers supplemented the state's analytical capacity did the data reflecting the failure of FTAS influence its politics. Prior to 2011, the treasure trove of data on Texas's student outcomes sat unanalyzed. By 2011, researchers had started publishing analyses, and public officials then started to pay attention. Perhaps most notably, Chief Justice of the Texas Supreme Court Wallace Jefferson took note of the findings of *Breaking Schools' Rules* and made addressing the criminalization of school-based behavior the signature policy focus of the Texas Judicial Council beginning in 2013 (the subsequent legislative session in which policy change could actually happen). In his 2012 article written for the National Center for State Courts, Jefferson references his realization of the deleterious and devastating impacts of FTAS, among other policies that criminalized school-based misbehavior. As described in Chapter 4, Jefferson cited

Breaking Schools' Rules and *Class Not Court* multiple times as justification for his focus on ending the criminalization of truancy and other school-age behaviors.

In response, hearings about revising the policy were grounded in data. Furthermore, the debates no longer centered on making the policy more stringent, as they had been during the early 2000s, but on whether or not the policy should exist at all.

Group Dynamics: Clear Evidence Shifts Power Dynamics

Echoing the process of policy revision for Washington's R&D tax credits, the availability of compelling data and clear analysis created the opportunity for more diffusely organized and less resourced constituencies (families and students) to outweigh the pressure of more powerful vested interests (judges and business owners) to successfully achieve policy revision. Furthermore, the compelling evidence on the policy's impacts also attracted attention from both small government conservatives and equity-minded liberals. This coalition, in turn, cooperated to support revising FTAS.

Coalitions Form with Different Rationales but Same Goal

Texas has long been a conservative state, and its policies in the 2010s were no exception. The governors were Republican, and the State Senate and House of Representatives had strong conservative majorities. And while the 2010s saw the beginnings of a decline in conservative support for tough-on-crime policies and support for mass incarceration (Dagan & Teles 2014), it was still quite common—and electorally popular—for conservative public officials to support such policies. This makes it all the more puzzling how Texas managed to revise its truancy policy. The clarity of the data on FTAS's outcomes shifted the policy conversation away from abstract partisan preferences to a concrete reaction to Texas's own outcomes. Clear findings on how FTAS affected Texas youth shifted the debate away from theoretical and ideologically grounded notions of how communities and schools should treat wayward students and toward responding to the systematically documented evidence that FTAS was exacerbating more problems than it was solving. These clear findings also allowed advocates for reform to develop an array of narratives that appealed to groups with different ideological reasons for opposing the growth of a carceral state.

Once state officials had access to *Breaking Schools' Rules*, both liberals and conservatives took issue with FTAS. Liberals and criminal justice advocates in the state took issue with the draconian involvement of the criminal justice system in schools and argued for a more therapeutic and preventive response to student misbehavior. *Breaking Schools' Rules* confirmed the liberals' persistent arguments that ratcheting up consequences ineffectively addressed undesirable criminal behavior because it failed to acknowledge or address the root causes—poverty, homelessness, and a weak social safety net. Further exacerbating inequality, the data also showed that students of color, students in poverty, and students with disabilities were disproportionately likely to receive court-based sanctions through FTAS (Fowler et al. 2015). (See Table 7.2 for a summary.)

In 2011, conservatives were on the precipice of a widespread reevaluation of their support for tough-on-crime policies (see Teles & Dagan 2016)), of which FTAS could be considered one. The new logic for conservative opposition to mass incarceration stemmed from a reaction to the exorbitant cost and increases in government infrastructure and personnel needed to sustain the carceral state. While the investments in the carceral state may have been worth the increase in spending and government had it worked, *Breaking Schools' Rules* clearly showed that reactive and punitive consequences for young people not only failed to prevent future rule-breaking, but it also resulted in greater involvement in and dependence on the state in the long run (as measured by criminal justice involvement and joblessness).

Perhaps most shockingly for both liberals and conservatives was the sheer number of students who were being run through truancy proceedings each year. Appleseed showed that over 100,000 students per year had received truancy charges. Combined with the clear evidence that early involvement in the criminal justice system was likely to result in continued involvement, as per the findings of *Breaking Schools' Rules*, the findings from Appleseed were once again concerning to conservatives from a financial and efficiency standpoint.

The reputation and timing of TPPRI's involvement may have played an important role in facilitating the bipartisan coalition to support revising FTAS. While both Texas Appleseed and TPPRI describe themselves as nonpartisan, TPPRI likely held this title more credibly in the eyes of

Table 7.2 Research relevant to Failure to Attend School, 1995–2015

Date	Report	Evidence	Findings
July 2011	*Breaking Schools' Rules*	Texas Education Agency data from longitudinal study of universe of Texas middle schools combined with juvenile justice data	• Almost 60% of Texas students had been suspended at least once during their 6–12 school years, with African American students disproportionately represented • Being suspended increased chances of dropping out and being held back two-fold, and made future involvement in the criminal justice system three times as likely • Suspension & expulsion rates varied significantly across schools with similar characteristics
March 2015	*Class Not Court*	Data from individual school districts obtained through Freedom of Information Act Requests and Texas Office of Court Administration	• Texas prosecutes more than twice the number of truancy cases of all other states combined • 80% of children sanctioned for truancy are from low socioeconomic status families, and the most common sanction is fines • Over 6000 students were ordered to drop out of high school and take the GED over three years • Despite variable reporting, rates of truancy prosecution do not align with improved attendance or graduation rates

Source : author's summary based on Breaking Schools' Rules (Carmichael et al. 2011) and Class Not Court reports (D. Fowler et al. 2015).

skeptics. Unlike Texas Appleseed, TPPRI was an organization of professionally trained scholars housed at Texas A&M, the more conservative of the state's two flagship universities. Furthermore, the Council on State Government and the Republican governor had encouraged the Texas Education Agency to grant TPPRI access to their data (Carmichael et al. 2011), giving the research a credible foundation of conservative support.

Researchers and administrators from TPPRI did not habitually lobby the legislature on behalf of specific policies. Appleseed and its executive director, Deborah Fowler, on the other hand, had been more involved in building political support for shrinking the size of the carceral state in the past, and therefore she was likely more skeptically viewed as nonpartisan. In fact, *Breaking Schools' Rules* directly acknowledges Fowler's "tireless" efforts which "not only helped put school discipline issues on Texas policymakers' radar, but have prompted improvements to policy and state law" (Carmichael et al. 2011, v). At one point during public hearings for revising FTAS, Senator Bill Hagerty (R) charged that Appleseed was simply a front group for national, liberal efforts to change Texas policy (*SB 106 Open Testimony* 2015).

The sequencing of events is just as important as whether they occurred at all (Pierson 2011). In this case, the earlier release of *Breaking Schools' Rules*, which came from researchers at Texas A&M University, was locally produced, more credibly nonpartisan, and based on the more comprehensive data. This in turn played an important role in building both liberal and conservative confidence that FTAS was failing to meet its objectives.

Although their ideological rationale for ending FTAS may have differed slightly from Texas Appleseed and other liberal-leaning groups, conservative groups supporting reform relied on the same data points to make their case to the legislature. Derek Cohen, a policy analyst for the conservative Texas Public Policy Foundation and Texas Right on Crime, also emphasized the absurdity, from his organization's perspective, of annually charging more than 115,000 students with truancy: "we are saying that 115 thousand is saying but for the grace of the coercive power of the state, we wouldn't be able to deal with these kids, and all we have is the 'hammer'" (*Senate Committee on Criminal Justice* 2015). Cohen cited the same types of peer-reviewed research that other supporters referenced to characterize FTAS as a failed policy. He argued that incarceration and court appearances were more likely to retraumatize a child rather than build their investment in attending school:

> Now today you are going to hear a lot about this mythical hammer is the needed coercive force simply needed to keep kids in school and there is going to be anecdotal evidence that this actually does, in some cases, work. However, study after study of peer-reviewed research has shown this is not the case, and often times this medicine is often more harmful than doing

> nothing at all. Now some of the judges and Justices of the Peace here to testify are not part of the problem. They care about the kids that come through their courts. However this bill as its laid out will still allow those courts to maintain jurisdiction over those kids . . . .this would be under child in need of supervision with robust protections. . . . This begs the question about the actual use of the state in this specific venue. . . . We are saying that skipping school as little as three times is tantamount to that.
>
> (*Senate Committee on Criminal Justice* 2015)

Using both state-specific research and peer-reviewed studies, Cohen undermined the arguments of opponents to revision before they were even able to make them. Supporters of revision leveraged data not only to highlight the policy's current failures, but also to advertise the success of possible alternatives to the status quo. For example, during the 2015 hearings for reforming FTAS, a representative from Round Rock Independent School District shared the community-based solution that the district implemented and described how the district's focus on addressing the root causes of truancy rather than punishing the student had resulted in a 50 percent decrease in truancy in three years.

Interestingly, while *individual* judges and justices of the peace vocally opposed revising FTAS, the data caught the attention of the larger judicial system organizations, and they actively acknowledged policy failure and supported revision (see Table 7.3). The Justices of the Peace and Constables Association supported revising FTAS. Furthermore, the chief justice of the Texas Supreme Court, Wallace Jefferson, made reforming school-based ticketing, including FTAS, a top priority for the Texas Judicial Council in 2013. The subsequent chief justice, Nathan Hecht, continued the court's support for reforming FTAS, after Governor Perry's accidental veto. In his testimony before the Senate Criminal Justice Committee in March 2015, Chief Hecht explained the pervasive use of FTAS and the negative consequences for young people, and thus, the judiciary's focus on reforming the policy. In addition, he once again cited the reports and data that emerged from *Breaking Schools' Rules* and *Class Not Court* as important evidence of the damage being done to Texas children.

FTAS may not have emerged in response to a crisis, but by 2013, there was an urgent crisis in the eyes of many liberals and a growing number of conservatives in the nation and especially in Texas: mass incarceration. Though the failures—equity and racial injustice or big government and

Table 7.3 Supporters and opponents registered at FTAS hearings, 1995–2015

Support status quo	Support policy revision
Individual judges	Texas Judicial Council
Individual school administrators	Texas Public Policy Foundation
Truancy class providers	Texas Appleseed
Individual superintendents	Texas Parent Teacher Association
	Individual students and families
	Youth justice organizations
	Texas Association of Business
	Texas Criminal Defense Lawyers Association
	Texas Association of School Administrators

Source : Author's summary of witness lists for FTAS hearings found in the Texas legislative archives.

spending—varied by ideology, powerful individuals on both sides of the aisle agreed that the rapid growth of the carceral state (and the subsequent adverse consequences for communities and government spending) needed to be addressed. Revising school-based ticketing for truancy was seen as a step in the right direction. While there was no certain alternative, an increasing number of constituencies argued more convincingly that the status quo was untenable. Twenty-five members of the House of Representatives were in office in both 1995 and 2015. Fourteen of the twenty-five voted *for* FTAS in 1995 but voted to revise the policy in 2015 (four of these members were Republicans and ten were Democrats); nine of the representatives opposed FTAS in both 1995 and 2015 (see Table 7.4). Even more overwhelming support for revising FTAS emerged among the senators who were in office during the same period. Six senators who had been in office in 1995 remained in 2015. All six of them had voted to pass SB 1 and to reform it by supporting HB 2398 (*Senate Journal: 74th Legislature, Eighteenth Day* 1995, 3346; *Senate Journal: 84th Legislature, Sixty-Third Day* 2015, 3496).

Clear Evidence of Failure Shifts Burden of Proof to Status-Quo Supporters

As policy feedback theories would predict, once constituencies acquired new powers and resources, they were hesitant to give it up. In the case of

Table 7.4 Support for criminalizing truancy over time among representatives in office, 1995–2015

Changed position: (Voted for SB 1 and HB 2398)		Maintained Opposition to FTAS (Nay on SB 1 and Yea on HB 2398)		Maintained Support for FTAS (Yea for SB 1 and Nay for HB 2398)		Changed position: (Nay on SB 1 and Nay on HB 2398)	
Allen	D	Alonzo	D	Kuempel	R	Dutton	D
Coleman	D	Alvarado	D				
Cook	D	Davis	D				
Craddick	R	Farrar	D				
Elkins	R	Longoria	D				
Giddings	D	Oliveira	D				
Gutierrez	D	Price	D				
Hernandez	D	Raymond	D				
Howard	R	Turner, S	D				
Johnson	D						
King, T.	D						
Naishtat	D						
Pickett	D						
Smithee	R						

Source: Author's summary of legislative records.

FTAS, judges, justices of the peace, and attendance officers accrued additional powers, and truancy bootcamp operators had access to a stream of guaranteed clients. Likely motivated to protect these resources and powers, in debates about FTAS, judges presented a litany of success stories for the state's approach to truancy. Young people, on the other hand, pleaded for a more supportive and therapeutic approach. Both of these narratives could have been equally compelling to legislators. However, thanks to high collection capacity and the analytical efforts of TPPRI and Texas Appleseed, only those supporting revision had large-scale, statewide data on their side, suggesting that their stories represented the trends across the state. This compelling data elevated these voices as a credible counternarrative to the compelling stories judges and bootcamp operators told about reformed youth.

According to the judges who argued for continuation of FTAS in legislative committee hearings, it was important to remind young people of the judges' ability to charge, arrest, and imprison young people as leverage with particularly obstinate students. Judges repeatedly attended the House of Representative and Senate committee hearings for bills attempting to decriminalize truancy. The main hearing on March 31, 2015 drew thirteen people testifying against amending FTAS, and nine of these were judges, justices of the peace, or attendance officers (*Witness List for SB 106*, 2015). The testimony from these constituents shared a consistent narrative: jailing and ticketing students should be a last resort, but taking away the officials' ability to threaten these things would undermine respect for the court. For example, in March 2015 during a Senate Criminal Justice Committee hearing on revising FTAS, Judge Wayne Mack argued as follows:

> Us being able to summon them [teenagers] to court, bring them to court, it is the sole leverage we have to try and get them in school. We are citing systems and schools and judges that don't work, but what I hear down here and concern from gentleman that spoke earlier . . . .what I am here to tell you that there are systems and judges within the current bill as they do work.
>
> (*Senate Committee on Criminal Justice* 2015)

Judge Mack also held that decriminalizing truancy, which would remove the potential to threaten students with jail time and tickets, would result in an increase of not only truancy but also risky adolescent behavior, evoking the "superpredator" fears of the 1990s:

> In this current form, Senator, you are throwing the baby with the bathwater . . . by failing to discipline parents and students associated with truancy this bill surely is creating a society where a higher percentage of at-risk children are getting into the pipeline.
>
> (*Senate Committee on Criminal Justice* 2015)

Over the course of the 2015 hearings, several judges, justices of the peace, and attendance officers told stories of individual students who claimed they turned their lives around in response to either the threat of or actual exposure to time in jail and a criminal charge. These officials argued that these individual data points suggested the policy was working (*Witness List for SB 106*, 2015). Several parents also testified, stating that without the substantial intervention of the court, their child would not have changed their destructive habits of skipping school and engaging in other risky behavior. Though evidence from Appleseed suggested that Dallas, in fact, implemented FTAS most widely, one judge suggested that the policy was failing only in Houston, the district of Senator Whitmire, who was leading the revision effort. The judge argued that while Senator Whitmire's hometown of Houston might be struggling, the rest of the state was leveraging FTAS effectively, arguing, "we don't need a solution for the entire state because of the triage in Houston" (*Senate Committee on Criminal Justice* 2015). Backed by data provided by Texas Appleseed, Whitmire quickly rebutted this claim, reminding his fellow committee members that this was in fact a statewide problem and that the Dallas metro area actually exceeded the Houston metro area for total ticketing.

In addition to judges and a handful of parents, a small boutique industry of running for-profit truancy bootcamps had emerged in some of the cities with higher truancy numbers. Some judges regularly sentenced truant students to attend these bootcamps, with the (theoretical) goal of having the students learn discipline and time management skills to facilitate more regular school attendance (*SB 106 Open Testimony* 2015). Unsurprisingly, the owners of these bootcamps testified ardently in favor of continuing FTAS before the state legislature (*Witness List for SB 106,* 2015). They also argued that the threat of harsh consequences improved students' behavior. In support, they shared multiple anecdotes about students who, they claimed, improved their attendance and academic performance after completing a bootcamp course. However, these bootcamp owners had no systematic data to back up their claims about the widespread benefit of their services.

During the 2013 and 2014 revision attempts, supporters of revision relied on anecdotal evidence to demonstrate FTAS's failure. Young people and, occasionally, their parents too, testified to the devastating impacts of ticketing, incarceration, and jail time on their self-worth and motivation to succeed in school. Several students argued that going to court and jail made them feel that adults thought they were worthless and incapable of success, which further entrenched their aversion to school. Other young people who were in the foster system argued that ratcheting up consequences did not factor into their decision making, especially when they were trying to cope with more urgent needs, such as surviving in an unsupportive foster home or juggling the effects of chronic homelessness.

The available data from *Breaking Schools' Rules* and *Class Not Court* informed Senator Whitmire's introductions to hearings on FTAS related bills, which often included diatribes about the widespread impact of FTAS, citing data on the number of schools and the number of citations recently handed out. In the whole chamber hearing on the decriminalization of

FTAS, Whitmire began with the following description of the extensive impact of FTAS, "Texas last year in its 1050 school districts wrote over a hundred thousand criminal citations to students and parents. This effort has been to decriminalize student behavior" (*Senate Committee on Criminal Justice* 2015).

In their testimony before the Senate and House of Representative committees, as evidence of the widespread impact of the policy's failure, supporters of revision frequently cited the data point that, under FTAS, over 100,000 students had been charged in 2013 alone. For example, Manny Nazami, a juvenile justice attorney from the Earl Carl Institute in Houston, testified in support of reforming FTAS, arguing that it did not allow for the nuance and therapeutic services often needed when dealing with young people. Instead of just relaying his experience in defending young people in truancy court, he was able to contextualize his experience as being common across throughout the state:

> You all know the statistics, 115,000 were prosecuted in 2013, two times as many as all other states combined, four out of five children taken to truancy court were economically disadvantaged and there was a disproportionate impact on Latino and special ed students.
>
> (*Senate Committee on Criminal Justice* 2015)

The comparison to other states and the disproportionality of the impacts of the policy's failure emphasized the generalizability of Nazami's personal experience with the policy's failure.

Although individual judges and some school administrators painted a bleak picture of the chaos to come if the legislature decriminalized truancy, the legislature voted not once, but twice, with bipartisan support to revise FTAS.[3] By 2015, the revision passed with near universal support across both houses of the state legislature (see Figure 7.2). Supporters of revision were able to combine the heart-wrenching stories of students traumatized by their time in court or in jail with clear evidence that these circumstances were

[3] Revision of FTAS, along with two other bills decriminalizing school-based behaviors, passed the legislature with bipartisan support in the 2013 legislative session. Although Governor Perry declared his intention to sign it, according to multiple sources he accidentally vetoed the decriminalization of FTAS, while signing the other two similar bills. In turn, the legislature had to reintroduce the bill in 2015.

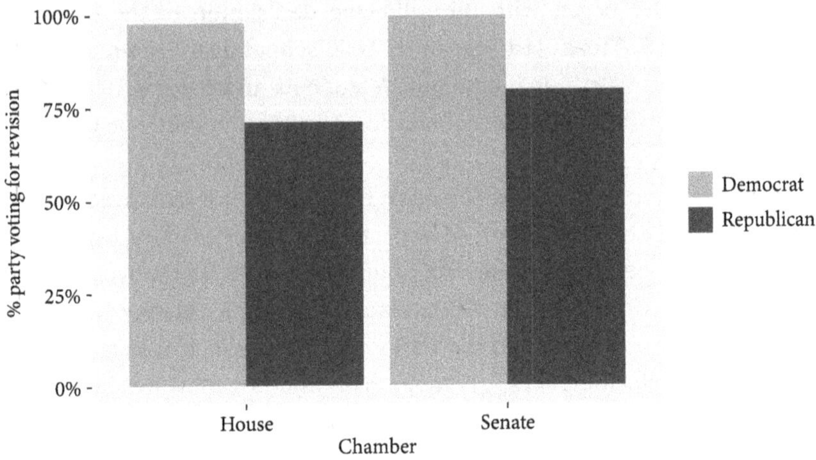

Figure 7.2 Support for revising FTAS, 2015

Source: Author's calculations based on roll-call votes in the House and Senate Journals. Party affiliation taken from the Texas Legislative Archives' list of membership lists and partisan affiliations. The *y*-axis represents the percentage of each party in each chamber that supported passage of HB 2398.

not aberrations, but rather a common norm across the state, and, thus, one worthy of an explicit ban from the legislature.

Conclusion

In both the Texas FTAS case and Washington's R&D tax credits, state-collected data informed transformative research that highlighted the failures of each policy. Unlike the experience in Washington, the data collection efforts for FTAS were not specific to the program. Instead, the state had initiated an ongoing, comprehensive data collection effort that had relevant data for evaluating FTAS. While this data sat unused for several years, it did exist. Thus, in 2009 researchers were able to collaborate with the Texas governor and legislators to pressure the Texas Education Agency to release the data for analysis.

The dynamics surrounding the revision of FTAS demonstrate the power of state-backed, broad-based data collection efforts. Furthermore, a comparison of attention to and support for revising FTAS pre- and post-2011, when TPPRI published *Breaking Schools' Rules*, suggests the power of data to draw the attention of public officials to a policy failure. It may be that universal data collection is more immune to resource threats than targeted collection efforts.[4] In this case, the Texas Education Agency had initiated a longitudinal study unrelated to FTAS, but the information facilitated careful study of the impacts of school-based discipline. Prior to the analysis of the educational, disciplinary, and juvenile justice data, there was limited acknowledgment of policy failure. The acknowledgment and subsequent policy revisions came once TPPRI and, later, Texas Appleseed, were able to analyze the data the state had collected. The clear outcomes regarding suspension, expulsion, and criminal justice exposure, in turn, meant political discussions that centered on whether the documented outcome of the existing policy was acceptable, rather than on what outcomes the policy was producing and how the state should go about studying such outcomes. Judges, along with a handful of school administrators and the original policy sponsor, continued to support FTAS. However, those calling for revision of the policy had reliable information to counteract anecdotal narratives of policy success. With clear data on the side of policy failure, the power dynamics shifted from the judges supporting the status quo to the families, students, legislators, and youth advocates arguing for a change.

Unlike Washington State, access to the data on FTAS and the subsequent analysis resulted from the efforts of nonstate actors. The Texas Public Policy Research Institute cooperated with the governor and several legislatures eager to learn more about juvenile justice trends in the state to gain access to the Texas Education Agency data. Texas Appleseed had to access a portion of the needed data more forcibly through Freedom of Information Act requests, but overall, both organizations were able to conduct their analyses with resources (both the data itself and political support) from the state. The state data collection efforts created the possibility of policy analysis, once there was the political will and analytical expertise to do so.

The power of data to generalize and dramatize the widespread impacts of the policy in the FTAS case echoes that in the Washington R&D tax

[4] This reflects the logic of findings about targeted versus universal welfare state programs. Scholars have shown that targeted programs are much more vulnerable to retrenchment and political attack than universal programs because of constituents' ability to identify and stigmatize the recipient group of a targeted program (Fording et al. 2007).Universal programs, on the other hand, build a wide base of support (Skocpol 1995). While stigma is not necessarily operating in the case of data, the inability of bureaucrats and other political actors to precisely identify *which* programs may be evaluated with any given dataset may somewhat insulate the data collection process from shirking or sabotage that might interfere with its usefulness.

credit case. This data supported students, families, social justice advocates, and conservatives eager to shrink the size and spending of the state government to convincingly argue that the excess cost and harms of the policy were widespread.

Both R&D tax credits and FTAS reflect relatively anonymous and preemptive origins. While public officials had a particular public policy problem in mind when they were crafting the original bill, it was an *anticipated* problem rather than a crisis dominating the headlines during the policy development phase. What happens when there is no reliable data for research organizations to analyze? The next chapter examines how the dynamics change when there is strong analytical capacity but no quality data to be analyzed.

8

The Hollow Case (Washington Truancy)

In the ideal and treasure trove cases, the state has collected usable data that, once analyzed, can credibly corroborate narratives of policy failure. Becca's Bill—a failed truancy policy in Washington State—represents the hollow case type in this study. In this case, there is robust analytical capacity without meaningful investments in data collection capacity. Accordingly, Washington had invested in analytical capacity for Becca's Bill but failed to establish robust collection capacity. Its failure to pair collection capacity with analytical capacity rendered investments in analytical capacity impotent to corroborate narratives of failure. Consequently, those advocating for reform were unable to convince Becca's Bill supporters that revising the policy was necessary. The hollow case is the first of the two cases in which the state failed to collect usable data.

Becca's Bill offers an illuminating contrast to FTAS, highlighting the importance of having statewide data to contextualize anecdotal reports of the benefits and harms of a policy. With its many research bureaucracies, Washington's analytical capacity is higher than Texas's (see Chapter 5 for a more detailed discussion). State research organizations alone published more than ten reports on the implementation and outcomes of Becca's Bill prior to 2017. Interestingly, far more than in Texas, lawmakers, advocates, and judges explicitly articulated their respect for science research and data. Yet, after two decades of experience with the policies, only Texas had revised its failing truancy policy.

Without a precise and comprehensive data collection plan, the findings from state research organizations on the impacts of Becca's Bill were contradictory and inconclusive. This variation in outcomes facilitated the claim of both supporters and opponents of revision that state evidence corroborated their perspective. The persistence of the status quo in the Becca's Bill case suggests that in the face of uncertainty about a policy's outcomes, supporters of reform may struggle to frame their narratives of failure as anything but an aberration to be lamented but not addressed. The hollow case shows the

The Politics of Failed Policies. Sarah James, Oxford University Press. © Oxford University Press (2025).
DOI: 10.1093/9780197813645.003.0009

challenge of relying on nonstate actors to supplement collection capacity, and, in turn, demonstrates how the state is uniquely suited to collect usable data on policy outcomes. Compared with the Washington R&D tax credits and Texas's Failure to Attend School, Becca's Bill also suggests that a policy's origin in crisis breeds additional uncertainty about revising failed policies without clear evidence.

Policy Origins: Crisis Breeds Policy Resilience

Even more so than Failure to Attend School in Texas and the R&D tax credits in Washington, the case of Becca's Bill highlights the importance of policy origins for understanding the potential for failure recognition. Two contextual factors stand out: first, the policy was created in response to a (at least perceived) crisis, and the original legislation abdicated decision making and control over data collection to local authorities. I will show that elected officials are more hesitant to recognize the failure of policies crafted to address a specific crisis. Second, limited investment in data collection capacity exacerbates the hesitancy to abandon a failed policy. The absence of clear data and compelling findings makes politically justifying the risk of abandoning a known policy for a new policy less palatable to (re)election-oriented public officials.

In 1993, Rebecca Hedman, a 13-year-old with a history of truancy, drug addiction, and prostitution, ran away from her home in Seattle, Washington, and fled to Spokane. She was found several days later, raped and murdered by the john that had been taking advantage of her desperation to feed her drug addiction. In the aftermath of the murder, Hedman's parents argued that they had repeatedly sought support for their daughter prior to her murder, but state laws did not allow them to detain Rebecca, despite her history of truancy and running away from home. Her parents argued that, had they been able to keep Rebecca in a safe place—school, home, or a treatment center—then they could have helped her recover from her mental health and addiction issues. Understandably, Washington officials were horrified by the tragedy, and both elected officials and the public responded to the Hedmans' explanation for how the state had failed them. Senator Jim Hargrove (D), in particular, took up the cause and was the leading legislative advocate for addressing the gaps in the state's response to runaways and truants.

In April 1995, the Washington State legislature passed SB 5439, which was officially titled Becca's Bill in honor of the slain teenager. While Democrats did control the executive and legislative branches in the state, the bill passed with bipartisan support[1] and was lauded as an overall improvement to the state's juvenile policies, as it created a consequence—detention in a crisis residential center (CRC)—for young people who violated court orders to remain at home or attend school.[2] At the time of passage, policymakers, along with the Hedmans, hoped that allowing temporary detention would give parents, schools, and social workers time to meet with troubled young people and connect them with much needed social services to address the root causes of their truancy and runaway behavior (Murakami 1995). Prior to passage of Becca's Bill, parents could not commit children over the age of thirteen without the child's consent; the law raised this age to eighteen (Murakami 1995).

As described in Part I, the legislature included specific mandates for the state research bureaucracy to study the impacts of Becca's Bill to determine whether it was accomplishing its goal of providing parents, schools, and community members, with "better tools to help at-risk, runaway, and truant youth. In the area of truancy, the law was designed to put teeth into compulsory attendance laws by requiring schools to take certain steps to help students and parents eliminate unexcused absences and then to take legal action if students or parents do not respond to school efforts" (Truancy Case Processing Practices 2004, 3). However, decentralized and undefined data collection practices undermined the effectiveness of Washington researchers' ability to accurately assess the impact of the policy. A handful of senators introduced bills to revise Becca's Bill in 2015 and 2017, but neither made it out of committee.

Analytical Capacity Is Insufficient on Its Own

As the namesake of Washington's truancy legislation, Rebecca Hedman and her struggles with attendance, drugs, and prostitution and her horrific rape

[1] Notably, the governor did weaken certain consequences for running away in the bill prior to passage. Specifically, he vetoed the provisions that would have allowed the state to take away teenagers' driver's licenses for truancy and to detain children for up to six months for running away from foster care.

[2] Note that the policy implemented several other changes for runaway children and children in need of services (CHINS), but the truancy piece is the main focus of this project, and also became the most contested feature of Becca's Bill.

and murder were never far from mind during discussions of the policy. As a direct response to Hedman's disappearance and death, the policy was symbolically, at least, a public effort to avoid such tragic circumstances from occurring again. This response stands in stark contrast with the inconspicuous origins of Failure to Attend School (FTAS) in Texas and Washington's own R&D tax credit. Washington public officials' concern with preventing a similarly horrific event suggests that in the face of uncertainty about a policy that emerged from a crisis, public officials are more likely to revert to the status quo.

A major component of the original vision for Becca's Bill was the creation of several crisis residential centers—safe spaces that were *not* juvenile detention centers or jails where young people detained under Becca's Bill could go to get social services and reconnect with trusted adults before returning home and to school. Senators Jim Hargrove and Franklin (two of Becca's Bill's original sponsors) developed a diagram (see Figure 8.1) outlining the paths from court to support that truant students were supposed to experience under the policy, including a prominent role for the CRCs in policy implementation. Shortly after passage, however, the policy's implementation ran afoul of their vision. Hargrove and Franklin intended for every county to have a CRC that was not a jail, but could provide shelter for juveniles while their legal and family challenges were sorted out. But most counties could not afford to create or staff a CRC, leading some students to be placed in juvenile detention or jail (Santos 2015). Despite this major change in implementation, Hargrove continued to support the policy.

During committee meetings on Becca's Bill, Hargrove would regularly recall the origins of the policy, and even project a picture of himself and Senator Rosa Lee Franklin, explaining the various responses the courts could take to students who were truants or runaways (see Figure 8.1). In describing the picture, Hargrove would remind the committee about the original intent of the bill and would usually follow this reminder with a description of how he believed the policy was still effective. During the discussion of revising the policy to remove detention as an option, Hargrove noted the complexity of the system while also indicating his continued support, describing it as a "fairly complicated system and it may have a few holes in it today" (Public testimony on HB 5651 and HB 5745 2015).

In 2002, Norm Mailing, then the King County prosecutor, and Justice Bobbe Bridge, a former King County Superior Court judge, co-founded

In March 1995, Democratic state Sen. Jim Hargrove, left, of Hoquiam explains to other Senate Democrats how runaways would be treated under the Becca Bill, which the Legislature approved later that year. Joining him at right is former state Sen. Rosa Franklin, D-Tacoma. (Washington State Archives, Senate Photograph Collections.)

Figure 8.1 Senator Hargrove and Senator Franklin explaining Becca's Bill

The diagram in the photo represents Hargrove and Franklin's vision for the various supports available to young people struggling with truancy. The diagram represents both state supports and county-based supports that Hargrove and Franklin anticipated would be established once Becca's Bill was passed. The diagram represents both paths from the Crisis Resource Centers back to a young person's home (the left side of the diagram) and the resources, like Family Preservation Services (represented by FPS in the diagram) that could connect young people with mental health, addiction, and other resources.

the Becca Task Force to connect judges, educators, service providers, and juvenile court administrators. Mailing and Bridge hoped that creating an informal network for information sharing would help address some of the challenges of the state's decentralized court system and spread best practices for implementing Becca's Bill. Over time, the group became more professionalized, receiving grant money to hold annual conferences and informing research agendas related to truancy in Washington. Aware of the power of a name, Justice Bridge encouraged Mailing to incorporate Hedman's name into the task force title, calling it the Becca Task Force instead of the Truancy Task Force (Interview with Washington State Judge 2018). Naming the Task Force after Becca once again kept the horrors of the raped and slain teenager front of mind during all Task Force business. The majority of the Becca Task Force, in turn, supported continuation of detention as part of Becca's Bill. Notably, the 2015 revision attempt resulted from the *minority* report that came out of the Task Force.

Hedman's horrific death and the potential for another such death seemed to fuel legislators' wariness of substantially revising the policy until there was more clear evidence on what type of alternative would be more effective than Becca's Bill. In 2008, during a discussion of whether truancy and detention notices should be delivered to the students in person, one school truancy officer invoked Hedman's story to say that she was far from the first student who needed more support and services. The truancy officer continued to describe a pregnant young woman she had worked with who died in a similar situation as Hedman had years earlier. The officer concluded by insisting that by requiring young people to be served with their court orders in person, the state was undermining the effectiveness of the consequences (Public hearing on HB 6429 2008). During this same hearing, a King County defense attorney and member of the Becca Task Force described how the Task Force was unable to reach a consensus on the bill, and directly acknowledged the fear of making changes, given the limited information available to public officials, "We really don't know what works, so to cast a wider net, and maybe do something that is even counterproductive is scary to us" (Public hearing on HB 6429 2008). Public officials conveyed uncertainty about making even minor revisions to Becca's Bill without clear information about its impact.

Those who supported revisions to Becca's Bill also evoked Hedman's memory, suggesting that they too recognized the emotional power of reminding public officials about the horrors of the catalysing event for the policy. During the failed revision attempt in 2015, Commissioner Jaclyn Jesky testified that the committee needed to reconsider Becca's Bill to incorporate new understandings of youth trauma and teen decision making. In doing so, she tried to invoke the Hedman case as a cautionary tale of what could happen when *not* revising the policy: "Becca is still here. She is still here. We lost children this past year just the way Becca was lost. There is no difference" (Public hearing on 5651 2015). Nonetheless, Jesky failed to convince the committee. Moreover, bringing up Hedman may have even further emphasized the importance of continuing with the status quo until a clear, evidence-backed alternative emerged.

During this same hearing, Senator Jeannie Darnielle, who sponsored the 2015 bill to eliminate detention as an option for truancy, questioned Justice Bobbe Bridge, a member of the Becca Task Force, former judge and longtime supporter of the policy. The exchange highlights the tension that likely paralyzed many of the public officials involved:

SENATOR DARNIELLE: Where is the evidence Justice Bridge, that a child with mental health issues should be placed in incarceration, have their clothes removed . . . hands behind their back?

JUSTICE BRIDGE: There is none. Its contra-indicated . . . the research is really clear.

DARNIELLE: Why are we still doing it? How are we continuing it 20 years later?

BRIDGE: Danger to self or others and lack of alternatives. . . . Judges will say they have all too little recourse. (Public hearing on 5651 2015)

Bridge's response suggests that while there is strong, albeit more general, evidence that Becca's Bill is not age- or situation-appropriate, some public officials saw no other alternatives. Thus, they supported maintaining the status quo even though it was "contra-indicated" by scholarly research and national data.

Policy and Institutional Design: Decentralized Data Collection Precludes Meaningful Evaluation

Despite Becca's Bill's built-in mandate for state research organizations, specifically the Washington State Institute for Public Policy (WSIPP) and the Joint Legislative Audit and Review Committee (JLARC), to regularly examine policy outcomes, anaemic data collection capacity for Becca's Bill precluded meaningful evaluations of its impact. While the courts were charged with collecting data on implementation of the bill, vague definitions and the judicial system's decentralization made collecting usable data impossible (see Chapter 4 for a more detailed discussion). Thus, Washington's elected officials had a robust analytical team capable of analyzing policy outcomes but only extremely limited and faulty data to analyze. Without usable data on the policy's implementation, researchers could not infer any clear findings about the impact of the policy. This problem in turn allowed public officials to maintain their preexisting opinions of Becca's Bill and to focus their debate on whether and how to collect better information, rather than debating how to revise Becca's Bill itself. The unclear evidence on Becca's Bill also allowed the fear of instigating a second horrific crisis with an amended bill to persist among lawmakers.

Legislative documents show that elected officials themselves sensed the need for better data on Becca's Bill. Between 1995 and 2015, the Senate and House committees responsible for education and juvenile justice debated at least twenty bills that would have expanded, refined, or revised Becca's Bill (see Table 8.1). Of these bills, at least four specifically addressed refining data collection and analysis for Becca's Bill. While these bills involved varying degrees of debate, research, and public testimony, the fact remained that instead of discussing whether and how to revise the bill—as public officials were able to do with FTAS in Texas—at least 10 percent of the legislation discussed in committee focused on whether and how to collect information.

The first efforts to systematically amend data collection were made before the Senate Committee on Human Services and Corrections in 2008. HB 6429 represented the most direct indication that public officials saw a need for more information about Becca's Bill. It directed WSIPP to analyze the local practices for implementing Becca's Bill. In public testimony before the Senate Committee, Justice Bridge articulated the need for more information on the impact of Becca's Bill:

> We have really wanted to have the kind of study that HB 6429 reflects. It is time now to be more rigorous. . . . There is a real need for the baseline identification of the actual practice going on. We know it is variable. Maybe that is good maybe it is not.
>
> (Public hearing on HB 6429 2008)

As was clearly the case with most elected officials and service providers testifying for and against revisions to Becca's Bill, Bridge articulated a strong desire to do what was best for kids, but she also admitted that given the lack of information about the policy, it wasn't clear what the best approach was. During the same testimony, Bridge described this challenge more directly:

> I hope we can learn through 6429. Find out what works to make kids comply. How can we give incentives, the right resources, the right tools to be the right ones without collapsing under its own weight? We have a lot of anecdotes and a lot of gripes of how oppressive the system can be . . . but we also have a lot of great stories from kids and families.
>
> (Public hearing on HB 6429 2008)

Table 8.1 Proposed legislation impacting Becca's Bill, 1994–2015

Year	Bill #	Content	Status
1995	5439	Created Becca's Bill	Signed into law
1995	1417	Increased consequences for running away multiple times in a twelve-month period; clarified detention requirements	Retained in present status
1995	6646	Technical and clarifying amendments	Died in Senate committee
1999	6570	Provided additional judicial authority	Signed into law
2001	5500	Made adjustment to programs and proceedings for children; clarified detention procedures	Left in X in Senate proceedings
2003	2391	Designed incentive policy to decrease truancy	Referred to committees
2005	5426	Found a need to review current laws and rules that govern school attendance requirements; convened a Washington State task force to evaluate the implementation of the Becca Bill, and related definitions and data collection efforts.	Left in X in Senate proceedings
2005	5834	Required JLARC to study juvenile offender rates	Retained in present status
2007	6398	Provided that the courts remit 50 percent of the fine collected in truancy court actions to the child's school district.	Signed into law
2008	6429	Directed WSIPP to analyze the effectiveness of the truancy law	Retained in present status
2008	6600	Required that students be served in person (via certified mail) with notice of summons for truancy. Students could be arrested if they failed to appear in court.	Retained in present status
2009	2449	Ordered payments to school districts from truancy fines	Retained in present status
2009	3039	Streamlined the truancy process to reduce the costs to courts and school districts.	Retained in present status
2009	3058	Required a school to collaborate with the community truancy board on the ongoing implementation of research-based diversion programs shown to reduce truancy rates.	Retained in present status

Continued

Table 8.1 *Continued*

Year	Bill #	Content	Status
2009	6519	Streamlined the process for school districts required to file truancy petitions in the juvenile court when middle and high school students accumulated a specific number of unexcused absences.	Retained in present status
2011	1064	Addressed school truancy diversions and school reengagement programs; petitions to juvenile court; requirements of the court; finding a child in contempt; and warrants for arrest of a child.	Retained in present status
2011	1530	Made certain truancy provisions discretionary rather than mandatory	Retained in present status
2011	2536	Addressed the use of evidence-based practices for the delivery of services to children and juveniles. Expanded the duties of various state departments and research agencies to examine best-practices	Signed into law
2011	6494	Prohibited issuance of a bench warrant for a child who failed to appear at a hearing on an initial truancy petition.	Signed into law
2013	1477	Provided flexibility to school districts when addressing truancy to reduce the administrative and paperwork load for school districts and the court system.	Left in committee
2015	1243	Reduced the administrative and paperwork load for school districts and the court system by providing flexibility for how school districts address truancy.	Retained in present status
2015	5745	Implemented the truancy reform recommendations of the Becca Task Force.	Retained in present status
2015	6497	Promoted attendance and reduced truancy by providing court-based and school-based intervention and prevention efforts; automatic stay for truancy charges	Retained in present status

Green rows indicate legislation that was passed and implemented; yellow rows indicate legislation that was introduced but never passed into law. There were no measures that were proactively voted against.

Source: Author's summary of Washington State legislative archives.

Faced with compelling personal anecdotes from young people about the horrors of being detained and with testimonials from parents of the value of having their child in a safe place, elected officials were bombarded with emotionally compelling, yet conflicting, information regarding the effectiveness of Becca's Bill.

Contradictory and uncertain findings from the state research agencies further complicated public officials' understanding of the policy's effectiveness. In 2015, when Senator Darnielle proposed the Becca Task Force's minority report as a revision to Becca's Bill, researchers from WSIPP testified on their research on the policy's outcomes. The WSIPP executive director and a researcher explained the usual research process they went through in order to rigorously assess policy outcomes. They then followed this explanation by admitting that they did not have any rigorous research on Becca's Bill:

> [O]n those lists, you won't find Becca [Becca's Bill]. There have been three studies of Becca, two done by the Institute and one done by the courts. And none of those studies, even our own, make our traveling squad here (referring to list of evidence-based practices). That is, the methods we were able to employ couldn't separate, in our judgement, causation from correlation, so we don't have those studies on this list. It may be possible in the future to do some work on that with some of the variation, the truancy variation, but we don't have those programs on our list today.
>
> (Public testimony on HB 5651 and HB 5745 2015)

The researcher continued, stating that because they were not confident in their evaluation of Becca's Bill, they instead "review[ed] trends in juvenile justice and K-12 [education]" (Public testimony on HB 5651 and HB 5745 2015). In the discussion of major revision to Becca's Bill, twenty years after its passage, professional researchers are still unable to accurately assess the policy's outcomes, and they openly admit as much. This ambivalence plausibly set the stage for supporters and opponents of revision to remain in their separate camps, as even the researchers argued they could not be sure of the actual outcomes. Those who did acknowledge the policy's failure could point to suggestive evidence from their own county or state and evidence from related fields to deduce that detention of truants and runaways was not an effective practice. Those who continue to support Becca's Bill as an important tool for helping young people could rely on the fact that there was no concrete evidence that *this* specific policy was not producing the intended outcomes.

Revisiting Data

In the face of uncertainty about the effectiveness of a policy, elected officials are likely to support the known, albeit problematic, policy, given that they have even less information about untested alternatives. In other words, policy change is risky—changes in policies can quickly and radically change politics—and without clear evidence suggesting change is needed, reelection-oriented elected officials are likely to support the status quo. Clear data and analysis can disrupt this preference for the status quo, and in Texas, the nonstate organizations were able to supplement analytical capacity and do so. Becca's Bill shows how nonstate actors are more constrained in their ability to supplement collection capacity, and, how without credible data, those harmed by policy failure struggle to achieve recognition and revision. Recognizing that they did not have adequate information to evaluate the impact of Becca's Bill, the Becca Task Force had applied for grant funding to support identify better data sources, improve data collection, and evaluate the impact of the policy. In 2007, the MacArthur Foundation chose Washington State to participate in their Models for Change program, which offered financial and logistical support to states interested in developing alternatives to formal court proceedings for truant youths (George 2011). Through the efforts of the Becca Task Force, Washington received $12 million between 2007 and 2014 to improve data collection on truancy and juvenile justice practices.

In 2008, during a hearing on HB 6429, which aimed to expand the reporting requirements for Becca's Bill, Justice Bobbe Bridge recognized that Washington had enlisted the help of the MacArthur Foundation through one of their Models for Change grants. In the hearing, she articulated her hope that "through the MacArthur Foundation we are hoping we can get real hard data on what is working" (Public hearing on HB 6429 2008). Here Bridge was suggesting that the involvement of a nonstate actor, the MacArthur Foundation, could help supplement the state's evaluations and reveal more decisive insight than was currently available to public officials. Although the partnership did facilitate revisiting and revising data collection and evaluation of Becca's Bill, the Models for Change researchers and their Washington State-based partners still faced the limitations imposed by the erratically collected data that existed for Becca's Bill. Notably, HB 6429 did not pass, and the Models for Change researchers and their state-based counterparts had to continue to rely on ad hoc, county-by-county data collection in the first few years of the grant program. Without addressing the gaps in data capacity, attempts to analyze the programs were limited.

In 2011, the Washington State Center for Court Research (WSCCR) published its first report that resulted from the collaboration with MacArthur. The Models for Change team had supported the WSCCR in using approximately one million student records from the state's Educational Research Database in a propensity score[3] matching research design. The researchers used the database to create two groups of students that were similar in their gender and racial composition, school disciplinary history, academic achievement, and history of absences. Students in both groups exhibited chronic truancy, but the students in the treatment group had received court petitions, while the students in the control group had not. The study found that court-petitioned youth generally fared worse than their nonpetitioned peers on subsequent attendance rates, likelihood of graduating, and academic achievement. While certainly a more comprehensive data source than the mismatched definitions and file types was available from the courts, the WSCCR researchers remained hesitant about the validity of their findings. The authors cautioned that they did not have an explanation for why some chronically truant youths were not petitioned to court. Therefore, they cannot be certain that their research design accounted for all of the variables necessary to truly assess the causal impact between Becca's Bill and long-term student outcomes:

> However, the possibility remains that being petitioned to the juvenile courts, either by itself or combined with an actual court appearance, could reduce the chances that students will engage in delinquent behavior.
>
> (George 2011, 35).

[3] As described by the report, propensity score matching is a statistical method in which a researcher "uses predicted probabilities of group membership in the treatment versus control conditions to match the two groups on a large set of observed variables. This ensures that the groups are similar in terms of the available information related to the likelihood of receiving a truancy petition" (George 2011, 31). There is significant debate regarding the effectiveness of this approach in achieving causal inference (Dehejia 2005; LaLonde 1986; Smith and Todd 2005), providing those unhappy with the findings from the study with an opportunity to dismiss it as lacking credibility.

The report concluded with a reminder that the researchers were only able to access data from students between 2004 and 2007 and that the implementation of Becca's Bill had changed in the intervening four years to include several experimental adjustments that a handful of counties pioneered. The report reiterates that rigorous quantitative evaluations will require detailed social, emotional, and academic data for all students over a substantial period—a luxury WSCCR researchers did not have.

The variation and uncertainty about the outcomes of Becca's Bill offered a plethora of options for different groups looking for empirical evidence to support their preferences for the future of the program. The next section examines how the opportunity to cherry-pick findings from the array of reports the state published undermined opponents' ability to build the political will for revision.

Group Dynamics: Inconclusive Evidence Preserves Status Quo

The incomparable and sporadically collected data produced inconsistent findings on Becca's Bill. Vacillating findings fueled opportunities for supporters and opponents to craft narratives that were most sympathetic to their perspectives on Becca's Bill's. Without clear findings regarding the policy's impacts, the more powerful groups—in this case the supporters—won out and maintained support for the program. Following is a description of how supporters and opponents of Becca's Bill leveraged state-produced data. Unlike Texas, however, there was no clear data to back up the claims of families, young people, and concerned senators. Thus, conversations about whether Becca's Bill should continue devolved into exchanges of anecdotal evidence and hearsay. Without clear data and therefore compelling analyses, existing power dynamics dominated the politics of revision for Becca's Bill.

The groups supporting and opposing the continuation of Becca's Bill closely align with the patterns of support for Failure to Attend School in Texas (see Table 8.2). On the whole, juvenile justice organizations, judiciary professional associations, and youth organizations supported amending Becca's Bill. In contrast with their professional organization, however, several individual judges and school and court administrators opposed removing detention as a consequence from Becca's Bill. In examining Texas, I found that the clear evidence presented in *Breaking Schools' Rules* and *Class Not Court* shifted the power dynamics, confirming and elevating the

Table 8.2 Groups supporting policy revision for FTAS and Becca's Bill

Case	Support status quo	Support policy revision
FTAS	Individual judges Individual school administrators Truancy class providers Individual superintendents	Texas Judicial Council Texas Public Policy Foundation Texas Appleseed Texas Parent Teacher Association Individual students & families Youth justice organizations Texas Association of Business Texas Criminal Defence Lawyers Association Texas Association of School Administrators
Becca's Bill	Individual judges Individual juvenile court administrators Individual school administrators	Individual students and families Mockingbird Society (representing homeless and foster-involved youth) Association of Washington Business Washington Principals Association ACLU Washington Public Defenders' Association

Source : Author's analysis of groups registered on, for, and against during public testimony on behalf of bills in each respective state legislature.

narratives from diffusely organized groups like students and families and criminal lawyer defense associations. Without clear data in Washington State on Becca's Bill, vested interests—like the judges and the original sponsors of the bill—dominated the narratives about the effectiveness of the policy.

Judges tended to support the sanctions created by Becca's Bill, arguing that, based on their anecdotal experience, it gave them a range of tools to help students and provided a powerful consequence for the most intransigent students unwilling to change their behavior. According to a 1998 WSIPP report, court commissioners and judges generally believed that

> in the majority of cases, a court order compelling school attendance reduced future unexcused absences for truant students. The courts surveyed, however, believed more could be done for students who violated court orders and exhibited serious attendance problems. While administrators stated that detention is an important final consequence for truants, most believed a graduated system of sanctions is necessary. Courts with

> established community service programs referred some truant students to work crews or community service.
>
> (Santos 2015, 21)

Supporters also argued that detaining students through Becca's Bill "peeled back the layers of society, exposing a whole stratum of dysfunctional families that we had not seen before. Bringing these youth back to school and providing additional services where necessary can help break the cycle of dysfunctionality and connect these young people to a brighter future" (Truancy Case Processing Practices 2004, 4). Importantly, both supporters and opponents maintained that their motivation was to ensure the best outcomes for young people and their families, but they disagreed on whether Becca's Bill was the most effective way to accomplish this goal.

Even when the national mood began to shift away from punitive carceral policies for juveniles, judges continued to support Becca's Bill. In 2014, the Office of Juvenile Justice and Delinquency Prevention (OJJDP) identified Washington as the number one state for detaining youth in the country. Scandalized by this ranking, several public officials looked for an explanation, and turned to Becca's Bill as a prime driver of the increased detention rates. Senator Jeannie Darnielle, in particular, became a vocal opponent of Becca's Bill, arguing that detention was being used too frequently and that the practice was harmful to students and excessively expensive for the state (Santos 2015). Hedman's parents also withdrew their support for the bill, saying that it was no longer working to connect young people and their parents with resources and support (Santos 2015).

Many judges, however, argued that declining juvenile crime rates were the result of Becca's Bill, despite state research agencies' clear statement that they did not have enough information to assess the impact of the bill. This logic pointed to Rebecca Hedman's death as just the start of the negative effects of what would happen if detention were removed as a consequence for repeated truancy. Because there was no clear evidence of direct harm from the policies, judges' anecdotal experiences and interpretations of their courtroom proceedings stood as credible evaluations of the policy.

Senator Hargrove, and other Becca's Bill supporters, however, continued to cite judges' arguments for keeping the program as an important tool for preventing other young people from the dangers that took Hedman's life. According to one *Seattle Times* article:

> Sen. Jim Hargrove, D-Hoquiam and the original Senate sponsor of the Becca Bill, said that without the threat of detention, judges "would have no leverage" to make kids follow court orders to attend school or come home at night. "Becca was put together to keep kids from getting hurt—to keep kids from getting into the criminal justice system," Hargrove said. "It was to protect the kids, not to punish them."
>
> (Santos 2015)

Given their status in state politics and their likely familiarity with state legislators and members of the executive branch, individual judges reasonably had more political clout than the average citizen, and certainly more clout and resources than many of the poor and minority families that bore the brunt of Becca's Bill.

Even when legislators directly questioned the value of Becca's Bill, the lack of clear findings stymied their ability to sway skeptics. By 2015, Senator Darnielle had introduced a bill to revise Becca's Bill to preclude detention for young people. Judge Jaqueline Jesky, the King County Superior Court commissioner, testified in favor of revising the policy, acknowledging that the policy had been implemented in good faith, but new information suggests that revision was necessary:

> We lost children this year the same way we lost Becca. I think Senator Hargrove and others were frankly ahead of their time. Ahead of the curve when they crafted this law. But it is 20 years later, and we know some things now that we didn't know back then, and there is still a lot of work to do.
>
> (Public hearing on 5651 2015)

Jesky was careful to praise Hargrove, the current chair of the Senate Human Services, Mental Health and Housing Committee and original sponsor of Becca's Bill, while still recommending that the committee take into account new research on teen decision making and the effects of trauma and detention. Despite this praise, Hargrove quickly retorted, "Do you have data on that assertion?"(Public hearing on 5651 2015). Without clear evidence on the outcomes of Becca's Bill specifically, Jesky was forced to support her argument with anecdotal evidence:

> No, I didn't, but I know of youth in my own caseload who lost their lives within the last year or so. I have talked to other commissioners throughout the state. We know that there are many youth that are still seriously at

> risk . . . how important it is that we focus and continue to improve on the work we started 20 years ago. Young people are still losing their lives.
>
> (Public hearing on 5651 2015).

The paucity of data specifically documenting Becca's Bill's outcomes thereby maintained the dominance of judges' and Hargrove's narrative. Hargrove asked Jesky to provide more specific evidence for her doubt in Becca's Bill, but Jesky was unable to provide specifics given the lack of reliable data on implementation of Becca's Bill.

Those in charge of implementing Becca's Bill argued that they could not be expected to prevent other horrific outcomes for truant youth without the threat of detention in their back pocket. By 2010, once findings from WSIPP and JLARC were becoming more convincing, the legislature did begin to encourage more preventive measures, such as the use of Community Truancy Boards, but the use of detention remained intact at the request of supporters who argued that the courts needed the threat of detention as a backstop to address the most desperate cases. Unlike the situation in Texas, the lack of clear data and analysis specifically on Becca's Bill more reasonably permitted public officials to leverage anecdotes as acceptable forms of evidence for the policy's average impact. Thus, Becca's Bill supporters, like Senator Hargrove, could continue pointing to correlational trends and individual judicial experiences suggesting that the policy was keeping students in school and offering an important safety net for getting them back on track. Opponents, on the other hand, were left to argue that correlation was not causation, and that multiple scholarly disciplines concurred that involvement in the judicial system and detention was counterproductive for students struggling to stay in school.

Revisting Becca's Bill: the Power of Collection Capacity

While this study examined the years 1995–2017, the policy context for Becca's Bill continued evolving. The policy's trajectory from 2017 to 2019 offers additional evidence that data collection has critical importance for acknowledging and revising policy failure.

In 2016, with the support of the Models for Change and the MacArthur Foundation, the Washington legislature passed HB 2449, which mandated that all districts report all juvenile detention and truancy data to the Administrative Office of the Courts and that all districts establish Community Truancy Boards (CTBs) to develop prevention strategies appropriate to their student population. This change enhanced reporting requirements by facilitating the production of coherent reports based on statewide data—something that was not possible with the reporting rules prior to 2016 and HB 2449. The Washington State Center for Court Research then published annual reports in 2016, 2017, and 2018 analyzing the juvenile detention patterns in the state.

In the very first report published with the newly collected data, the introduction recognizes the significance of this change, reminding the legislature that "a significant portion of the time used to develop this report was devoted to data acquisition, management, and cleaning" (Gilman and Sanford 2017, 1). The report explained how all juvenile courts would be using the Administrative Office of the Courts as the clearinghouse for their data collection moving forward. This change in data collection capacity gave researchers access to usable data, and thus shifted Becca's Bill from the hollow case to the clear-cut case. In May 2019, three years after the first updated report was published Washington State followed Texas's lead and banned the detention of juveniles for truancy. Notably, the MacArthur Foundation helped *the state* develop better data collection capacity, rather than attempting to manage the collection itself. This further emphasizes the unique role the state plays in administering meaningful data collection, particularly for sensitive, individual-level data.

In addition to being the first year with additional high-quality data on juvenile detention in Washington, 2017 brought a new committee chair to the Senate Human Services, Mental Health and Housing Committee: Senator Darnielle, who had originally supported Becca's Bill, but had changed her position after learning more about its effectiveness, was one of the first senators to suggest reforming Becca's Bill. As chair, she struck a notably different tone from Hargrove's casual (and causal) analysis of observational data. Instead, Darnielle oriented her committee to the value of high-quality data and evidence at the beginning of committee meetings. In one of the first hearings on the renewed attempt, Senator Darnielle offered an introduction that reminded the committee of the existing research on juvenile detention, trauma, and recidivism, along with the state's culture for evidence-based policymaking:

> This is not a new issue for me. We have been trying to promote the change reflected in 5290. My goal, my mission, with this bill I guess, is to end the incarceration of youth who have committed a status offense. . . . I view this as state-imposed trauma. It is right up there as a trauma because they are shackled, strip searched, removed from their schools and communities. They are traumatized, isolated; they are stigmatized, and they are incarcerated alongside youth that are actually criminalized and committing crimes in our community. . . . I am extremely proud of things Washington is doing to turn the corner. We now realize that prevention is better than curative kinds of work.
>
> (Senate Human Services, Reentry & Rehabilitation Committee Work Session & Public Hearing on SB 5290 2019)

She then went on to emphasize the importance of relying on evidence to make decisions on policy:

> We've even passed laws saying we are going to use evidence-based practices in the implementation of our services. We are not just fond of science, we embrace science in the state of Washington, and we really respect research. So this detention of children for status offenders is contrary to science. There is no pathway to ending trauma in children's lives by creating more trauma, especially state-imposed trauma.
>
> (Senate Human Services, Reentry & Rehabilitation Committee Work Session & Public Hearing on SB 5290 2019)

By creating a comparable and coherent data collection system and developing statewide definitions of concepts critical to measuring the impacts of Becca's Bill, the legislature's newly orchestrated data collection helped enhance the data collection capacity for the policy.

While this shift in leadership from the policy's most ardent supporter to its most vocal critic certainly played a role in the shifting possibility of policy revision, it also took an improvement in data collection capacity to catalyze a change in the state's evaluation of Becca's Bill's effectiveness. Senator Darnielle herself changed her mind over time as she learned more about the policy. She also explicitly centered high-quality data in her committee meetings and built political support for change. In 2019, supporters of reform were able to bring data to bear on their testimony, bolstering their anecdotal evidence of how the policy was failing, and the legislature responded, repealing the possibility of detention for truant youth.

Conclusion

By 2015, a handful of Washington State public officials had acknowledged the failures of Becca's Bill. Senator Darnielle and a minority of the Becca Task Force partnered to introduce this legislation that would have removed detention as a consequence for truancy and running away and instead emphasized preventive truancy practices and therapeutic responses. However, the legislature not only failed to revise Becca's Bill, the Human Services, Mental Health, and Housing Committee refused to pass a direct amendment to the detention clause in Becca's Bill out of committee. Senator Hargrove, one of the original sponsors of the bill and a strong advocate for its continued use, backed by individual judges, continued to narrate the overall positive impacts of Becca's Bill, though Hargrove, at least, did acknowledge some need for minor revisions. Supporters of revision did not have clear evidence to elevate their narratives over those propagated by Hargrove and the judges.

Although Washington as a state wielded significant analytical capacity with its many state-backed research agencies, the paucity of data collection on Becca's Bill specifically denied the policy's opponents the clear tools necessary to convince the legislature that revising the bill would improve outcomes compared with the status quo. Further reinforcing the barriers to revision, the origins of Becca's Bill as the response to a horrific crisis made revising the policy even less palatable to most public officials. Without clear evidence that the status quo was failing, fear of being blamed for another horrific death of a child reigned as a key decision maker.

In Texas, the state lacked the tools and motivation to analyze its truancy data, but nonstate actors were able to supplement this capacity and produce meaningful information that highlighted the failures of the status quo and shifted the power dynamics to those demanding revision. In the hollow case, however, nonstate actors cannot supplement data collection capacity to the same effect. No amount of resources or expertise can turn back time to collect high-quality data on policy outcomes.

However, while in Texas, the independent researchers could dig into data as soon as they got a hold of it, Washington public officials had to work with the MacArthur Foundation to establish a plan for improved data collection, lobby for implementation of more centralized collection and then wait for the plan's implementation for long enough to provide usable, longitudinal data. Even after state legislatures supported bringing in the

MacArthur Foundation team to help address concerns about policy evaluation, they failed to pass legislation introduced to bring data collection for Becca's Bill up to the standards advocated by the Foundation's researchers. This dynamic further demonstrates that the unique role the state played in establishing data collection capacity for a given policy and that investing in reliable and clear data collection from the outset is critical for enabling the recognition of failure.

Without clear evidence that Becca's Bill was producing the opposite of the intended results for young people, judges and the original supporters of the policy could wield their political power to protect the status quo, justifying their inaction by reminding everyone that there was no clear evidence that any alternative would be better than the one already in place. Fearful of being held responsible for another tragedy, a the potential of being blamed for another tragedy as horrific as Hedman's murder further discouraged elected officials from supporting policy reform.

9

The Status-Quo Case (Texas's Tax Incentives)

Tax credits and truancy policy in Washington and truancy policy in Texas highlight the political dynamics of policy revision when there is some semblance of data collection or analytical capacity. Texas's Chapter 313 (Ch 313) tax credits round out the typology described in Chapter 2 by examining the politics that rein in the status quo case, where there is low data collection and low analytical capacity.

Texas's Ch 313 tax abatement program demonstrates supporters' opportunity to frame a policy's worth in the absence of clear and consistent documentation of the policy's outcomes. The Texas Ch 313 case also provides insight into the importance of the original policy context for influencing public officials' openness to acknowledging policy failure. As a policy created in direct response to a perceived impending economic crisis, Ch 313 has remarkable immunity to revision, as policymakers feared triggering another crisis. Finally, in comparison with Washington's R&D tax credit, Ch 313 demonstrates how, without robust data collection and analysis, sunset provisions cannot fully perform their intended role of forcing elected officials to comprehensively reevaluate expensive government programs.

Policy Origins: Responding To Crisis

The Texas Ch 313 provides a second example, along with Washington's Becca's Bill, of the long shadow of crisis for policies forged in their wake. It was created in response to what turned out to be a nonexistent threat to the state's economy. And yet, vested interests were able to continually leverage the fear of a crisis to protect Ch 313. The combination of low collection *and* low analytical capacities made it unlikely that elected officials would

The Politics of Failed Policies. Sarah James, Oxford University Press. © Oxford University Press (2025).
DOI: 10.1093/9780197813645.003.0010

be pressured to acknowledge its failures: the program's emergence as a crisis response and the low collection and analytical capacity available for the program.

Site Selection magazine, as the name suggests, offers insight into the intricacies of choosing the location for new and expanding businesses by evaluating the tax climate, the policy landscape, and the natural and human resources available across the country. The magazine publishes annual rankings of the business friendliness of each state. Throughout the 1990s, Texas had been the proud recipient of the Governor's Cup, an award given each year to the state with the most capital investment projects in the previous year. Thus, when *Site Selection* published its business-friendliness rankings in 2000, Texans were astounded: not only had the state lost the Governor's Cup, Texas had also come in at a whopping 37th—far from a spot in the top three to which they had been accustomed. As it later turned out, this drop in rankings had been a mistake in calculation on behalf of *Site Selection* magazine and was subsequently corrected a year later. Not knowing at the time that it was purely the result of a calculating error, elected officials hurried to address the crisis and ensure that they would not be outdone by other states in their attractiveness to companies. In 2001, the Texas legislature passed HB 1200 with substantial bipartisan support (see Table 9.1), the Texas Economic Development Act, known more commonly by its location in the Texas tax code, Chapter 313 (Ch 313).

Ch 313 allowed school districts to offer property tax abatements to companies that were locating within their district. Companies had to invest an agreed-upon minimum and create at least twenty-five new jobs in order to qualify for an abatement, and they had to pay taxes during the first two years after a company relocated (or was created). Then they would receive an abatement for the next eight years, at which point, in theory, the business would go back on the tax rolls at its full value and, again in theory, begin contributing to the district's tax base. Ch 313 also held school districts financially harmless for agreeing to tax abatements, as any amount of money that school districts lost in property tax funding through Ch 313 would in turn be reimbursed by the state.[1] Although districts were held financially harmless, providing such financial support and reimbursement still strained the state budget and education resources.

[1] Holding schools financially harmless for lost property tax revenue was a critical component of this bill, given that there is no state income tax in Texas and the vast majority of school funding comes from local property taxes.

Table 9.1 Legislation related to Ch 313, 2001–2017

Year	Bill	Status	Impact	House	Senate
2001	HB 1200	Passed	• Created Texas Economic Development Act (Ch 313)	**61%** D-45% R-98%	**77%**D-64%R-88%
2007	HB 1470	Passed	• Extended program through 2011 • Need for comptroller to provide an economic impact evaluation of proposed deals to the school district and a recommendation	100%	100%
2009	HB 3676	Passed	• Extended expiration through 2015 and expanded eligibility • Named specific components of what the comptroller's evaluation has to include • Required discovery of appraised value limitations • Clawback provisions	**100%**	**84%**D-67%R-95%
2011	SB 1590	Left pending in committee	• Would have capped the amount at $225M • Eliminated one of the tax credit categories • Required comptroller to approve agreements, before school districts	Left pending in committee	

Continued

Table 9.1 *Continued*

Year	Bill	Status	Impact	House	Senate
	SB 829	Left pending in committee	• Would require the comptroller to verify information provided on applications and compliance forms for Ch 313	Left pending in committee	
2014	HB 3390	Passed	• Required projects to show they would pay more in taxes than benefit • Restricted to projects that could prove taxes were pivotal in location decision making • Extended the act through December 2024	**96%**D-91%R-99%	**66%** D-9% R-100%
2017	SB 600	Left pending in committee	• Would have repealed Ch 313	Left pending in committee	

Key: Yellow rows indicate bills left pending in committee; green rows indicate legislation that passed Without clear reporting.
Source: Author's summary based on Texas legislative archives, which can be accessed at https://lrl.texas.gov/legis/billSearch/index.cfm

Between 2001 and 2011, Ch 313 received wide bipartisan support from public officials and local media, including the first two renewals of the policy in 2007 and 2009 (see Table 9.1). The original bill passed with the support of over 85 percent of Republicans and a majority of Democrats in the Texas legislature. In fact, support for Ch 313 grew after its implementation, with 100 percent of the Texas legislature supporting its first renewal in 2007. In stark contrast to Washington's R&D tax credit, this support continued through the second renewal vote in 2009, which extended the program through 2015, with 100 percent of the House supporting the renewal and over two-thirds of Democrats and 95 percent of Republicans in the Senate voting to continue the policy (see Table 9.1).

While the legislature did hold hearings every four to six years to reevaluate Ch 313, without clear information on its outcomes, the conversation remained mired in anecdotal evidence from deeply invested (and therefore biased) stakeholders. Beginning in 2012, however, both Texas and national media outlets, along with a small handful of elected officials, raised concerns about the exorbitant cost of the program and questioned whether it was producing the intended outcomes (Chasnoff 2012). Despite several attempts to increase the requirements for participation in the program and one attempt in 2017 to repeal Ch 313 entirely, the program remains in place owing to three different bipartisan-supported renewals, the last of which pushed the sunset date back to 2024.

Policy and Institutional Design: Compliance Monitoring is not Evaluation

One purpose of sunset provisions is to trigger an examination of policy outcomes. If the policy is working, then future legislators can vote to continue the policy, and if it is failing then, without taking direct action, they can allow it to expire. While this is certainly a useful tool for forcing policymakers' hands in confronting policy outcomes (as happened in Washington), data collection and analytical capacity play a critical role in whether failed policies are successfully acknowledged and revised. The regular reconsideration provided by sunset clauses creates predictable political opportunities for supporters and opponents to vie for their preferred policy outcomes. In Washington State with the R&D tax credits, high collection and analytical capacity originated with the program in question. These capacities, in turn, generated increasingly convincing and consistent findings about the effects of the tax credits. In Texas, without usable data, renewal debates were a prime opportunity for vested interests to reinforce support for the program that benefited them.

First, the requirements and guidelines for data collection and the inclusion of mandatory policy evaluation establish the collection and analytical capacity for a given state policy. These design features in turn influence the likelihood that public officials will acknowledge and respond to policy failure. Second, the inclusion of sunset provisions can force reconsideration of a policy, as public officials are required to reevaluate and take proactive steps to renew a policy at regular intervals.

This section explores both of these design features in Texas Ch 313. While the original policy did establish some minimal reporting requirements for participating companies, the information gathered was geared toward ensuring compliance with policy requirements rather than evaluating policy outcomes. Similar to Washington's R&D tax credits, Texas's Ch 313 did include sunset provisions. However, at each policy renewal opportunity, the dynamics reflected the preferences of those who were benefiting the most from the policy—big business and public officials with school districts that had received the tax abatements. In what follows, I justify my claim that Texas had low collection and analytical capacities for Ch 313. I then show how failure to invest in these capacities created long-term structural advantages for those who benefitted from the continuation of Ch 313, despite its failure to achieve its intended outcomes. Each of these design features is examined in more detail, and how they influenced the political incentives for public officials to support (or oppose) revising the policy is explored.

Compliance Rather than Evaluation

Unlike Washington's R&D tax credit, the original Ch 313 legislation lacked any robust requirements for data collection or regular analysis. Self-reported data from recipient companies was the only source of data mandated for Ch 313, and this in turn fundamentally undermined the reliability and effectiveness of data collection for the program. The limited data collection that the policy did require focused exclusively on self-reported compliance metrics. With the data reporting process in the hands of those who were most interested in preserving the program (aka the benefiting school districts and companies), there was limited capacity for credible and critical evaluations. As a condition of receiving an abatement, companies were required to self-report certain metrics about job creation, wages, and benefits to the school district in which the business would be located. The school district in turn was responsible for certifying to the Texas comptroller that any participating companies had met the job creation metrics required by law. School districts, especially in Texas, are notoriously underresourced and underfunded. When self-reporting data, organizations (and individuals for that matter) have an incentive to report information selectively to frame their performance as favorably as possible (Milgrom and Roberts 1988). Given the incentive structure of Ch 313, in which school districts are held financially harmless for entering into an agreement with a company, schools had little reason to invest precious resources or expertise in auditing a company's self-reporting. A 2014 report from the Texas State Auditor's office reviewed the Ch 313 reporting practices from four participating school districts and noted that "Chapter 313 does not require school districts to verify that information, and the school districts audited did not perform verifications" (Keel 2014).

Through self-reporting job growth, value-add, and cost to the local school districts with limited threat of audit, companies had the incentive and power to positively frame their contribution to the local economy. A boutique industry of Ch 313 consultants emerged in response to these regular compliance reporting requirements. The recipient companies hire the Ch 313 consultants, who specialize in completing Ch 313 compliance paperwork, presumably in ways that highlight the positive economic contributions of their clients. These consultants testified in opposition to any revision to Ch 313 that would either cut the available benefits or expand reporting requirements beyond simple compliance (HB 3390 Witness List 2013).

Ch 313 did require the state comptroller to audit at least three companies per year to ensure compliance with the law's growth, costs, and estimated value-add to the local economy (Brimer 2001a). However, like the required data sharing, these audits focused entirely on compliance rather than on policy evaluation. This design choice assumed that the policy works if the companies meet the original policy requirements. Furthermore, low collection capacity directly resulted from the absence of any mandate for a regular, systematic, and objective comparison between the actual and intended outcomes of the Ch 313 tax credits.

By 2015, a handful of legislators had expressed their opposition to continuing the program and called for revising it. As early as 2015, Senator

Lois Kolkhorst (R-Brenham) proposed capping or shrinking the program several times but to no avail (Michels 2016). She also argued that the program's biggest issue was the lack of verification for the self-reported outcomes that recipient businesses shared with the school districts each year. And in 2016, Senator Kirk Watson (D-Austin), called for more robust financial analysis to more conclusively determine whether the program was cost-effective. He argued that the burden of proof should be on the businesses and supporters of the program to show that it was effective, rather than on opponents having to prove it isn't (Michels 2016).

In 2015, attempts at oversight, and the subsequent efforts to analyze the outcomes of the Ch 313 were limited and ineffective. The 84th legislature did create the Texas Economic Incentive Oversight Board in 2015. This board was composed of community members, legislators, and policy experts appointed through the Governor's Office and the Texas legislature and was charged with evaluating the effectiveness of the many tax incentives available to companies doing business in the state. However, the Oversight Board had little actual power and so could not mandate additional data collection. While the Oversight Board may eventually be able to scavenge useful data to evaluate Ch 313, they were unable to do so immediately, and thus their evaluations remained at the mercy of anemic data availability. Thus, as explained in Part I, without reliable data and analysis on the program's outcomes, the Board could do little aside from asking questions and demanding more oversight.

Thus far, Ch 313 has seen three successful renewals and two failed repeal attempts. The included sunset clause combined with the lack of credible analysis of Ch 313's outcomes to create regular opportunities for ardent supporters of Ch 313 to tout the success of the program and continue its existence. As the following section discusses, without clear evidence suggesting otherwise, groups opposing the continuation of Ch 313 were unable to frame the policy as a failure and as a drain on the state budget and anemic education resources.

Group Dynamics: Beneficiaries Dominate the Narrative

In Texas, without established definitions of the key components of the policy, such as job creation, or an established schedule for evaluating policy outcomes, the data yielded contradictory findings. The truth about the actual effects of the program was difficult to separate out from the glowing self-reported findings produced by the companies. When disparate stories are presented about the impact of a policy, lawmakers choose whichever suited their ideological preferences and financial supporters.

Enthusiastic support from recipient companies, school district leaders, and legislators dominated the agenda about Ch 313. While some elected officials and advocacy groups opposed the continuation of Ch 313, no meaningful coalition formed to oppose it. Without clear evidence that Ch 313 is failing, Ch 313's highly organized and well-resourced supporters won out in the policy debate. While there have been occasional protests from those most impacted by the limited tax revenue (e.g., individual communities, families, students, and other local public service recipients) against the continuation of Ch 313, there has been no sustained opposition to Ch 313.

The negative impacts of tax breaks are diffuse and difficult to trace. Without clear information from companies about their costs and benefits, it was hard for policymakers, let alone the average citizen, to understand whether the glowing narrative the policy supporters' shared was true. Unlike the situation with Texas's Failure to Attend School or Washington's R&D tax credit, no broader coalition ever formed to oppose Ch 313. This in part explained its resistance to revision despite acknowledgment from at least some public officials that it had failed to produce the economic growth and jobs that the policy originally promised.

The first time the legislature took up Ch 313 after the publication of some negative press about the policy was in 2013, and it did so not with a threat to repeal the policy but with the goal of imposing more stringent reporting requirements. HB 3390, which required Ch 313 recipients to show that they had paid more in taxes than they had received in benefits and restricted the tax incentive to projects that could prove taxes were pivotal in choosing a location, did pass. However, it kept the debate focused on reporting requirements rather than on whether the policy should remain on the books. HB 3390 also proposed *extending* the policy another ten years through December 2024. Supporters and opponents of revision disagreed about what would likely happen after a project was phased out of Ch 313 after ten years (e.g., would it go on the books at full and fair value and contribute to the tax base, or would the technology be obsolete and therefore not actually contribute to the tax base in the school district?)

Recipient companies received close to $5 billion in reduced property taxes, and, in turn, strengthened political support for the program over time (Toohey 2015). Except for a handful of editorial pieces in the *Austin American-Statesman* (e.g., Editorial Board, 2001), Ch 313 received near-universal support from elites and the public alike on both sides of the aisle. Without usable data, opponents had few resources to combat the dominant narrative from big business: Texas would lose out economically without the tax credits.

Similar to the dynamics in Washington's R&D tax credit case, the witness lists from public testimony regarding renewing, revising, and repealing Ch 313 reflected the substantial support from the technology, manufacturing, and energy (renewable and nonrenewable) industries, along with several different business associations and Chambers of Commerce (see Table 9.2). Interestingly, two individuals also testified on behalf of LLCs set up to help companies apply for and maintain compliance with Texas tax abatements (HB 3390 Witness List 2013).

Opposition began materializing among public officials soon after this second renewal. In 2011, Senators Juan Hinojosa (D) and Steve Ogden (R) initiated SB 1590, which would have limited the program through reducing eligibility and capping the funds available for Ch 313. However, the legislation was left pending in committee. Soon thereafter, local journalists took up the cause and began publishing pieces critical of Ch 313's structure and economic impact on the state. As early as December 2011, the *New York Times* published a piece about the "bonanza" for businesses in Texas, including an entire section labeled "Companies gain, Schools lose" (Aaronson 2011). A year later, Texan journalists wrote about Ch 313 as offering far too much to large corporations in exchange for limited benefits for schools and residents (Texas' tax abatement program too broad 2012) and as draining the state coffers. Opposition among a minority of public officials continued, with Senator Konni Burton introducing a measure to repeal Ch 313 in 2017; however, similar to the 2011 attempt, SB 600 was also left pending in committee.

The paucity of data resulting from limited collection capacity and the resulting unreliable and sparse analyses of Ch 313's outcomes rendered its few organized opponents powerless in the face of big businesses and powerful public officials supporting its continuation. The impotence of Ch 313's opponents was twofold: first, they had to spend their political power and resources arguing for better data collection and evaluation and, second, without this clear information on the policy's outcomes, they did not have any evidence to back up their claim that the policy had failed.

Table 9.2 Groups testifying during select Ch 313 public hearings, 2001–2017

Bill/Year	Supporting Ch 313	Opposing Ch 313	Neutral on Ch 313
HB 1200, 2001	Ft. Worth City Council National Federation of Independent Business The Greater San Antonio Chamber of Commerce Texas Economic Development Council Fort Worth Chamber of Commerce The Greater Houston Partnership	Center for Public Policy Priorities	Office of the Comptroller of Public Accounts Texas Department of Economic Development
HB 1470, 2007	Eastman Chemical Corporation Texas Taxpayers & Research Association Dow Chemical		Center for Public Policy Priorities Comptroller of Public Accts
HB 3390, 2014	Phillips 66 Texas Assn of Manufacturers Texas Taxpayers & Research Association Cummings Westlake LLC Dow Chemical *TxOGA, AECT, Texas Chemical* Council City of Corpus Christi Lyondell Basel Texas Association of Mexican American Chambers of Commerce SHI Government Solutions Texas Association of Business Texas Technology Consortium The Metro 8 Chambers of Commerce Valero Dupont Huntsman Corp., Sherwin Alumina Co., and BASF Corp.) Occidental Petroleum Corporation Chevron USA Greater Austin chamber of commerce TechAmerica Texas Economic Development Council (Enterprise Products, LLC) Hewlett Packard Exxon Mobil Corporation Arlington Chamber of Commerce (Dallas Regional Chamber) TechNet	Center for Public Policy Priorities Texas AFT Greg Poole	Moak, Casey & Associates The Wind Coalition American Wind Energy Association Raise your Hand Texas Texas Renewable energies Association Comptroller Texas Association of School Boards

Continued

Table 9.2 *Continued*

Bill/Year	Supporting Ch 313	Opposing Ch 313	Neutral on Ch 313
SB 600, 2017	Sweetwater Economic Development Texas Association of Manufacturers The Wind Coalition Texas Taxpayers & Research Association Victoria Economic Development Corp. Samsung Austin Semi-Conductor Texas Association of Business Texas Chemical Council Texas Economic Development Council Conroe Economic Development Council Enbridge Energy Greater Irving, Las Colinas Chamber of Commerce BP America Avangrid Computing Technology Industry Association Greater San Marcos Partnership Texas Association of Community Schools Texas 2050 Group Austin Chamber of Commerce Texas Solar Power Association ELON Climate & Renewables Cypress Creek Renewables Pattern Energy Solar Energy Industries Association Environmental Defense Fund TechNet Public Citizen Texas Texas Healthcare & Bioscience Institute AET, TXOGA Dallas Regional Chamber of Commerce AES Generation Longview Chamber of Commerce BASF Corporation Texas Advanced Energy Business Alliance Sierra Club, Lone Star Chapter Texas School of Coalition Corpus Christi Regional Economic Development Council ConocoPhillips San Antonio Chamber of Commerce Apex Clean Energy Greater Houston Partnership EDF RE Dow Chemical Freeport LNG Lincoln Clean Energy EDPR Gregory Portland ISD Metro 8 Chambers of Commerce Texas Economic Development Council	Center for Public Policy Priorities Texas Public Policy Foundation City of Corpus Christi	Nathan Jensen (professor at UT-Austin) Comptroller

Source: Author's summary of witness lists from Texas legislative archives.

Furthermore, without clear documentation and analysis of the policy's outcomes in Texas, acknowledgment of the policy's failure was limited to those already committed to opposing tax cuts for big businesses, with limited opportunity to convince additional stakeholders of the policy's failure. Additionally, without clear evidence suggesting that the state economic and education systems were suffering from a shrinking tax base, supportive political elites could manage the messaging around the impact of Ch 313, highlighting the benefits a handful of individual schools were accruing.

School districts play a central role in doling out Ch 313 funds, but educational actors and organizations were surprisingly absent from the public testimony on Ch 313. The Texas Association of School Boards registered as neutral on 3390. Greg Poole, the superintendent of Blackwell Independent School District, represented the most successful school districts under this tax system, and he was often featured in media accounts as a prime example of how school districts could finesse the policy to get major financial support for their school district (e.g., Michels 2016). Poole testified for the continuation of Ch 313 multiple times, and, in 2016, he also began organizing fellow superintendents to lobby on behalf of Ch 313 deals (Poole, personal communication, January 21, 2016).

Unlike the situation with Failure to Attend School, no cross-partisan coalition formed to oppose continuation of Ch 313. Though fiscally conservative Republicans and Democrats supportive of funding education and social services might have both agreed that Ch 313 was failing (albeit for different reasons), there were no compelling findings to catalyze such a coalition. At Ch 313's inception, only the Center for Public Policy Priorities (CPPP),[2] a self-described independent public policy organization that prioritizes data and analysis in decision making, opposed the creation of the tax credit. The CPPP opposed continuation and expansion of the program, and Dick Lavine, a senior fiscal analyst with CPPP, consistently testified whenever it came up for public hearing. The Texas Chapter of the American Federation of Teachers registered in opposition to the 2014 policy clarification and expansion attempt but never testified. In 2017, the Texas Public Policy Foundation, a conservative public policy research organization that prioritizes "academically sound research and outreach," also registered in

[2] As of 2020, the CPPP changed its name to Every Texan, though it maintains the same mission.

opposition to continuation of Ch 313. Unlike with FTAS, no coordination or consistent messaging from those groups supporting revision ever coalesced.

Supporters and opponents of Ch 313 focused on different problems in the 2013 renewal debates. The 2013 debate in the Senate and House testimony on 3390 centered on the outcomes of the policy (from the companies) and the need for better data collection (from the opponents). Ch 313 supporters—businesses, chambers of commerce, and tax lawyers—relied on the impossible-to-prove counterfactual that businesses would not have located in Texas without the tax subsidies. For example, Bob Adair, the tax advisor for Phillips Gas, said that Ch 313 was "very significant" in "mov[ing] the needle towards approval." He continued with the following remarks:

> Chapter 313 I believe is, it is my experience, that it is well named as the Texas Economic Development Act. It is achieving its purposes the way it is now. My concern, and I think yours is too, is that we are trying to improve the process and the economic development capability of Chapter 313, not distract from it and lose projects to other states and other countries.
>
> (House Ways & Means Committee Public Hearing on 3390 2013)

Those opposing revision argued that the comptroller's assessments of the impact of Ch 313 did not account for the number of service sector and construction jobs that Ch 313 projects brought to a school district. Given the reliance on self-reporting from companies and the lack of additional data collection on additional benefits accrued from the tax abatements, there was no way to ground the conversation in what had happened. The chairman of the committee, Representative Harvey Hildebrand, responded to Levine's testimony with an argument, not based on any hard data, but with speculation in line with his ideological stance on the policy by asking the following question:

> would these projects come to Texas if we didn't have this? I think some would have but most would not have come. We need to tweak and refine this bill, so it performs the objectives and helps us preserve this program, addressing the biggest barrier to economic development.
>
> (House Ways & Means Committee Public Hearing on 3390 2013)

Without clear evidence regarding the counterfactual on company location, employment opportunities, and economic growth, those opposing revision could evoke fear of another drop in rankings and economic growth.

Ch 313 opponents struggled to win support for their narratives of the policy's failure. Without clear information, opponents of the program were left to argue that the state should collect better data to confirm the policy's failure, rather than arguing for the policy's revision. Dick Levine, from the Center for Public Policy Priorities, pointed to a study done by the comptroller Carol Strayhorn in 2003, arguing that she showed that there was over a 75 percent chance that companies would have located in Texas regardless of tax abatements. He then acknowledged that this was "difficult to prove" but that asking whether companies would have come anyway was the most important question to ask. Levine followed this observation up with the following plea to at least *collect information* on the tax program so that policymakers could better evaluate its impact in the future:

> We do have every four to six years a chance to come back and discuss this, and I certainly hope if there is an extension, I do hope it is not longer than another 6 years, but it has never been audited. A lot of the information that comes into the program is supplied by school districts that have absolutely no incentive to double check the companies to see if the jobs are being created, what the benefits are, what the wages are, etc. And the Comptroller just takes the school districts' word for it and repeats it. There is a lot of data in there that is very useful data *if it's true* (emphasis added), but we don't even know if it's true, because no one has ever gone back and audited it. A lot of these companies you just heard testify from major publicly traded companies, they probably have their own audits and obviously the SEC and whoever would require it so it should not be hard to go back or use unemployment insurance numbers and to see who is working there and how many people and what do they get paid. None of that has been done. That is why I suggest if you renew this program, you do it on a very short basis and have a thorough audit.
>
> (House Ways & Means Committee Public Hearing on 3390 2013)

Levine went on to point out that his current calculations for the cost per job was quite high, and even higher if one considered that only two companies—Toyota and Caterpillar—were responsible for the vast majority of jobs created, though many other tax credits were distributed. Those arguing for revision thus had to spend their testimony time and political capital lobbying for the documentation of failure, rather than focusing solely on building a case for revision. This further divided an already less resourced opposition, decreasing the chances of revision.

Those testifying neutral on the bill also focused their arguments on the lack of data on the success of the program. Jeff Clark testified that his organization, the Texas Wind Coalition, wanted to support the bill, but that they also firmly believed that the state needed a better metric for measuring job creation (House Ways & Means Committee Public Hearing on 3390 2013). In particular, he pointed to the discrepancies in job measurement for natural resource companies that received tax credits, arguing that some metrics accounted for temporary construction jobs while others ignored the long-term service jobs that were created.

Without any meaningful change in collection since the previous renewal, attempts to eliminate Ch 313 continued to flounder. The 2015 attempt at a full revision of Ch 313 failed to garner any meaningful support from public officials. The 2017 legislative session brought a second attempt to revoke Ch 313. In this second revision attempt, Senator Burton (R) sponsored SB 600, which would have repealed Ch 313, preventing any future abatements, but leaving the existing ones intact. Senator Burton introduced the bill with an impassioned speech about the cost of Ch 313 for taxpayers and argued that it was a distortion of the free market that was preventing the state from more comprehensively reforming a failed property tax system (Senate Committee on Natural Resources & Economic Development, Part I, Public Hearing on SB 600 2017). She cited the committee's own Interim Report on Economic Development Incentives as evidence that Ch 313 was costing the state over $7 billion in lost education funds. Burton also relied on this single report to argue that an estimated 85–95 percent of companies that received the Ch 313 abatements would have located in Texas without a Ch 313 agreement. However, the bill did not make it out of committee. The debate between SB 600 supporters and opponents in the public testimony in the Natural Resources and Economic Development Committee demonstrated how politics as usual, with big businesses winning out, plays out when there is not sufficient acceptable evidence to counter anecdotal narratives about the success of a failed policy.

Senator Burton and the representative from the Texas Public Policy Foundation both cited the Interim Report to the 84th Legislature from the House

Committee on Economic Development Incentives as evidence that the program was expensive and not necessary for attracting business. A scholar from the University of Texas at Austin also testified as a resource witness and described a causally identified analysis he had conducted using supplemental payments as a proxy for how much a company was able to pay in taxes (i.e., how pivotal were the tax breaks to making locating in Texas financially feasible). He found that 80–85 percent of companies would have located in Texas without Ch 313 credits.

Those testifying in opposition to the reform included representatives of various business associations (e.g., Texas Chemical Council, Sweetwater Enterprise Institute, Texas Economic Development Council), all of whom argued that without the continuation of Ch 313, Texas would lose out on future businesses and economic growth (House Ways & Means Committee Public Hearing on 3390 2013).

The lack of consistent, reliable, and comparable data on business investments and decisions in this case presented opponents to reform with the opportunity to deny the findings from both the state comptroller's office and local scholars studying Ch 313's impact.

Opponents of SB 600, however, dismissed the findings as irrelevant calculations that did not reflect the reality of doing business in the state. Instead, they pointed to anecdotal evidence about the value of the program. When confronted with numbers, every opponent to the bill shared a story about some company that their county would have lost had it not been for the abatements. For example, Ken Becker, the executive director of the Sweetwater Enterprise Institute, a local economic development organization in Sweetwater, Texas, discussed the positive impact of Ch 313 on the Rosco Independent School District. He described Rosco as a low-resourced area that transitioned to having 90 percent of their students earning associate degrees after a wind farm settled in the area. Without any citation of methodology or sources, Becker argued that this was a direct result of the company's investing because of Ch 313. He then also cited the Texas Taxpayers Research Association's claim that Ch 313 was the "single most important economic development tool" in the region, but he failed to explain how this determination was reached (Senate Committee on Natural Resources & Economic Development, Part I, Public Hearing on SB 600 2017).

A senior fiscal analyst from the Texas Taxpayers' Research Association, Dale Craymer, framed all of the state's data as an unreliable measure of the program's cost. Senator Burton and Hinojosa, both supporters of SB 600, questioned Craymer about the cost of the program to the state (House Ways & Means Committee Public Hearing on 3390 2013). Craymer responded that it only *looked* like the state was losing money because of the "static fiscal notes" which didn't account for what the new projects added to the tax base long term. Several other opponents to SB 600 reinforced the inaccuracy of the state's data by arguing that their measures of job creation failed to account for the service and supplier jobs that were created to support Ch 313 recipients.

Perhaps most telling was the testimony from Jeffrey Clark of the Texas Wind Coalition. He went a step further and, when asked directly about his response to the analysis provided by the University of Texas researcher, responded that "his [referring to the researcher] study was based on mathematically derived concepts, not talking to people . . .bottom line is this is a spreadsheet, a calculation" (Senate Committee on Natural Resources & Economic Development, Part II, Public Hearing on SB 600 2017). That dismissal of systematic research in favor of strategically chosen anecdotes shows the power of the businesses benefiting from the program to craft the narrative without clear and compelling data to contradict them.

In Texas, public officials had two stories to choose from: either that Ch 313 was draining the state coffers and was bleeding the state education funds dry through a $400 million structural deficit, or that it was a great deal, costing only $3,000 per job, which then created over $20,000 in new tax revenue per job annually, with the ancillary benefits of creating thousands of additional service sector jobs. With pressure from the organized and well-resourced big oil and energy industries, as well as unclear evidence suggesting that the policy was failing, elected officials adopted the more optimistic narrative and opted to continue supporting the policy.

Policy Origins Revisted: Crisis Breeds Policy Resilience

To further cloud the already uninformed discussions surrounding Ch 313, public officials also had to contend with the memory of the originating crisis that, in large part, inspired Ch 313: a substantial drop in Texas's ranking as a business-friendly state in a well-regarded national business publication. While it later turned out that this downgrade had been the result of a mistaken calculation by the magazine (Senate Committee on Natural Resources

& Economic Development, Part I, Public Hearing on SB 600 2017), the effect on Texas public officials was immediate.

This acute crisis stands in stark contrast to the policy origins of Washington's R&D tax credits and Texas's Failure to Attend School. Notably, while the general goal was the same for both Ch 313 and this R&D tax credit, Washington's tax program was launched in response to a general sense that the state could be doing more to proactively encourage the growth of the tech sector, rather than a response to a specific crisis. The introduction to Washington's R&D tax credit legislation states, "The legislature finds that high-wage, high-skilled jobs are vital to the economic health of the state's citizens, and that targeted tax incentives will encourage the formation of high-wage, high-skilled jobs" (Engrossed Second Substitute Senate Bill 6347 1994). The legislation framed the bill as building on an already strong foundation for the growth of the tech sector: "Investing early in these businesses will build upon the state's established high-technology base, creating additional research and development jobs and subsequent manufacturing facilities" (Engrossed Second Substitute Senate Bill 6347 1994, 2). Language justifying Ch 313, on the other hand, specifically references the change in *Site Selection* rankings as a key rationale for the new policy. The House Research Organization Bill Analysis for HB 1200 specifically states the following:

> Texas is falling behind other states in attracting major new industrial projects. According to the authoritative *Site Selection* magazine, Texas has dropped from first in 1990 to 37th in 2000 in terms of new manufacturing facilities. Since 1997, Texas has lost at least 12 major projects to other states that would have invested more than $4.5 billion and created approximately 5,200 new jobs.
>
> (HB 1200 House Research Organization Bill Analysis 2001, 7)

In 2001, both Intel and Boeing pulled out of deals to locate in the Dallas/Ft. Worth area (Senate Committee on Natural Resources & Economic Development, Part I, Public Hearing on SB 600 2017). The *New York Times* announced Boeing's decision to locate in Chicago, over Dallas and Denver, with the headline "Chicago, Offering Big Incentives, Will Be Boeing's New Home," explicitly crediting tax incentives as the rationale for the choice, though the details of any incentives were kept confidential (Barboza 2001). Furthermore, Austin, and the state more broadly, had been one of the biggest beneficiaries of the 2000 tech boom, but it was now facing the bursting of the bubble and all of the economic adversity that comes with a pop.

While there are several similarities between the intents provided for the Washington and Texas legislation, including expanding high-paying jobs and capital investments, Washington's description for the purpose of the legislation was both internal (i.e., focused on changes and context within the state like the changing nature of the lumber industry) and forward-looking (i.e., anticipating a likely change of the economic opportunities in the state) compared to the rationale provided by the Ch 313. The Texas legislation explicitly states the need to lure business away from other states in its third and fourth intentions:

> (3) attract to Texas large-scale businesses that are potentially planning to locate in other states/countries;
> (4) enable state/local governments to compete with other states by authorizing economic development incentives that are comparable to incentives being offered. (Brimer 2001b)

The Washington purpose, on the other hand, articulated the need for proactively developing new economic opportunities given the decline of natural resources and the importance of technology.

As the literature on policy feedback would suggest, once in place, Ch 313 created beneficiaries who then fought to protect the program. They often did so by involving the memory of the original *Site Selection* crisis. In 2008, during the beginning of the Great Recession, Representative David Swinford (R-Amarillo) pointed directly to Ch 313, citing it as the reason Texas was "so economically powerful in this so-called depression" (Michels 2016, 9). He implied that any revocation of the program could plunge the state into the deeper economic crisis facing the rest of the country at the time.

In 2014, the Legislative Committee on Economic Development argued that the program was overall a net positive for Texas (Interim Report to the 84th Legislature: House Select Committee on Economic Development Incentives 2015; Toohey 2015). This report also specifically referenced the possibility of losing out on economic development and weakening Texas's reputation as a hotbed for businesses, given the incentives available in other states:

> With this in mind, the answer to whether tax incentives are necessary is incredibly important. Overwhelmingly, testimony and other sources

> indicate that Texas sells itself; without incentive plans, the state leads the country in multiple elements necessary to compete for any business. That said, incentives are *increasingly prevalent and aggressive from many states* [emphasis added]. In the fight for Toyota's North American headquarters, North Carolina offered over $100 million to the company in return for locating within its borders—though already high on Toyota's short list, Texas needed to answer with a $40 million package to win the bid. In terms of resources, Texas is unrivaled, but North Carolina proved that other states are going to great lengths to overcome their own shortcomings. As a result, incentives are the icing on the cake Texas needs to retain its competitive advantage over the rest of the country.
>
> (Interim Report to the 84th Legislature: House Select Committee on Economic Development Incentives 2015, 9)

Business-oriented think-tanks and lobbying firms echoed this finding, continually reminding legislators that eliminating the tax incentive would fundamentally undermine Texas's ability to attract investment, recalling the panic that the (mistaken) slip in rankings in *Site Selection* from several years prior.

Those who supported revision of Ch 313 attempted to leverage a crisis documented on a different list: Texas had been in the bottom ten for the worst education in the country for several years. Advocates for revision argued that it was draining already strained state coffers and that an underfunded education system needed more funding to effectively meet the needs of students. In 2011, Senator Steve Ogden (R-5th District) tried to limit state reimbursement funds to schools for abatements when he served as the chair of the financial committee, but again to no avail (Copelin 2012; Randall 2011, 38). The Legislative Budget Board echoed the finding that the program represented a limitless cost to the state (Michels 2016). However, the concern about maintaining Texas's reputation as a business-friendly state continued to discourage supporters from allowing the program to expire.

Conclusion

Without clear information, vested interests, along with a conservative and pro-business ideology, dominated the discussion of Ch 313. Business interests testified heavily in favor of continuing the policy at every opportunity.

School districts that hosted Ch 313 recipients along with the consultants the businesses hired to prepare their annual compliance reports also testified strongly in favor of preserving the policy. Although a handful of organizations opposed it, their perspectives had little effect on the political agenda. Calls to move beyond compliance reporting also went unheard.

The only data collected by the state was self-reported by participating companies, and it served to monitor companies' compliance with the law's participation requirements, rather than stringently evaluate its impact. Although local scholars did attempt to evaluate it, they were limited by the quality of the available data—which consisted of compliance data self-reported by the companies themselves. The use of complex statistical methods created opportunities for supporters of Ch 313 to dismiss the findings as contrived. Unlike the situation with Failure to Attend School in Texas, there was no plausibly credible data to analyze, nor were there researchers tasked with analyzing policy outcomes. Therefore, there was also limited evidence to bolster the claims of those arguing that the policy was failing. In fact, few organizations were even actively aware of the policy's failure, let alone were mobilized against it. While some school officials did protest the rosy picture of the program expanding funding for education in the state, they had no clearly credible evidence to back up their anecdotal experiences.

Further enhancing the resilience of Ch 313, the policy resulted directly from a crisis (albeit a manufactured one, given that it was the result of a calculating error). Memory of this crisis was enough to spook public officials from supporting the removal of the tax credit, and it offered supporters of the credit a compelling talking point, as they could point back to the concern about the original fall in the *Site Selection* rankings whenever public officials seriously discussed policy revision.

The juxtaposition of Ch 313 with both Failure to Attend School in Texas and Washington's R&D tax credits demonstrates the power of collection and analytical capacity to shift perspectives and the political dynamics of failed policies. In these other two cases, clear evidence interrupted the traditional power dynamics and accepted narratives among political elites about the policies. The failure of those calling for revising Ch 313 shows just how strong these status quo forces can be, especially when there is no convincing data to bolster alternative narratives about the policy's impact.

10

Experimentation and Failure as Opportunities

This book began with a contemporary example of policy experimentation: Utah tried a radically different approach to address its homelessness crisis. At least initially, the program produced remarkably positive results, reducing rates of unhoused people and curbing relapse among those struggling with addiction. In more recent years, however, Utah's evaluations of its housing approach have been less glowing. A 2021 audit of the program applauded the effectiveness of the program but warned that rising costs and increasingly limited space—especially in the Salt Lake City area—for building new units could jeopardize the long-term success of the program (Rodgers 2021). Rising inflation has also put additional financial pressures on state government and those dependent on its resources. Time will tell if Utah's experiment can continue to empirically reduce homelessness. But in the meantime, changing social, economic, and political conditions—like the rise in far-right extremism, unprecedented affective polarization, and the aftershocks of a worldwide pandemic—will also influence the perceived viability of this policy approach and the political power of stakeholders affected by the policy. How state elected officials balance the empirical realities of the program and the political pressures they face will dictate the longevity of Utah's housing program.

As with everything in politics, data and analyses do not exist in a void. Even the most objectively collected and analyzed information can be interpreted through the lenses of reputation, ideology, and experiences with existing policies. The takeaway from this book is not that data and analysis can erase politics, but rather that there are ways to craft and evaluate policies and design state institutions that can increase the likelihood that future public officials will be constrained by the realities of policy outcomes.

The Politics of Failed Policies. Sarah James, Oxford University Press. © Oxford University Press (2025).
DOI: 10.1093/9780197813645.003.0011

What We've Learned

A review of policy failure and the policy feedback effects of state capacity for data collection and analysis may be useful. The puzzles tackled in this book are as follows: When do state elected officials recognize that a policy experiment has failed? And what do they do about it? When are public officials willing to recognize policy failure when it contradicts their a priori expectations or partisan preferences? To fully understand the politics of policy failure, a state's capacity for research or policy evaluation should be examined as the product of two distinct features: data collection capacity and analytical capacity. The interaction of these two capacities produces predictable patterns of responses to policy failure.

In this book, I used two policy domains—criminalization of truancy and business location tax incentives—with a strong empirical record of ineffectiveness to study the politics of policy failure. Six state policy trajectories—three tax incentive policies and three truancy policies—were traced in Kansas, Texas, Washington, and Wyoming to show how collection and analytical capacity interact to influence the politics of acknowledgment and revision of policy failure. Although the focus in this book is on two specific types of policies, they are representative of the types of policies that many states have in place.

Part I demonstrates that data collection capacity is distinct from analytical capacity and that state investment in collection capacity is necessary for recognition of evidence-informed failure. Analytical capacity, while also necessary, can be supplemented by nonstate actors. Part II explores the dynamics of revision once at least some public officials have acknowledged policy failure. Specifically, examined here are how high-quality policy evaluation interacts with a policy's origins (whether it was passed in response to a crisis or in a proactive attempt to prevent a problem), a policy's original design (whether the policy required evaluation from the outset), and group dynamics (which groups support and oppose revising the policy and what power they have to implement their political will). I analyze the efforts to revise each of the policies, and the ways credible data analysis shifted the burden of proof from a failed policy's supporters to its opponents. Strong data collection and analysis jointly (but not separately) have the potential to disrupt stakeholder dynamics in ways that empower a policy's opponents over its beneficiaries. The availability of clear evidence about the failure of a reactive policy can alter public officials' calculus about the risks of revising the policy.

The two cases with high collection capacity—Washington's R&D tax credits and Texas's Failure to Attend School—have achieved both widespread recognition and revision of policy failure, while the two policies with low collection capacity—Washington's Becca's Bill (pre-2015) and Texas's Ch 313—failed to generate consensus of failure among public officials. The comparison between the Washington and Texas tax cases (Chapters 6 and 9, respectively) showed how an alignment between high collection and high analytical capacity (and its opposite, low collection, and low analytical capacity) influence the debate about the opportunities and perils of revising policies.

Chapters 7 and 8 examined the two cases with mismatched capacities (high collection/low analytical capacity and low collection/high analytical capacity) through the Texas and Washington truancy cases. The truancy cases offer insight into how opponents of a policy can take advantage of clear data to change the burden of proof in the policy discussion, thereby shifting power dynamics away from supporters of the status quo. Furthermore, these cases demonstrate that the opportunity to shift the burden of proof to policy supporters is not a viable strategy when there is low collection capacity. This is the case because political debates become mired in disputes about data quality and become invested in more accurate policy evaluations, rather than debating the policy's actual outcomes.

Collectively, the juxtaposition of these cases highlights four important themes about the establishment and intersection of collection and analytical capacity. First, when, where, and by whom the capacities get established are political choices that have long-term impacts on the resiliency of a failed policy. The earlier the capacities are established and the more investment the evaluation efforts receive, the more likely the information will affect later policy revision efforts. Compelling policy evaluations examine longitudinal outcomes in local contexts. No matter how well resourced the researcher, there is no way to acquire data from the past that was not collected. Early investments in data collection matter. Investments in data analysis can occur later in the policy's trajectory and can be more effectively supplemented by nonstate actors.

Second, capacities matter because of the substantial effect credible information has on which narratives are most compelling. Clear findings about policy outcomes can trigger both resource and interpretive policy feedback effects. Well-resourced and organized interests have enormous power in the American political economy. When they are harmed by policy failure, they have multiple avenues and venues through which to demand policy revision and are likely to get their way. When the tables are turned, however, and policy failure benefits entrenched interests and harms marginalized or more diffusely organized groups, credible information, especially that generated with state resources, can bolster the narratives of constituencies harmed by the failure. This in turn can help elevate failure on the political agenda.

The quality of the available data and analysis can upend the power differentials of politics-as-usual by shifting burden of proof from supporters to opponents of reform. This shift, in turn, changes the power dynamic between organized and resourced groups and less organized and underresourced groups. More specifically, the availability of high-quality data and subsequent analysis (present in the clear-cut case and the treasure trove case, assuming outside actors step in to conduct the analysis) give reformers a counternarrative to compelling anecdotal evidence that reform opponents present to lawmakers. Data and analysis also give lawmakers a basis for questioning both supporters and opponents of a policy. In the hollow and the politics-as-usual cases, the narratives are more susceptible to carefully handpicked data, analysis, and framing from high-resourced and politically powerful groups (i.e., businesses could generate their own data about their economic value add and judges supervising truancy could offer anecdotal evidence about the success of their scared straight model) that emphasize the value of the status quo. Data and analysis constrain the extent to which powerful interest groups opposing reform can shape the narrative. Furthermore, clear data can shift the burden of proof to the opponents of reform, while also bolstering the universality of seemingly anecdotal claims from weaker groups (e.g., families and students).

Third, the original political, social, and economic context of a failed policy interacts with investments in collection and analytical capacity to influence the likelihood of revision and failure. In particular, the cases show that whether a policy is passed as a proactive solution or a retroactive response to a crisis influences elected officials' calculus about the electoral risk of reforming a failed policy.

Policies can be created in response to a range of events, including a specific and salient crisis. Policies implemented to prevent or address such a crisis will be more impervious to reform than those passed in response to anticipated problems. When public officials, interest groups, and the public have memories of a specific crisis, the cost of uncertainty associated with policy change will more powerfully dissuade support for reform. When there is either low collection or analytical capacity, the fear of a crisis repeating itself will heighten the sensitivity of public officials to possible bias or flaws in the policy analysis, thus making reform less likely. Policy findings resulting from high collection and analytical capacities, on the other hand, will be more likely to facilitate reform because iron-clad findings shift the burden of certainty: not acting in the face of clear information can result in blame for a future crisis rather than fear of re-creating a past one.

Fourth, mandating reconsideration of policies through sunset provisions alone is insufficient to prompt evidence-based reconsideration of policy failure. Sunset provisions are often seen as tools for triggering policy evaluations and as a fail safe for eliminating an ineffective policy and preventing policy stagnation (a condition, unsurprisingly, that often benefits elites; Kelly and Morgan 2022). However, sunset provisions alone do not guarantee an objective reaction to a policy's outcomes. My comparison of Texas and Washington suggests that without a pairing of sunset provisions with high analytical and collection capacity, politics as usual can dictate the renewal process just as much as the original policy process. Sunset provisions do not automatically result in outcomes responsive to real policy outcomes. In other words, policy features that require revisiting the policy are only as good as the evidence available to researchers and lawmakers at the time of reconsideration. Legislators serious about provisions that require policy reconsideration should also ensure that they enhance the data collection and analytical capacity for the policy area in question.

Building in sunset provisions and clear guidelines for evaluating the success of the policy may provide convincing evidence that a policy should continue, but if the policy is failing, high-quality analysis should lead to the demise of the policy. Thus, public officials face a dilemma. Preemptively designing policy to be vulnerable to evidence has the potential to constrain your future self to the findings. However, it can also constrain your political opponents to findings that support your policy preferences. More examination of when and how public officials are willing to build in sunset provisions and agree to carefully outlined policy evaluation is needed, but my findings do suggest that incorporating such features into policy has the potential to enhance the recognition of and response to policy failure.

While many factors affect the willingness of elected officials to acknowledge policy failure, we can empower evidence-based policymaking in the cacophony of partisan politics if the procedures, expertise, and resources for collecting and analyzing data are enshrined in well-resourced state agencies.

Policy Feedback and Failure

Although elected officials and activists may earnestly believe (or at least hope) their policy solutions will work, they cannot possibly know for sure in advance. Thus, requiring evaluation in the original policy may present a double-edged sword for public officials: committing to being data driven brings useful political cachet but can also complicate future efforts to maintain support for a preferred policy. Committing to data collection and analysis before knowing the outcomes is a political choice that both supporters and opponents of a new policy can consider, and their decision has downstream consequences for the recognition of policy failure. As Pierson and Hacker point out, one of the biggest prizes of politics is institutionalizing policies and procedures:

> In a political world with policy at its core, durable outcomes are not just possible; they are the biggest prize of all. Winners get to impose their policy preferences on losers. Often, this means imposing arrangements to which losers must adjust even if their side wins future elections.
>
> (Hacker & Pierson 2014, 651)

There is yet another way policy winners can impose their preferences on losers. Winners can get their way not only by winning in the original policy battle, but also through influencing the degree to which the state invests in evaluating the policy over time. The availability of information—which is the result of data collection capacity and analytical capacity—influences the extent to which elected officials will feel compelled to revisit an existing policy at a later point. In other words, decisions about data collection and analysis have policy feedback effects on elite support for failed policies.

Government may find more information complicating rather than illuminating. Elected officials may not always have either the incentive or the anticipated resources to thoroughly evaluate every single policy they pass. And yet, my research shows that there are important long-term consequences—policy feedback effects—for whether a state invests in its capacity to collect and process information. While more information can be frustrating for reelection-minded political elites looking to appease the most powerful constituencies, it may also be empowering to those experiencing the consequences of a failed policy.

When elected officials are passing policies, they may incorporate processes by which those policies are reevaluated (e.g., through sunset provisions and established evaluation schedules and procedures). These policy features, in turn, can constrain future public officials to react to documented policy outcomes, instead of prioritizing their preferred interpretation of the policy's impact. This makes it all the more important to be intentional with who has a seat at the metaphorical table during the policy design process. The voices that participate in policy design and implementation—and subsequently what gets studied as part of the policy evaluation—have implications for whether failure will get recognized (assuming it occurs). Interests supporting the passage of a policy will have little incentive to evaluate it, particularly if they are confident that, regardless of the alignment with the stated goals, they will benefit from the policy's effects. To increase the chances that the policy feedback effects of information will draw attention to the genuine policy outcomes, incorporating individuals with a wider range of perspectives on and stakes in the policy domain can inform a more robust evaluation plan for potential new policies. There are many reasons to include more perspectives—particularly those that have historically been excluded from decision making in American politics. My research adds yet another reason to ensure that more voices are represented in places of power.

Policies as the Prize in the American Political Economy

This book also offers further evidence of a return to "policy-focused analysis" (Hacker & Pierson 2014) in which the true prize of politics is influencing the design and implementation of enduring policies, regardless of whether one (or one's party) wins elections. My findings on the power of the state institutional landscape and the original designs of individual policies to empower certain policy demanders over others offer further evidence that those creating and implementing policies have substantial influence over not only the original policy itself, but also its resilience to evaluation, revision, and changing preferences.

Unsurprisingly, the businesses that stand to receive tax credits tend to be the most ardent supporters of renewing tax incentive policies. In both Texas and Washington, businesses, business associations, and chambers of commerce narrated the critical importance of tax breaks for companies continuing to invest in and hire from each state. On the other side, however, are educators, students, families, and social justice advocates—those who are usually most affected by the absence of robust and reliable funding for vital public services. The resources, centralization, and organization of these two groups are starkly different. Businesses have resources to hire lobbyists, gather and analyze friendly data, donate to political candidates, and dedicate time to cultivating relationships with relevant public officials. School administrators, teachers, and students, on the other hand, do not generally have access to any of these resources. Furthermore, there are substantial barriers to organizing busy families, young students, and overworked teachers to build relationships with public officials. Thus, as many scholars have already shown, we should expect that political elites' and big business's policy preferences are likely to win out (Gilens 2009; Gilens & Page 2014; Hacker & Pierson 2011). However, the case of R&D tax credits in Washington demonstrates that coherent and reliable data analysis of a policy's outcomes can help balance some of these power differentials by shifting the burden of proof to the opponents of reform. In Washington State, with access to state-collected data, students and teachers were able to build a narrative about the public harm of the R&D tax credits to counter the positive narrative pushed by the benefiting tech companies. This allowed supporters of reform to move beyond anecdotal evidence of the harms of the tax credit, building a more persuasive picture of the widespread negative consequences of tax breaks. Furthermore, this narrative connected the tax breaks to a more present harm: the financial and budget crisis. A similar dynamic occurred in Texas with FTAS, though in this case, families and social justice advocates were able to overcome the political power of elected judges.

In their argument for a return to policy-focused analysis, Hacker and Pierson point out that "whether counter-mobilization is successful, in short, depends heavily on how policy structures affect the prospects for group mobilization" (Hacker & Pierson 2014a, p. 646). I show another dimension along which policy structures affect the ability of opponents to organize effectively to demand reform. The degree of data collection capacity and analytical capacity included in the original policy design and, more generally, available in the state, affects the information available to a policy's supporters and opponents. In turn, this information can influence who can frame policy outcomes and how they can reasonably structure them.

Marginalization and Policy Failure

Not all groups in American society are equally likely to be counted. Political scientists have long noted disparities in political power and voice in American politics. As the scholars behind the COVID Tracking Project showed, these disparities extend to data collection and analysis. They explicitly cited the harms of not knowing how the virus was affecting the marginalized (e.g., people living in poverty and racial and ethnic minorities) as a severe injustice. The effects of the virus were not uniform. Those who could afford to stay home, access quality health care, and use private transportation were more likely to avoid COVID. Without evidence of the racial and socioeconomic trends, the public and public officials could more easily keep addressing these issues off the political agenda. The "data heroes" of the COVID Tracking Project drew attention to important disparities in the effects of COVID for the most marginalized (Armstrong 2020) and inspired equity-focused policy responses to address the disparities (American Rescue Plan Equity Learning Agenda 2022).

This book was inspired by my own observation that groups that have traditionally faced discrimination and disenfranchisement may also be most harmed by the continuation of failed policies. One important implication of my findings is that more data collection, rather than less, will lead to more frequent recognition and revision of policy failure. However, astute observers of race, inequality, and data in American history may rightfully point out that data has often been used to stymie, rather than expand, racial and economic inequality. There is a long history of data, particularly as it relates to people of color, being manipulated to further inequality, discrimination, and racism and to justify racist ideologies (see, for example, Muhammad 2010).

The wealth, social status, race or ethnicity, and historical political involvement of a constituency affects the extent to which voices are heard in American politics (Gamble & Stone 2006; Gilens 2009; Hacker et al. 2021).

In other words, accusations of policy failure may be taken seriously by elected officials depending on who is making the claims. The quality and reliability of the data and the analysis can enhance the narratives of politically marginalized groups to help bring about reform, despite opposition from well-resourced companies or interest groups, both of which tend to dominate political narratives in American politics (Bawn et al. 2012; Gilens 2009; Hacker and Pierson 2011).

Data collection is not a panacea for inequality, particularly racially disparate outcomes and inequality stemming from racist practices and systems. Public officials and activists should be wary of claims using state-collected data that justify an unequal status quo. However, fear that data *may* be used improperly does not eliminate the possibility that systematically collected information can also be used to identify disparities and empower those arguing for targeted policy change (just as occurred with the COVID Tracking Project). Advocates concerned with the disparate impacts of a policy's failure should view the data collection and analysis procedures as important as the policy itself. Demanding accurate and robust data analysis that accounts for the impact on traditionally marginalized communities can help advocates and public officials recognize and address disparities faster. Developing the data collection and analytical procedures that guard against backwards and unjust interpretations of policy data will require involving more diverse perspectives in the design of policy evaluation and research institutions, not just in the design of the original policy.

Clear data and analysis can act as a mitigating force for the resources that we often think of as empowering the strongest political actors. Weaker political groups can leverage credible data and analysis to bolster their narratives of the policy outcomes. When the data or the analysis is disputed, however, the resources and political power of traditionally powerful groups can win out, as the uncertainty of changing away from the status quo is more appealing than addressing a questionably documented problem.

Federalism, Polarization, and Data

The United States' experience with COVID-19 presents a recent example of the complicated relationship among data, politics, experimentation, and recognition of failure. Some states had established procedures and infrastructure they could mobilize to collect and disseminate data about the virus, while others remained (either willingly or not) in the metaphorical dark about just how severel the virus had affected their residents. As described in Chapter 5, journalists, scholars, and volunteers in turn spent thousands of hours creating a more credible COVID-19 database to produce a more reliable picture of the pandemic. Even as scientists learned more about how the virus worked and which mitigation strategies would be effective, public health officials were lambasted for "changing their minds" on the best guidelines for avoiding COVID (Brewster 2020; Helm and Spicuzza 2020; Romero 2020).

Having the resources to collect and analyze COVID data was far from the only obstacle to taking a data-driven approach to pandemic responses. Some states preemptively set thresholds that were tied directly to data on cases and deaths for when they would open up or close back down, while others refused to implement mask mandates, shut down orders, or vaccination requirements (James, Tervo, and Skocpol 2022). Scholars have now shown that by and large implementation of data-driven mitigation strategies depended on the partisan control of state governments (Adolph et al. 2022; Capano et al. 2020; Fischer et al. 2021; James, Tervo, and Skocpol 2022). Elected officials employed different narratives about the measures of success to rally the public and justify their approach. Democrats cited the unprecedent virulence of COVID-19, the reduction of harm (i.e., cases and deaths from COVID-19), and the importance of limiting strains on the health care system as justifications for stay-at-home orders and other mitigation strategies (Luna and Willon 2021; Stolberg 2020a, 2021). Republicans, on the other hand, questioned both the severity of the virus and the legitimacy of the health research, and emphasized protecting the economy and individual freedoms from government regulation, while insisting that the rates of infection and death were no more concerning than the annual flu (Bump 2020; Montanaro 2020). Republican officials—President Trump included—limited the collection of COVID data and cherry-picked statistics to craft a narrative about the low risk of the virus (Deconstructing Georgia's Dubious COVID-19 Data Dashboard 2020; Helm and Spicuzza 2020; Qiu 2020; Stolberg 2020b).

This is all to say that collecting and analyzing data alone is not the answer: scientists knew conclusively that COVID was more dangerous than the flu, and yet saying otherwise was perfectly acceptable in many political circles. But there were *some* voices, even in the most conservative states, that used data to point to the realities of the pandemic. In states with governors or legislators opposed to mitigation strategies, local officials and public health experts attempted to implement data-informed public health measures, albeit usually with less success and substantial pushback (Bauer 2021; Helm and Spicuzza 2020; Vetterkind and Schmidt 2020).

Credible evidence is both a product and a producer of politics. Partisan polarization and ideological vitriol existed before the arrival of COVID-19 in the United States, and it fundamentally influenced the process of responding to data during the pandemic. The investments states make in institutionalizing the creation and use of data can have important downstream impacts for which narratives can dominate a policy debate, what people see as credible information, and whether there is a culture of prioritizing data in making public policy decisions.

COVID is certainly a unique example, but it indicates that we are in a world where Democrats and Republicans are utilizing and talking about data in very different ways. The current climate of state and national politics—with the rise of extremism, ideological polarization, rejection of norms, questioning facts—makes understanding the politics of recognizing and responding to objective policy failures especially important. In Chapter 1, I shared Paul Ryan's justification for evidence-based policymaking. In his vision of the world, "if we do this right, we'll stop having debates over what's Republican and what's Democrat . . . or what's liberal and conservative. . . . And we'll start having debates over what works and what doesn't work" (Congressional Record—House 2015, H5488). Even with data, the debate over what works and what doesn't work is still susceptible to the politics of ideology and strategic alliances among elected officials and the wealthy and powerful. Elected officials, activists, and lobbyists will (likely) always fight for policies that align with their ideological preferences, and, currently, the wealthy and better organized interests win most political contests. Strategic investments in a state's resources and procedures for collecting data and analyzing it play important roles in whether these powerful players can permanently dominate the narratives on policy outcomes. Investing in data collection and analysis has differential effects on the chance that those harmed by policy failure can successfully organize and justify their claims of failure and convince policymakers to change course.

As elected officials increasingly and strategically invoke "evidence" and "data" on behalf of their preferences, my research suggests that public officials need to be attentive not only to where data and analysis come from, but also whether and when the state invests in generating and processing its own data. Failure to acknowledge the essential role that state investment plays in data collection and analysis further relegates traditionally marginalized groups to further disadvantage in a political system dominated by organized interests.

Directions for Future Research

An important next step for this research agenda is to expand the measurement of collection and analytical capacity beyond the six state policy trajectories studied here. I juxtapose the case studies to identify data collection and analytical capacity as critical components of a state's institutional landscape for encouraging public officials to acknowledge and respond to policy failure. The comparisons also suggest several features that are essential to high collection and analytical capacity. Centralized data collection, clearly defined key terms, and concepts, and overlapping and ongoing data collection efforts characterize state policy areas with high collection capacity. Through my cases I also find that state-sponsored research institutions, legislation mandating evaluation, a history of regularly published policy evaluation reports, and the presence of universities and other nonstate research organizations characterize robust analytical capacity. An important followup to this project will be to study these features systematically across more states and policy areas.

The cases presented here also suggest that building collection and analytical capacity can be accidental, or, at the very least, an unintentional consequence of other government actions. Further investigation should probe the extent to which intentional data collection is more effective than accidental (or incidental) collection. There are also unanswered questions about analytical capacity. Are there ways in which a state might unintentionally establish analytical capacity? In an era of extreme affective polarization and increasing skepticism in universities on the far right, it will be important to continue to study the kinds of nonstate research organizations that offer the most political powerful analyses.

The policy analysis movement (and subsequent iterations) touted data as a panacea for ineffective policies. Instead of lamenting the unfulfilled promises of greater data availability, my findings suggest that supporters of policy analysis can lobby for specific policy and institutional design choices that will enhance the potential of our increased statistical knowledge, computing power, and data storage abilities.

Policy Failure as Opportunity

In his landmark study of social policy and policy learning, Hugh Heclo astutely noted the perpetual process of policymaking:

> Policy is not made once and for all; it is made and re-made endlessly. Policymaking is a process of successive approximation to some desired objectives in which the desired itself continues to change under reconsideration.
>
> (Heclo 1974, 86)

Much of political science, public policy, and political administration research has rightfully focused on understanding the factors that explain the passage and implementation of new policies. Yet, the full effects of a new policy are nearly impossible to predict ahead of time. Thus, even for the best-intentioned public servants, policy enactment is only one stop on a continual cycle of implementation, experience, learning, and revision. In this book, I explored a specific subset of public policies: those that fail to live up to their stated purpose. I examined the conditions that can facilitate the recognition and revision of failed policies. Rather than presuming, as the original policy analysis movement once did, that increasingly sophisticated data and analysis will eventually yield perfect policy out of the gate, this book assumes that predicting the myriad ramifications of any given policy—or the politics that new policies produce—is next to impossible. We saw in real time just how challenging and fraught it is to make policy in response to crises during COVID. We should not, and cannot, expect our elected and appointed public officials to be omniscient about how their policies will work. In fact, policy failure is a permanent, and perhaps even important, feature of governing in societies as rich and complex as the contemporary United States.

As Edison noted in the introduction's epigraph, learning something new often requires learning through thousands of small failures. We cannot, and should not, seek to lambaste those responsible for well-intentioned policy experiments that fail. Instead, we should hold our public officials accountable to investing in capacity, resources, and procedures that facilitate the recognition of failure when it occurs and praise public officials who are willing to innovate, learn, admit mistakes, and revise policy to the best of their knowledge. As Americans grapple with the long-term impacts of the past half-century's meteoric rise in inequality and the recent devastating impacts of a worldwide pandemic, we need public officials to be creative and bold and take policy risks. But we also need them to see failure as an opportunity to learn and try again.

APPENDIX

Building Policy Trajectories

Finding Legislative Archives and Legislation

Tracing the many legislative actions related to each of the policies in question formed the backbone of this book. To find all legislative records related to each policy, I used several strategies. First, I used keyword searches in each state's legislative archive search engine. I then read the returned legislation to determine whether the results were related to the policies in question. I iteratively cross-checked legislative records with news media searches to ensure that I had captured all legislative developments.

For each instance of legislative action, I collected the texts of any introduced, amended, or enacted bills. I also collected witness lists from committee hearings, House and Senate journal entries, and videos of committee hearings and floor debates. The House and Senate journal entries provided, when appropriate, documentation of roll-call votes, transcripts of statements made on the floor, and final vote totals. State legislative archives could then be used to identify important information about specific legislators, including their partisan affiliation, district, tenure, and committee assignments.

I watched (or listened to in a few cases) all committee hearings and floor debates for each policy trajectory. I transcribed the portions of each video or audio file that were relevant to the policies in question. Using the transcripts, I then coded for instances of invoking data or evidence in support of the arguments presented. I also documented the arguments that different actors made for and against the policies.

News Media Searches

I used Nexis Uni and major state newspapers to find news stories related to each policy. Keyword searches on Nexis Uni included major national newspapers (i.e., *The New York Times*, *The Washington Post*). Nexis Uni has uneven coverage of state and local newspapers, though keyword searches did turn up some subnational stories on some of the policies. To supplement the returns from Nexis Uni, I also conducted keyword searches in each state's major news outlets (see Table A.1 for a list of specific publications).

Media stories played several important roles in my research of the policy trajectories. First, they provided a starting point for identifying relevant policies in each state. I was then able to use dates, bill numbers, and other keywords provided in news stories to search for specific legislation in each state's archives. Second, news stories provided an initial list of key actors and organizations in the passage, reform, and resistance to reform for each policy. Interview quotes also offered insight into the arguments that supporters and opponents used for each policy. Discussion of public reaction (or lack thereof) offered clues to how the broader public was engaging with the process of acknowledging and addressing policy failure.

Table A.1 Keyword search terms and media outlets by state

	Case	Keyword Search Terms	Subnational Media Outlets
Texas	Failure to Attend School	• Texas AND Truancy • "Failure to Attend School"	*Austin-American Statesman* *Houston Chronicle* *Texas Monthly* *San Antonio Express News*
	Chapter 313	• Texas AND "tax incentives" AND "school" OR "school district" • "Chapter 313" OR "Ch 313"	
Washington	Becca's Bill	• Washington AND truancy • "Becca's Bill"	*The Seattle Times* *The Columbian*
	R&D Tax Credits	• Washington AND tax incentives • "R & D tax credits" OR "research and development tax credits" OR "research and development tax incentives"	
Wyoming	Juvenile Justice Act	• Wyoming AND truancy • "Juvenile Justice Act" AND Wyoming	*The Casper-Star Tribune* *Wyoming Tribute-Eagle*
Kansas	PEAK	• Kansas AND tax incentives • "PEAK" AND Kansas • "Promoting Employment Across Kansas"	*The Wichita Eagle* *The Topeka-Capital Journal*

Interview Sampling Techniques & List

Individual lawmakers, activists, and constituents can be important instigators of policy change (or resilience). Using legislative archives and the news stories I collected, I created a list of people who were directly involved in the activism, research, and political processes involving the cases (see Table A.2). Broadly, I aimed to speak with legislators who sponsored the original bills or any subsequent changes. I also sought out those who vocally opposed changes in committee hearings or floor debate.

Table A.2 Interview List

Position	Organization/position	Case Study
Government relations coordinator	Wind Energy Corporation	KS taxes
Executive and member	Kansas City Chamber of Commerce	KS taxes
Senator and Member	Kansas Senate and Commerce Committee	KS taxes
Executive	Kauffmann Family Foundation	KS taxes
Executive	Wind industry Corporation1	TX taxes
Researcher	University of Texas at Austin	TX taxes
Policy Expert at	Center for Public Policy Priorities	TX taxes
Wind industry executive	Wind Energy Corporation2	TX taxes
Tax Expert	Good Jobs First	TX taxes
Policy Expert	Texas Taxpayers Association	TX taxes
Executive Director	Texas Appleseed	TX truancy
Policy expert	Senator Whitmire's office	TX truancy
Policy expert	Texas Judicial Council	TX truancy
Lead Researcher	Texas Public Policy Research Institute	TX truancy
Leader	Texas Association of School Boards	TX truancy
Policy Expert	Texas Right on Crime	TX truancy
Member and Committee Leader	Washington Association of Juvenile Court Administrators	WA truancy
Organizational leader	Center for Child and Youth Justice	WA truancy
Organizational leader	Team Child	WA truancy
Senior Researcher	Washington State Center for Court Research	WA truancy
Organizational leader	Mockingbird Society	WA truancy
Policy expert	Washington State Institute for Public Policy	WA truancy
Senator	Washington Legislature	WA truancy
Policy expert	Governor's Office	WA truancy
Member	WA House of Representatives	WA truancy
Judge	State Supreme Court	WA truancy

Continued

Table A.2 *Continued*

Position	Organization/position	Case Study
Member	Washington Association of Juvenile Court Administrators	WA truancy
Researcher and advocate	Wyoming State Government	WY truancy
Representative	WY Children's Law Center	WY truancy
Policy expert	WY Juvenile Law Center	WY truancy
Policy expert	Member of the Juvenile Detention Alternative Initiative	WY truancy
Researcher and advocate	Wyoming State Government	WY truancy
Senior Researcher and Lawyer	Wyoming Children's Law Center and National Juvenile Justice Network	WY truancy

I conducted semistructured interviews, usually over the phone or through zoom. I offered my interviewees the opportunity to be identified only by their organization and position. In the cases of individuals who belonged to a for-profit business, I also offered to preserve the anonymity of the company names. I concluded each interview with a request for suggestions regarding other people I should consult to learn more about the policy in question. In three of the four cases, I reached saturation—with interviewees recommending people I had already spoken with. I was unable to reach saturation in the Washington R&D tax credit case given the extremely limited responses I received for my interview requests for this case.

In total, I made more than 100 interview requests across the six case studies. I followed up with individuals who did not respond after two weeks and then again after four weeks, at which point I stopped contacting them if I received no response. When an interviewee offered to put me in contact with someone else, I took them up on the connection to increase the likelihood of getting a response (and subsequent interview). In total, I interviewed thirty-four researchers, policymakers, business leaders, and philanthropists.

I did not have even coverage across my cases, which reflects the variation in the saliency of each policy. I was unable to secure interviews with anyone directly involved in the Washington Research and Development tax case.

Organizational Records

Media stories, witness lists, and interviews provided an initial list of research organizations and public agencies involved in each case. I documented the mentions of organizations and then searched their websites for reports, press releases, and any other documents related to the relevant policies. I contacted researchers and policy experts at the organizations when the websites named a specific person as specializing in the given policy area. I also contacted executives and research directors at the organizations to request interviews.

I used two strategies to find relevant documents on organizational websites. First, if the organization hosted an internal search tool, I would search the broad policy area (e.g., truancy or taxes) and review the returned results for anything related to the specific policies in question. When a document was broadly relevant to the policy area in the state (even if it was not about the specific policy in question), I would also retain the document. Second, I would do a broader internet search of the organization's or agency's name in quotes, as well as the name of the relevant policy in quotes, to identify any other remaining documents.

Creating Policy Trajectories

Collecting the data described above was an iterative process. As I interviewed additional people and discovered more documents, I would find new relevant organizations, individuals, and documents. As I collected this data, I created timelines for each policy. These timelines noted the dates of important legislative events (such as passage of the original policy, introductions of proposed reforms, committee hearings, and votes). I noted actors that played prominent roles in each of these developments. I added in the dates of publications of any research findings, state agency policy evaluations, or nongovernment organizational reports. When relevant, I also included the dates and timelines for national policies or events that may have impacted public officials' responses to the policies in their own states.

To ensure that I was analyzing comparable information for each policy, I also created a policy "questionnaire" that I completed for each. These questionnaires (see Table A.3) probed key information about the timing, context, and actors involved in each policy. Documenting the answers to these questions across all cases made developments easier to compare. When answering the questions, I would include quotes, snapshots of documents, and source information to facilitate comparison of primary sources across cases.

Table A.3 Template questionnaire for case studies

CASE STUDY QUESTIONNAIRE
Background on state politics

- How professional is the state legislature?
- Partisan makeup
- Institutional background
- What research institutions exist at the state level?
- Which national institutions, if any, are involved in this policy area in the state?
- What advocacy organizations exist?
- Local level

Continued

Table A.3 *Continued*

Background on policy

- When was the original policy passed?
- What was the political context under which it passed?
- What is the original text of the legislation?
- What are the stated goals of the policy?
- How does the policy work?

Evidence of failure

- Who collects data on the policy's outcomes?
- What data suggest that the policy has failed to meet the stated intentions?
- Who collected the data and who published it?
- Is there contrary evidence? Who collected this data and published it?

Acknowledging failure

- Who has and has not acknowledged the failure of the policy? What justifications do they provide to support their argument?
- Specific textual evidence of acknowledged policy failure.
- What does local media tend to suggest about the policy?

Responding to failure

- Has the state attempted to reform the original policy? If so, how? Was it successful?
- Who supported the reforms?
- Who opposed the reforms?
- Were there multiple attempts at reform? Describe each and why each was successful or unsuccessful.

Timeline
Addi

References

74th Senate Education Committee Tape 1 of 5: Hearing on 2 of 5 before the Senate Education Committee, Senate 74 regular session (1995). https://tslarc.tsl.texas.gov/senaterecordings/74/740598b_01.mp3

2007 Full Tax Preference Performance Reviews (07–14). (2007). Joint Legislative Audit & Review Committee.

2008 Democratic Party Platform: Renewing America's Promise. (2008). The American Presidency Project. https://www.presidency.ucsb.edu/documents/2008-democratic-party-platform

2008 Republican Party Platform. (2008). The American Presidency Project. https://www.presidency.ucsb.edu/documents/2008-republican-party-platform

2012 Tax Preference Performance Reviews (13–1). (2013). Joint Legislative Audit & Review Committee. http://leg.wa.gov/jlarc/AuditAndStudyReports/Documents/2012TaxPreferenceReviewsProposedFinalPresentation_printver.pdf

2020 Democratic Party Platform. (2020). The American Presidency Project. https://www.presidency.ucsb.edu/documents/2020-democratic-party-platform

Aaronson, B. (2011, December 23). Yes, Perry has lured business to Texas, but how many jobs created is in dispute. *The New York Times*, 25A.

About WYSAC. (2019, October 29). Wyoming Survey and Analysis Center. https://wysac.uwyo.edu/wysac

Acemoglu, D., Moscona, J., & Robinson, J. A. (2016). State capacity and American technology: Evidence from the nineteenth century. *American Economic Review, 106*(5), 61–67.

Adolph, C. (2016, May). Washington companies got $500 million in tax breaks, and that's just the ones we know about. http://kuow.org/post/washington-companies-got-500-million-tax-breaks-and-s-just-ones-we-know-about

Adolph, C., Amano, K., Bang-Jensen, B., Fullman, N., Magistro, B., Reinke, G., & Wilkerson, J. (2022). Governor partisanship explains the adoption of statewide mask mandates in response to COVID-19. *State Politics and Policy Quarterly, 22*(1), 24–49.

Amenta, E., Clemens, E. S., Olsen, J., Parikh, S., & Skocpol, T. (1987). The political origins of unemployment insurance in five American states. *Studies in American Political Development, 2*, 137–182. https://doi.org/10.1017/S0898588X00000444

American Rescue Plan Equity Learning Agenda. (2022). Biden White House. https://www.whitehouse.gov/wp-content/uploads/2022/05/American-Rescue-Plan-Equity-Learning-Agenda.pdf

Andersen, L. M. F. (2013). *The Politics of Prohibition: American Governance and the Prohibition Party, 1869–1933*. Cambridge University Press.

Angelone, E. (2010). The Texas two-step: The criminalization of truancy under the Texas "Failure to Attend" Statute. *The Scholar: St. Mary's Law Review on Minority Issues, 13*, 433–481.

Aos, S. (2002). *Keeping Kids in School: The Impact of the Truancy Provisions in Washington's 1995 "Becca's Bill"* (02.10.2201). Washington State Institute for Public Policy. http://www.wsipp.wa.gov/ReportFile/809/Wsipp_Keeping-Kids-in-School-The-Impact-of-the-Truancy-Provisions-in-Washingtons-1995-Becca-Bill_Executive-Summary.pdf

Arceneaux, K. (2012). Cognitive biases and the strength of political arguments. *American Journal of Political Science, 56*(2), 271–285.

Armstrong, D. (2020, November 20). Data heroes of Covid Tracking Project are still filling U.S. government void. *Bloomberg.Com.* https://www.bloomberg.com/news/features/2020-11-20/covid-tracking-project-volunteers-step-up-as-u-s-fails-during-pandemic

Arthur, P., Rabinowitz, M., & Horvath, J. (2010). *A Call to Stop Child Prosecutions in Wyoming Adult Courts.* The National Center for Youth Law and The American Civil Liberties Union, Wyoming Chapter.

Atalay, S. (2012). *Community-Based Archaeology: Research with, by, and for Indigenous and Local Communities.* University of California Press. http://ebookcentral.proquest.com/lib/gonzaga/detail.action?docID=962591

Baker, J. A., Derrer, R. D., Davis, S. M., Dinklage-Travis, H. E., Linder, D. S., & Nicholson, M. D. (2001). The flip side of the coin: Understanding the school's contribution to dropout and completion. *School Psychology Quarterly, 16*(4), 406–426.

Balla, S. J. (2001). Interstate professional associations and the diffusion of policy innovations. *American Politics Research, 29*(3), 221–245.

Barboza, D. (2001, May 11). Chicago, offering big incentives, will be Boeing's new home. *The New York Times.* https://www.nytimes.com/2001/05/11/business/chicago-offering-big-incentives-will-be-boeing-s-new-home.html

Barnard, C. I. (1938). The economy of incentives. *Classics of Organization Theory*, 93–102.

Baron, J. (2013). *Randomized controlled trails commissioned by the Institute of Education Sciences since 2002: How many found positive versus weak or no effects.* Coalition for Evidence-Based Policy. http://coalition4evidence.org

Baron, J. (2018). A brief history of evidence-based policy. *The ANNALS of the American Academy of Political and Social Science, 678*(1), 40–50. https://doi.org/10.1177/0002716218763128

Bartik, T. J. (1992). The effects of state and local taxes on economic development: A review of recent research. *Economic Development Quarterly, 6*(1), 102–110.

Bartik, T. J. (2017). *A New Panel Database on Business Incentives for Economic Development Offered by State and Local Governments in the United States* (225; Labor Economics Commons). W. E. Upjohn Institute for Employment Research. https://research.upjohn.org/reports/225

Bauer, S. (2021). Republican-controlled Wisconsin Senate votes to repeal state's mask mandate. *Chicago Tribune*. https://www.chicagotribune.com/coronavirus/ct-nw-wisconsin-mask-mandate-20210126-e4bzbwayrrcgleyrezx5ppau4a-story.html

Baumgartner, F. R., & Jones, B. D. (2015). *The Politics of Information: Problem Definition and the Course of Public policy in America*. University of Chicago Press.

Bawn, K., Cohen, M., Karol, D., Masket, S., Noel, H., & Zaller, J. (2012). A theory of political parties: Groups, policy demands and nominations in American politics. *Perspectives on Politics*, *10*(3), 571–597.

Becca's Bill, Pub. L. No. E2SSB 5439, Chapter 312, Laws of 1995 1 (1995).

Béland, D., & Cox, R. H. (2010). *Ideas and Politics in Social Science Research*. Oxford University Press.

Bennett, A., & Checkel, J. T. (2015). *Process Tracing: From Metaphor to Analytic Tool*. Cambridge University Press.

Bennett, C. J., & Howlett, M. (1992). The lessons of learning: reconciling theories of policy learning and policy change. *Policy Sciences*, *25*(3), 275–294.

Berk, R. A. (1991). Toward a methodology for mere mortals. *Sociological Methodology*, *21*, 315–324.

Berry, F. S., & Berry, W. D. (1990). State lottery adoptions as policy innovations: An event history analysis. *American Political Science Review*, *84*(02), 395–415.

Berry, F. S., & Berry, W. D. (1999). Innovation and diffusion models in policy research. *Theories of the Policy Process*, *169*.

Best, J. (2012). *Damned Lies and Statistics: Untangling Numbers from the Media, Politicians, and Activists*. University of California Press.

Birkland, T. A. (1998). Focusing events, mobilization, and agenda setting. *Journal of Public Policy*, *18*(1), 53–74.

Bishop, M. W. (Director). (2012, December 1). Border War: Kansas City. *New York Times*. https://www.nytimes.com/video/business/100000001832941/border-war.html

Boatright, R. G. (2013). *Getting Primaried: The Changing Politics of Congressional Primary Challenges*. University of Michigan Press.

Bornstein, D. (2012, May 30). The dawn of the evidence-based budget. *New York TImes*. https://opinionator.blogs.nytimes.com/2012/05/30/worthy-of-government-funding-prove-it/

Boswell, C. (2009). The political uses of expert knowledge: Immigration policy and social research. In *The Political Uses of Expert Knowledge: Immigration Policy and Social Research*. https://doi.org/10.1017/CBO9780511581120

Bound, J., Braga, B., Khanna, G., & Turner, S. (2019). Public universities: The supply side of building a skilled workforce. *RSF: The Russell Sage Foundation Journal of the Social Sciences*, *5*(5), 43–66. https://doi.org/10.7758/rsf.2019.5.5.03

Brady, H. E. (2019). The challenge of big data and data science. *Annual Review of Political Science*, *22*, 297–323.

Brambor, T., Goenaga, A., Lindvall, J., & Teorell, J. (2020). The lay of the land: Information capacity and the modern state. *Comparative Political Studies*, *53*(2), 175–213.

Brehm, J., & Gates, S. (1999). *Working, shirking, and sabotage: Bureaucratic response to a democratic public*. University of Michigan Press. https://books.google.com/books?hl=en&lr=&id=KmJo8Y8HFyAC&oi=fnd&pg=PR9&dq=working+shirking+sabotage&ots=wqtazPliVH&sig=kezDAORveDxmlLoJUvO8LFx0VZ8

Brewster, J. (2020, October 20). Is Trump right that Fauci discouraged wearing masks? Yes—But Early On And Not For Long. *Forbes*. https://www.forbes.com/sites/jackbrewster/2020/10/20/is-trump-right-that-fauci-discouraged-wearing-masks/

Brimer, K. (2001). *Office of House Bill Analysis HB 1200*. Office of House Bill Analysis. https://capitol.texas.gov/BillLookup/Text.aspx?LegSess=77R&Bill=HB1200

Brown, T. (2011, October 18). Juvenile justice tracking system could cost $500k. *Wyoming Tribune Eagle*. https://www.wyomingnews.com/news/juvenile-justice-tracking-system-could-cost-k/article_f5e017ef-ec71-5269-8847-073c4a2e1b63.html

Brown, T. (2013, December 9). Gov. Mead looks to expand juvenile justice data program. *Wyoming Tribune Eagle*. https://www.wyomingnews.com/news/gov-mead-looks-to-expand-juvenile-justice-data-program/article_20cc1d09-613c-531f-ba00-d015e22c4661.html

Brownson, R. C., Chriqui, J. F., & Stamatakis, K. (2009). Understanding evidence-based public health policy. *American Journal of Public Health*, *99*(9), 1576–1583.

Brownson, R. C., Fielding, J. E., & Green, L. W. (2018). Building capacity for evidence-based public health: Reconciling the pulls of practice and the push of research. *Annual Review of Public Health*, *39*(1), 27–53. https://doi.org/10.1146/annurev-publhealth-040617-014746

Bump, P. (2020, March 25). Analysis | Trump again downplays coronavirus by comparing it to the seasonal flu. It's not a fair comparison. *Washington Post*. https://www.washingtonpost.com/politics/2020/03/24/trump-again-downplays-coronavirus-by-comparing-it-seasonal-flu-its-not-fair-comparison/

Burley, M., & Harding, E. (1998). *Truant Students: Evaluating the Impact of the "Becca Bill" Truancy Petition Requirements* (98-01–2201). Washington State Institute for Public Policy. http://www.wsipp.wa.gov/ReportFile/1271/Wsipp_Truant-Students-Evaluating-the-Impact-of-the-Becca-Bill-Truancy-Petition-Requirements_Full-Report.pdf

Burstein, P. (1991). Policy domains: Organization, culture, and policy outcomes. *Annual Review of Sociology*, *17*(1), 327–350.

Bursztynsky, J. (2023, March 10). *Organizational psychologist Adam Grant explains why we should normalize failure*. Fast Company. https://www.fastcompany.com/90862444/organizational-psychologist-adam-grant-explains-why-we-should-normalize-failure

Buss, T. F. (2001). The effect of state tax incentives on economic growth and firm location decisions: An overview of the literature. *Economic Development Quarterly*, *15*(1), 90–105.

Butler, D. M., Volden, C., Dynes, A. M., & Shor, B. (2017). Ideology, learning, and policy diffusion: Experimental evidence. *American Journal of Political Science*, *61*(1), 37–49.

Callen, M., Khan, A., Khwaja, A. I., Liaqat, A., & Myers, E. (2017, August 13). Analysis | These 3 barriers make it hard for policymakers to use the evidence that development researchers produce. *Washington Post*. https://www.washingtonpost.com/news/monkey-cage/wp/2017/08/13/these-3-barriers-make-it-hard-for-policymakers-to-use-the-evidence-that-development-researchers-produce/

Calvert, R. L., & Fenno, R. F. (1994). Strategy and sophisticated voting in the Senate. *The Journal of Politics, 56*(2), 349–376. https://doi.org/10.2307/2132143

Campbell, A. L. (2003). Participatory reactions to policy threats: Senior citizens and the defense of Social Security and Medicare. *Political Behavior, 25*(1), 29–49.

Canes-Wrone, B. (2015). From mass preferences to policy. *Annual Review of Political Science, 18*, 147–165.

Capano, G., Howlett, M., Jarvis, D. S., Ramesh, M., & Goyal, N. (2020). Mobilizing policy (in) capacity to fight COVID-19: Understanding variations in state responses. *Policy and Society, 39*(3), 285–308.

Carmichael, D., Marchbanks III, M. P., Booth, E., Fabelo, T., Thompson, M. D., & Platkin, M. (2011). *Breaking Schools' Rules: A statewide study of how school discipline relates to students' success and juvenile justice involvement.* Justice Center at the Council for State Governments & Texas Public Policy Research Institute.

Carpenter, D. P. (2001). *The Forging of Bureaucratic Autonomy: Reputations, Networks, and Policy Innovation In Executive Agencies, 1862-1928.* Princeton University Press.

Carpenter, D. P. (2014). *Reputation and Power: Organizational Image and Pharmaceutical Regulation at the FDA.* (Vol. 137). Princeton University Press.

Choi, B. C. K., Pang, T., Lin, V., Puska, P., Sherman, G., Goddard, M., Ackland, M. J., Sainsbury, P., Stachenko, S., Morrison, H., & Clottey, C. (2005). Can scientists and policy makers work together? *Journal of Epidemiology and Community Health (1979–), 59*(8), 632–637.

Coffey, D. J. (2011). More than a dime's worth: using state party platforms to assess the degree of American party polarization. *PS: Political Science & Politics, 44*(2), 331–337. https://doi.org/10.1017/S1049096511000187

Cohen, M., Karol, D., Noel, H., & Zaller, J. (2009). *The Party Decides: Presidential Nominations before and after Reform.* University of Chicago Press.

Cohen, R. (2022, December 15). *The most successful strategy for ending homelessness is under attack.* Vox. https://www.vox.com/policy-and-politics/23504323/housing-first-homelessness-houston-homes

Collier, D. (2011). Understanding process tracing. *PS: Political Science & Politics, 44*(4), 823–830.

Collins, B. K., & Gerber, B. J. (2006). Redistributive policy and devolution: Is state administration a road block (grant) to equitable access to federal funds? *Journal of Public Administration Research and Theory, 16*(4), 613–632.

Congressional Record—House. (2015). H5486-H5488. https://www.congress.gov/114/crec/2015/07/27/CREC-2015-07-27-pt1-PgH5486.pdf

Conway, M. A., & Pleydell-Pearce, C. W. (2000). The construction of autobiographical memories in the self-memory system. *Psychological Review, 107*(2), 261–288. https://doi.org/10.1037/0033-295X.107.2.261

Cook, S. J., & Fortunato, D. (2023). The politics of police data: State legislative capacity and the transparency of state and substate agencies. *American Political Science Review, 117*(1), 280–295.

Copelin, L. (2012, September 12). Samsung could double Austin investment, depending on incentives, official says. *Austin American Statesman.* http://www.statesman.com/business/technology/samsung-could-double-austin-investment-depending-on-incentives-2456790.html

Dagan, D., & Teles, S. M. (2014). Locked in? Conservative reform and the future of mass incarceration. *The ANNALS of the American Academy of Political and Social Science, 651*(1), 266–276.

Dagan, D., & Teles, S. M. (2015, October). *The Social Construction of Policy Feedback: Incarceration, Conservatism, and Ideological Change.* Studies in American Political Development.

Dahl, R. A. (1961). *Who Governs? Democracy and Power in an American City.* Yale University Press.

Davidson, R. H., & Oleszek, W. J. (1994). *Congress and Its Members.* CQ Press.

Davies, E., Dube, S., Farver, M., Silloway, T., Sutherland, K., & White, D. (2017). *How States Engage in Evidence-Based Policymaking.* PEW Charitable Trusts & MacArthur Foundation.

Defoe, I. N., Dubas, J. S., Figner, B., & van Aken, M. A. G. (2015). A meta-analysis on age differences in risky decision making: Adolescents versus children and adults. *Psychological Bulletin, 141*(1), 48–84.

Dehejia, R. (2005). Practical propensity score matching: A reply to Smith and Todd. *Journal of Econometrics, 125*(1), 355–364. https://doi.org/10.1016/j.jeconom.2004.04.012

Democratic State Senator in office in 1995. (2015, June 18). *Interview with Texas Democratic State Senator* [Phone Interview].

Department of Commerce: Evaluating the Department's Compliance with Statutory Caps for the PEAK Program (Limited Scope Performance Audit Report L-17-014). (2017). Legislative Division of Post Audit.

Derthick, M. (2011). *Agency under Stress: The Social Security Administration in American Government.* Brookings Institution Press. https://books.google.com/books?hl=en&lr=&id=N3LI4Jr8cZMC&oi=fnd&pg=PA3&dq=martha+derthick+social+security&ots=Rn2lcN-KkS&sig=ThRGjzRBvcaZHYV6P_4PKLG-CUg

Desmond, M. (2016). *Evicted: Poverty and Profit in the American City.* Crown.

Deutsch, K. (1966). *The Nerves of Government.* The Free Press.

Dishion, T. J., McCord, J., & Poulin, F. (1999). When interventions harm: Peer groups and problem behavior. *American Psychologist, 54*(9), 755.

Doberstein, C. (2017). Whom do bureaucrats believe? A randomized controlled experiment testing perceptions of credibility of policy research. *Policy Studies Journal, 45*(2), 384–405. https://doi.org/10.1111/psj.12166

Druckman, J. N., & McDermott, R. (2008). Emotion and the framing of risky choice. *Political Behavior, 30,* 297–321.

Economic Development: Determining Which Development Tools Are Most Important and Promoting Job Creation and Economic Growth in Kansas, Part 3 (Performance Audit Report R-14-011; pp. 1–49). (2014). Legislative Division of Post Audit.

Economic Development: Determining Which Economic Development Tools are Most Important and Effective in Promoting Job Creation and Economic Growth in Kansas, Part 1 (Performance Audit Report R-13-010; pp. 1–72). (2013). Legislative Division of Post Audit.

Economic Development: Determining Which Economic Development Tools are Most Important and Effective in Promoting Job Creation and Economic Growth in Kansas, Part 2 (Performance Audit Report R-14-003; pp. 1–49). (2014). Legislative Division of Post Audit.

Edin, K. J., & Shaefer, H. L. (2015). *$2.00 a Day: Living on Almost Nothing in America.* Houghton Mifflin Harcourt.

Editorial Board. (2001, May 26). Perry should veto school-tax giveaway. *Austin American-Statesman*, A14.

Einstein, K. L., & Glick, D. M. (2016). Does race affect access to government services? An experiment exploring street-level bureaucrats and access to public housing. *American Journal of Political Science*, n/a–n/a. https://doi.org/10.1111/ajps.12252

Elazar, D. J. (1972). *American Federalism: A View from the States.* Crowell.

Engrossed Second Substitute Senate Bill 6347, Pub. L. No. SB 6347, ESSB 6347 (1994).

Engrossed Substitute Senate Bill 5882, Pub. L. No. ESSB 5882 (2013).

Erikson, Robert S. (2015). Income inequality and policy responsiveness. *Annual Review of Political Science, 18*, 11–29.

Etheredge, L. S. (1981). Government learning. In *The Handbook of Political Behavior* (pp. 73–161). Springer. http://link.springer.com/chapter/10.1007/978-1-4615-9191-7_2

Eullit, D. (2016, August 26). *End the economic border war that is wasting KC area taxpayers' dollars.* Kansascity. http://www.kansascity.com/opinion/editorials/article98128057.html

Fiorina, M. P. (1981). *Retrospective Voting in American National Elections.* Yale University Press.

Fischer, C. B., Adrien, N., Silguero, J. J., Hopper, J. J., Chowdhury, A. I., & Werler, M. M. (2021). *Mask adherence and rate of COVID-19 across the United States.* https://doi.org/10.1101/2021.01.18.21250029

Fording, R. C., Soss, J., & Schram, S. F. (2007). Devolution, discretion, and the effect of local political values on TANF sanctioning. *Social Service Review, 81*(2), 285–316.

Fowler, D., Mergler, M. S., Johnson, K., & Craven, M. (2015). *Class not Court: Reconsidering Texas' Criminalization of Truancy.* Texas Appleseed. https://www.texasappleseed.org/class-not-court-reconsidering-texas-criminalization-truancy-full-report

Fowler, S., & Fleming, L. (Directors). (2020, May 19). Deconstructing Georgia's dubious COVID-19 Data Dashboard. In *Georgia Public Broadcasting-NPR.*

Franco, A., Malhotra, N., & Simonovits, G. (2014). Publication bias in the social sciences: Unlocking the file drawer. *Science, 345*(6203), 1502–1505. https://doi.org/10.1126/science.1255484

Franko, W. W. (2021). How state responses to economic crisis shape income inequality and financial well-being. *State Politics & Policy Quarterly, 21*(1), 31–54.

Freng, A., Rees, C., Siegel, G., Torbet, P., & Hurst, H. (2004). *Youth Case Processing in the State of Wyoming: An Analysis of Four Counties Report to the Wyoming Department of Family Services* (CJG-404; pp. 1–184). Wyoming Survey & Analysis Center.

Frey, D. (2011). *Truancy and Habitual Truancy: Examples of State Definitions.* Education Commission of the States.

Fullerton, T. (2002). Empirical evidence on the El Paso property tax abatement program: 1988-2011. *Journal of Law & Border Studies, 2*, 37–48.

Fullerton, T., & Aragones-Zamudio, V. (2006). *El Paso Property Tax Abatement Ineffectiveness* (Document MPRA Paper No. 626). Munich Perosnal RePEc Archive. http://mpra.ub.uni-muenchen.de/626

Gaines, B. J., & Jenkins, J. A. (2009). Apportionment Matters: Fair Representation in the US House and Electoral College. *Perspectives on Politics, 7*(4), 849–857. https://doi.org/10.1017/S1537592709991848

Gamble, V. N., & Stone, D. (2006). US policy on health inequities: The interplay of politics and research. *Journal of Health Politics, Policy and Law, 31*(1), 93–126.

Gardner, G. (2001). Unreliable memories and other contingencies: Problems with biographical knowledge. *Qualitative Research, 1*(2), 185–204. https://doi.org/10.1177/146879410100100205

George, T. (2011). *Truancy in Washington State: Trends, Student Characteristics, and the Impact of Receiving a Truancy Petition.* Washington State Center for Court Research, Administrative Office of the Courts. https://www.digitalarchives.wa.gov/do/3C985DB3F53948DE53EBF1E1672E4B8C.pdf

Gerring, J. (1999). What makes a concept good? A criterial framework for understanding concept formation in the social sciences. *Polity, 31*(3), 357–393. https://doi.org/10.2307/3235246

Gerring, J. (2012). *Social Science Methodology: A Unified Framework* (2nd Edition). Cambridge University Press.

Gilardi, F. (2010). Who learns from what in policy diffusion processes? *American Journal of Political Science, 54*(3), 650–666.

Gilens, M. (2009). Preference gaps and inequality in representation. *PS: Political Science & Politics, 42*(2), 335–341.

Gilens, M., & Page, B. I. (2014). Testing theories of American politics: Elites, interest groups, and average citizens. *Perspectives on Politics, 12*(03), 564–581.

Gilman, A., & Sanford, R. (2017). *Washington State Juvenile Detention 2016 Annual Report* (Washington State Juvenile Detention). Washington State Center for Court Research, Administrative Office of the Courts.

Gilmer, T. P., Stefancic, A., Katz, M. L., Sklar, M., Tsemberis, S., & Palinkas, L. A. (2014). Fidelity to the Housing First Model and Effectiveness of Permanent Supported Housing Programs in California. *Psychiatric Services, 65*(11), 1311–1317. https://doi.org/10.1176/appi.ps.201300447

Glickhouse, R. (2021, April 14). *Analysis & Updates | Measuring Our Impact at The COVID Tracking Project.* The COVID Tracking Project. https://covidtracking.com/analysis-updates/measuring-our-impact

Godwin, M. L., & Schroedel, J. R. (2000). Policy diffusion and strategies for promoting policy change: Evidence from California local gun control ordinances. *Policy Studies Journal, 28*(4), 760–776.

Gray, V. (1973). Innovation in the states: A diffusion study. *American Political Science Review, 67*(4), 1174–1185.

Greenberg, D. H., & Robins, P. K. (1985). The changing role of social experiments in policy analysis. *Journal of Policy Analysis & Management*, *5*(2), 340–362.

Greenblat, A. (2011, August). Kansas City businesses want to end the 'economic border war. *Governing the States and Localities.* http://www.governing.com/topics/economic-dev/kansas-city-businesses-want-end-economic-border-war.html

Grumbach, J. M. (2022). *Laboratories Against democracy: How National Parties Transformed State Politics.* Princeton University Press.

Haberman, C. (2014, April 6). When youth violence spurred 'superpredator' fear. *The New York Times.* https://www.nytimes.com/2014/04/07/us/politics/killing-on-bus-recalls-superpredator-threat-of-90s.html

Haberman, M., & Parker, A. (2016, January 13). New attack ads call Marco Rubio a flip-flopper on immigration. *The New York Times.* https://www.nytimes.com/2016/01/13/us/politics/new-attack-ads-call-marco-rubio-a-flip-flopper-on-immigration.html

Hacker, J. (2002). *The Divided Welfare State: The Battle over Public and Private Social Benefits in the United States.* Cambridge University Press.

Hacker, J., Hertel-Fernandez, A., Pierson, P., & Thelen, K. (2021). *The American Political Economy: Politics, Markets, and Power.* Cambridge University Press.

Hacker, J., & Pierson, P. (2011). *Winner-Take-All Politics: How Washington Made The Rich Richer–And Turned Its Back on the Middle Class.* Simon and Schuster.

Hacker, J., & Pierson, P. (2014). After the "Master Theory": Downs, Schattschneider, and the Rebirth of Policy-Focused Analysis. *Perspectives on Politics*, *12*(3), 643–662. https://doi.org/10.1017/S1537592714001637

Haider-Markel, D. P. (2001). Policy diffusion as a geographical expansion of the scope of political conflict: same-sex marriage bans in the 1990s. *State Politics & Policy Quarterly*, *1*(1), 5–26. https://doi.org/10.1177/153244000100100102

Halbfinger, D. M. (2004, September 30). Kerry says flip-flop image "doesn't reflect the truth." *The New York Times.* https://www.nytimes.com/2004/09/30/politics/campaign/kerry-says-flipflop-image-doesnt-reflect-the-truth.html

Hall Family Foundation study shows Missouri has lost $217 million in taxes in border war. (2014, February 7). *Missouri Chamber.* https://mochamber.wordpress.com/2014/02/07/hall-family-foundation-study-shows-missouri-has-lost-217-million-in-taxes-in-border-war/

Hall, P. A. (1993). Policy paradigms, social learning, and the state: The case of economic policymaking in Britain. *Comparative Politics*, 275–296.

Hall, P. A., & Taylor, R. C. (1996). Political science and the three new institutionalisms. *Political Studies*, *44*(5), 936–957.

Hartney, M., & Flavin, P. (2011). From the schoolhouse to the statehouse: Teacher Union political activism and U.S. state education reform policy. *State Politics & Policy Quarterly*, *11*(3), 251–268. https://doi.org/10.1177/1532440011413079

Haskins, R. (2018). Evidence-based policy: The movement, the goals, the issues, the promise. *The ANNALS of the American Academy of Political and Social Science*, *678*(1), 8–37. https://doi.org/10.1177/0002716218770642

Hayek, F. (1973). *Law, Legislation, and Liberty: Rules and Order.* Routledge.

HB 1200 House Research Organization Bill Analysis. (2001). House Research Organization. https://capitol.texas.gov/BillLookup/Text.aspx?LegSess=77R&Bill=HB1200

HB 3390 Witness List. (2013). Texas House of Representatives. https://capitol.texas.gov/tlodocs/83R/witlistmtg/pdf/C4902013040914001.PDF

Headrick, B., Serra, G., & Twombly, J. (2002). Enforcement and oversight: Using congressional oversight to shape OSHA bureaucratic behavior. *American Politics Research, 30*(6), 608–629.

Hearing on HB 1303, HB 2101, HB 2177, HB 2175: Hearing before the House Technology and Economic Development Committee, House of Representatives 2014 Regular Session (2014). https://www.tvw.org/watch/?eventID=2013011075

Hearing on Public: HB 1260, HB 1301, HB 1303: Hearing before the House Technology and Economic Development Committee, House of Representatives 2013–2014 (2013). https://www.tvw.org/watch/?eventID=2013011075

Heclo, H. (1974). *Social Policy in Britain and Sweden.* Yale University Press.

Heclo, H. (1977). Political executives and the Washington bureaucracy. *Political Science Quarterly, 92*(3), 395–424.

Helm, M., & Spicuzza, M. (2020, December 10). "I became a lightning rod": Wisconsin health officers have been vilified and threatened during COVID-19, and some have quit. *Post Crescent.* https://www.postcrescent.com/in-depth/news/2020/12/10/wisconsin-health-officers-quit-during-covid-19-pandemic-amid-pushback/6428607002/

Hennings, V. M., & Urbatsch, R. (2016). Gender, partisanship, and candidate-selection mechanisms. *State Politics & Policy Quarterly, 16*(3), 290–312. https://doi.org/10.1177/1532440015604921

Hertel-Fernandez, A. (2014). who passes business's "model bills"? Policy capacity and corporate influence in US state politics. *Perspectives on Politics, 12*(03), 582–602.

High Technology Tax Incentives, Pub. L. No. HB 2546, HB 2546 (2004).

Hirschman, A. O. (1970). *Exit, Voice, and Loyalty: Responses to Decline in Firms, Organizations, and States* (Vol. 25). Harvard University Press.

House Finance Committee Public Hearing on SB/HB 2546: Hearing before the House Finance Committee, Senate 2003-2004 Session (2004). https://www.tvw.org/watch/?eventID=2004011130

House Ways & Means Committee Public Hearing on 3390: Hearing before the House Ways & Means Committee, House of Representatives 83rd regular session (2013). https://tlchouse.granicus.com/MediaPlayer.php?view_id=28&clip_id=6791

Hout, M. (1999). Abortion politics in the United States, 1972–1994: From single issue to ideology. *Gender Issues, 17*(2), 3–34. https://doi.org/10.1007/s12147-999-0013-9

Howard, C. (1999). *The Hidden Welfare State: Tax Expenditures and Social Policy in the United States.* Princeton University Press.

Huh, K. (2017). *How States Are Improving Tax Incentives for Jobs and Growth: A National Assessment of Evaluation Practices.* PEW Charitable Trusts. http://www.pewtrusts.org/~/media/assets/2017/05/edti_how_states_are_improving_tax_incentives_for_jobs_and_growth.pdf?la=en

Idaho Policy Institute. (2023, May 23). Idaho Policy Institute. https://www.boisestate.edu/sps-ipi/

Ingram, H., & Mann, D. (1980). Policy failure: An issue deserving analysis. In H. Ingram & D. Mann (Eds.), *Why Policies Succeed or Fail* (pp. 11–32). Sage Publications.

Insley, A. C. (2001). Suspending and expelling children from educational opportunity: Time to reevaluate zero tolerance policies comments. *American University Law Review, 50*(4), 1039–1074.

Interim Report to the 84th Legislature: House Select Committee on Economic Development Incentives (pp. 1–49). (2015). [Interim Committee Report]. Texas House of Representatives. https://house.texas.gov/_media/pdf/committees/reports/83interim/House-Select-Committee-on-Economic-Development-Incentives-Interim-Report-2014.pdf

Interview with Policy Analyst at the Texas Public Policy Research Institute at Texas A&M. (2017, March 27). [Phone Interview].

Interview with Policy Expert on the Texas Judicial Council. (2017, March 8). [Phone Interview].

Interview with Washington State Judge. (2018, January 16). [Phone Interview].

Israel, B. A., Schulz, A. J., Parker, E. A., & Becker, A. B. (1998). Review of community-based research: Assessing partnership approaches to improve public health. *Annual Review of Public Health, 19*(1), 173–202.

Iyengar, S., Lelkes, Y., Levendusky, M., Malhotra, N., & Westwood, S. J. (2019). The origins and consequences of affective polarization in the United States. *Annual Review of Political Science, 22*, 129–146.

James, S., Tervo, C., & Skocpol, T. (2022). Institutional capacities, partisan divisions, and federal tensions in US responses to the COVID-19 pandemic. *RSF: The Russell Sage Foundation Journal of the Social Sciences, 8*(8), 154–180.

Jansa, J. M. (2020). Chasing disparity: Economic development incentives and income inequality in the U.S. States. *State Politics & Policy Quarterly, 20*(4), 462–488. https://doi.org/10.1177/1532440019900259

Jefferson, W. (2012). Recognizing and combating the "School-to-Prison" pipeline in Texas. *Future Trends in State Courts 2012.* https://ncsc.contentdm.oclc.org/digital/collection/famct/id/865/

Jenkins-Smith, H. C. (1988). Analytical debates and policy learning: Analysis and change in the federal bureaucracy. *Policy Sciences, 21*(2), 169–211.

Jensen, N. (2018). Opinion | Why are your state tax dollars subsidizing corporations? *The New York Times.* Retrieved April 16, 2018, from https://www.nytimes.com/2018/03/06/opinion/state-tax-dollars-subsidizing-corporations.html

Jensen, N. (2016). Job creation and firm-specific location incentives. *Journal of Public Policy, 37*(1), 1–28.

Jensen, N., Malesky, E. J., & Walsh, M. (2015). Competing for global capital or local voters? The politics of business location incentives. *Public Choice; Dordrecht, 164*(3–4), 331–356. http://dx.doi.org/10.1007/s11127-015-0281-8

Jervis, R. (1998). *System Effects: Complexity in Political and Social Life.* Princeton University Press.

Jones, B. D., & Baumgartner, F. R. (2005). *The Politics of Attention: How Government Prioritizes Problems*. University of Chicago Press.

Jones, P. E. (2011). Which buck stops here? Accountability for policy positions and policy outcomes in Congress. *The Journal of Politics, 73*(3), 764–782.

Juvenile Detention Alternatives Initiative. (2019, October 29). The Annie E. Casey Foundation. https://www.aecf.org/work/juvenile-justice/jdai/

Kansas Department of Commerce Department Overview and Special Initiatives. (2017). Kansas Department of Commerce.

Karch, A., & Cravens, M. (2014). Rapid diffusion and policy reform: The adoption and modification of three strikes laws. *State Politics & Policy Quarterly, 14*(4), 461–491.

Karch, A., & Rose, S. (2017). States as stakeholders: Federalism, policy feedback, and government elites. *Studies in American Political Development, 31*(1), 47.

Kaufman, H. (1976). *Are Government Organizations Immortal?* The Brookings Institution.

Keel, J. (2014). *An Audit Report on Selected Major Agreements under the Texas Economic Development Act* (15–009; pp. 1–113). State Auditor's Office. https://www.sao.texas.gov/reports/main/15-009.pdf

Keightley, E., & Pickering, M. (2013). *Research Methods for Memory Studies*. Edinburgh University Press. http://ebookcentral.proquest.com/lib/gonzaga/detail.action?docID=1962036

Kelly, N. J., & Morgan, J. (2022). Hurdles to share prosperity: congress, parties, and the national policy process in an era of inequality. In J. Hacker, A. Hertel-Fernandez, P. Pierson, & K. Thelen (Eds.), *The American Political Economy: Politics, Markets, and Power*. Cambridge University Press.

Kendi, I. X. (2021, May 2). We Still Don't Know Who the Coronavirus's Victims Were. *The Atlantic*. https://www.theatlantic.com/ideas/archive/2021/05/we-still-dont-know-who-the-coronaviruss-victims-were/618776/

Kiga, F. C. (1997). *Tax Incentives for Investment in Research and Development: Sales Tax Exemption & B&O Tax Credit* [Revenue Research Report]. Department of Revenue.

Kilma, T., Miller, M., & Nunlist, C. (2009). *hat Works? Targeted Truancy and Dropout Programs in Middle and High School* (09-06–2201). Washington State Institute For Public Policy. https://www.wsipp.wa.gov/ReportFile/1045/Wsipp_What-Works-Targeted-Truancy-and-Dropout-Programs-in-Middle-and-High-School_Full-Report.pdf

Kingdon, J. W. (1984). *Agendas, Alternatives, and Public Policies*.

Kirby, D. B., Laris, B. A., & Rolleri, L. A. (2007). Sex and HIV education programs: Their impact on sexual behaviors of young people throughout the world. *Journal of Adolescent Health, 40*(3), 206–217.

Koerth-Baker, M. (2012, August 15). The mind of a flip-flopper. *The New York Times*. https://www.nytimes.com/2012/08/19/magazine/the-mind-of-a-flip-flopper.html

Kraft, P. W., Lodge, M., & Taber, C. S. (2015). Why people "don't trust the evidence" motivated reasoning and scientific beliefs. *The ANNALS of the American Academy of Political and Social Science, 658*(1), 121–133.

Krehbiel, K. (1992). *Information and Legislative Organization*. University of Michigan Press. http://ebookcentral.proquest.com/lib/gonzaga/detail.action?docID=3414917

Lacombe, M. J. (2019). The political weaponization of gun owners: The national rifle association's cultivation, dissemination, and use of a group social identity. *The Journal of Politics*, *81*(4), 1342–1356. https://doi.org/10.1086/704329

LaLonde, R. J. (1986). Evaluating the econometric evaluations of training programs with experimental data. *The American Economic Review*, 604–620.

Lead Texas Education Researcher. (2015, June 22). *Interview with lead education researcher in Texas* [Phone Interview].

Leak, R. (2021). *Chasing Failure: How Falling Short Sets You Up for Success*. Thomas Nelson. https://www.amazon.com/Chasing-Failure-Falling-Short-Success/dp/0785261605/ref=asc_df_0785261605/?tag=hyprod-20&linkCode=df0&hvadid=509245866633&hvpos=&hvnetw=g&hvrand=4377178570480412681&hvpone=&hvptwo=&hvqmt=&hvdev=c&hvdvcmdl=&hvlocint=&hvlocphy=9033782&hvtargid=pla-1263187003908&psc=1

Lee, M. M., & Zhang, N. (2017). Legibility and the informational foundations of state capacity. *The Journal of Politics*, *79*(1), 118–132. https://doi.org/10.1086/688053

Legislative assistant. (2017, March 3). *Interview with Legislative Assistant to Senator Whitmire* [Phone Interview].

Legislative Budget Board Staff. (2011). *Texas State Government Effectiveness and Efficiency: Selected Issues and Recommendations* (pp. 1–10). Legislative Budget Board. http://www.lbb.state.tx.us/Documents/Publications/GEER/GEER01012011.pdf

Lester, P. (2018). Managing toward evidence: State-level evidence-based policymaking and the results first initiative. *The ANNALS of the American Academy of Political and Social Science*, *678*(1), 93–102. https://doi.org/10.1177/0002716218767839

Lindblom, C. E., & Cohen, D. K. (1979). *Usable Knowledge: Social Science and Social Problem Solving*. Yale University Press.

Lindvall, J., & Teorell, J. (2016). *State Capacity as Power: A Conceptual Framework*. STANCE Working Paper 1, Lund University.

Lowry, R. (2007). The political economy of public universities in the United States: A review essay. *State Politics & Policy Quarterly*, *7*(3), 303–324.

Luna, T., & Willon, P. (2021, January 31). Amid recall push, Newsom blasted by Democrats for COVID-19 response—Los Angeles Times. *The L.A. Times*. https://www.latimes.com/california/story/2021-01-31/newsom-covid-19-criticism-democrats-allies-possible-recall

Mahoney, J., & Thelen, K. (Eds.). (2010). A theory of gradual institutional change. In *Explaining Institutional Change: Ambiguity, Agency, and Power*. Cambridge University Press.

Mahoney, J., & Thelen, K. (2015). *Advances in Comparative-Historical Analysis*. Cambridge University Press.

Manna, P., & Harwood, T. (2011). Governance and educational expectations in the U.S. states. *State Politics & Policy Quarterly*, *11*(4), 483–509. https://doi.org/10.1177/1532440011421302

Martinez, S. (2009). A system gone berserk: how are zero-tolerance policies really affecting schools? *Preventing School Failure: Alternative Education for Children and Youth, 53*(3), 153–158. https://doi.org/10.3200/PSFL.53.3.153-158

Maxwell, J. C. (2007). *Failing Forward: Turning Mistakes into Stepping Stones for Success* (Reprint edition). HarperCollins Leadership.

May, P. J. (1992). Policy learning and failure. *Journal of Public Policy, 12*(4), 331–354.

McAdam, D., Tarrow, S., Tilly, C., & McAdam, D. (2001). *Dynamics of Contention.* Cambridge University Press. http://ebookcentral.proquest.com/lib/gonzaga/detail.action?docID=202055

McArdle, M. (2015). *The Up Side of Down: Why Failing Well Is the Key to Success* (Reprint edition). Penguin Books.

McCarthy, B. (2008, June 13). Kids in jail: Are we creating monsters? *Wyoming Tribune Eagle.* https://www.wyomingnews.com/news/kids-in-jail-are-we-creating-monsters/article_007c38dc-b108-509f-ac4b-f024bc92abc7.html

McCluskey, C. P., Bynum, T. S., & Patchin, J. W. (2004). Reducing chronic absenteeism an assessment of an early truancy initiative. *Crime & Delinquency, 50*(2), 214–234.

McCoy, T. (2021, October 27). Meet the outsider who accidentally solved chronic homelessness. *Washington Post.* https://www.washingtonpost.com/news/inspired-life/wp/2015/05/06/meet-the-outsider-who-accidentally-solved-chronic-homelessness/

McCubbins, M. D., & Schwartz, T. (1984). Congressional oversight overlooked: Police patrols versus fire alarms. *American Journal of Political Science,* 165–179.

McDonough, J. E. (2001). Using and misusing anecdote in policy making. *Health Affairs, 20*(1), 207–212.

McEvers, K. (2015, December 10). Utah Reduced Chronic Homelessness by 91 Percent; Here's How. *National Public Radio.* https://www.npr.org/2015/12/10/459100751/utah-reduced-chronic-homelessness-by-91-percent-heres-how

McQueen, S. (2021). Pipeline or pipedream: Gender balance legislation's effect on women's presence in state government. *State Politics & Policy Quarterly, 21*(3), 243–265. https://doi.org/10.1017/spq.2020.8

Mettler, S. (2005). *Soldiers to Citizens: The GI Bill and the Making of the Greatest Generation.* Oxford University Press on Demand.

Micheli, C. (2019). California courts and use of legislative intent materials. *The National Law Review, X(261).*

Michels, P. (2016, March 14). Meet Ch 313, Texas' Largest Corporate Welfare Program. *Texas Observer.* https://www.texasobserver.org/chapter-313-texas-tax-incentive/

Michener, J. (2018). *Fragmented Democracy: Medicaid, Federalism, and Unequal Politics.* Cambridge University Press.

Michener, J. (2019). Policy feedback in a racialized polity. *Policy Studies Journal, 47*(2), 423–450. https://doi.org/10.1111/psj.12328

Milan, S., & Velden, L. V. D. (2016). The alternative epistemologies of data activism. *Digital Culture & Society, 2*(2), 57–74. https://doi.org/10.14361/dcs-2016-0205

Milgrom, P., & Roberts, J. (1988). An economic approach to influence activities in organizations. *American Journal of Sociology, 94,* S154–S179.

Miller, D. Y. (1991). The impact of political culture on patterns of state and local government expenditures. *Publius, 21*(2), 83–100.

Miller, M., Kilma, T., & Nunlist, C. (2010). *Washington's Truancy Laws: Does the Petition Process Influence School and Crime Outcomes* (10-02–2201). Washington State Institute For Public Policy. https://www.wsipp.wa.gov/ReportFile/1066/Wsipp_Washingtons-Truancy-Laws-Does-the-Petition-Process-Influence-School-and-Crime-Outcomes_Full-Report.pdf

Mintrom, M. (1997). Policy entrepreneurs and the diffusion of innovation. *American Journal of Political Science*, 738–770.

Mintrom, M., & Vergari, S. (1998). Policy networks and innovation diffusion: The case of state education reforms. *The Journal of Politics*, *60*(1), 126–148.

Mitchell, M. D., Farren, M. D., Horpedahl, J., & Gonzalez, O. (2019). *The Economics of a Targeted Economic Development Subsidy* (H71, O1, R11). Mercatus Center.

Moe, T. M. (2011). *Special Interest: Teachers Unions and America's Public Schools*. Brookings Institution Press.

Moe, T. M. (2019). *The Politics of Institutional Reform: Katrina, Education, and the Second Face of Power*. Cambridge University Press.

Mongan, P., & Walker, R. (2012). "The road to hell is paved with good intentions": A historical, theoretical, and legal analysis of zero-tolerance weapons policies in American schools. *Preventing School Failure: Alternative Education for Children and Youth*, *56*(4), 232–240. https://doi.org/10.1080/1045988X.2011.654366

Montanaro, D. (2020, March 24). FACT CHECK: Trump compares coronavirus to the flu, but it could be 10 times deadlier. *NPR*. https://www.npr.org/sections/coronavirus-live-updates/2020/03/24/820797301/fact-check-trump-compares-coronavirus-to-the-flu-but-they-are-not-the-same

Morgan, D. R., & Watson, S. S. (1991). Political culture, political system characteristics, and public policies among the American states. *Publius*, *21*(2), 31–48.

Morris, F. (2015, September 4). *Applebee's Split from Kansas City Region May Help End Economic Border War*. http://kcur.org/post/applebee-s-split-kansas-city-region-may-help-end-economic-border-war

Muhammad, K. G. (2010). *The Condemnation of Blackness: Race, Crime, and the Making of Modern Urban America*. Harvard University Press.

Murakami, K. (1995, June 23). Would "Becca Bill" have saved becca?—named for runaway girl who was murdered, new law gives parents more control over kids. *Seattle Times*. http://community.seattletimes.nwsource.com/archive/?date=19950623&slug=2127830

Nathan, R. P., & Gais, T. L. (2001). *Is Devolution Working: Federal and State Roles in Welfare*. Brookings.

Nordlinger, E. A. (1982). *On the Autonomy of the Democratic State*. Harvard University Press.

Opportunities Suspended: The Devastating Consequences of Zero Tolerance and School Discipline. (2000). The Civil Rights Project at Harvard University.

Orfield, G. (2001). Why data collection matters: The role of race and poverty in American education. In *In Pursuit of Equity in Education: Using International Indicators to Compare Equity Policies* (pp. 165–193). Kluwer Academic Publishers.

Parilla, J., & Liu, S. (2018). *Examining the Local Value of Economic Development Incentives: Evidence from Four U.S. Cities* (Metropolitan Policy Program).

The Brookings Institution. https://www.brookings.edu/research/examining-the-local-value-of-economic-development-incentives/

Patashnik, E. M. (2008). *Reforms at Risk: What Happens after Major Policy Changes Are Enacted.* Princeton University Press.

Patashnik, E. M. (2023). *Countermobilization: Policy Feedback and Backlash in a Polarized Age.* University of Chicago Press. https://books.google.com/books?hl=en&lr=&id=mbbdEAAAQBAJ&oi=fnd&pg=PR7&dq=countermobilization+patashnik&ots=BDgPitdeGD&sig=6zG3K6MITTusYlWXJY-qoLT_m-A

Patashnik, E. M., & Zelizer, J. E. (2013). The struggle to remake politics: Liberal reform and the limits of policy feedback in the contemporary American state. *Perspectives on Politics, 11*(4), 1071–1087.

Patterson, S. C. (1968). The political cultures of the American states. *The Journal of Politics, 30*(1), 187–209. https://doi.org/10.2307/2128314

Pierson, P. (1993). When effect becomes cause: Policy feedback and political change. *World Politics, 45*(04), 595–628. https://doi.org/10.2307/2950710

Pierson, P. (2000). The limits of design: Explaining institutional origins and change. *Governance, 13*(4), 475–499. https://doi.org/10.1111/0952-1895.00142

Pierson, P. (2011). *Politics in Time: History, Institutions, and Social Analysis.* Princeton University Press.

Pinsker, J. (2019, August 21). Republicans changed their mind about higher education really quickly. *The Atlantic.* https://www.theatlantic.com/education/archive/2019/08/republicans-conservatives-college/596497/

Poole, G. (2016, January 21). *313 Coalition* [Personal communication].

Promoting Employment across Kansas Act, Pub. L. No. Senate Bill 97, Supp 79-3234 (2008).

Promoting Employment across Kansas Program Evaluation and Economic Impact Analysis (pp. 1–56). (2013). The Docking Institute of Public Affairs. http://kanview.ks.gov/EcoDev/Documents/PEAK%20Docking%20Report.pdf

Public: HB 1260, HB 1301, HB 1303 Executive: HB 1183 Work Session: Tax preferences for economic development purposes.: Hearing before the House Technology & Economic Development Committee, House of Representatives (2013). https://www.tvw.org/watch/?eventID=2013011075

Public Hearing on 5651: Hearing before the Senate Human Services, Mental Health & Housing Committee, Senate 2015 Regular Session (2015). https://app.leg.wa.gov/billsummary?BillNumber=5651&Year=2015&Initiative=False

Public Hearing on HB 6429: Hearing before the Senate Human Services, Mental Health & Housing Committee, Senate (2008).

Public Testimony on HB 5651 and HB 5745, Senate 2015 legislative session (2015). https://app.leg.wa.gov/billsummary?BillNumber=5651&Year=2015&Initiative=False

Qiu, L. (2020, August 5). Trump cherry-picks coronavirus data in briefing appearance. *The New York Times.* https://www.nytimes.com/2020/08/04/us/politics/coronavirus-trump-data-briefing.html

Randall, E. (2011, August 15). The origins of the "Texas Miracle." *The Atlantic.*

Randall, M. A. (2016). *The Effects of the Texas School Property Tax Abatement Program on Public School Finance* [Master's Thesis, The University of Texas at Austin]. https://repositories.lib.utexas.edu/handle/2152/41484

Rice, W. (2003). *High Technology Tax Incentives Study*. Department of Revenue.

Robinson, J. A., & Acemoglu, D. (2012). *Why Nations Fail: The Origins of Power, Prosperity and Poverty*. Profile London.

Rodgers, B. (2021, November 16). Utah's 'housing first' model is keeping people off the streets. So why are auditors worried? *The Salt Lake Tribune*. https://www.sltrib.com/news/politics/2021/11/16/utahs-housing-first-model/

Rom, M. C. (2006). Taking the Brandeis metaphor seriously: Policy experimentation within a federal system. *Promoting the General Welfare, Ed. AS Gerber* and *EM Patashnik. Washington, DC: Brookings Institution.*

Romero, S. (2020, October 1). Fauci pushes back against Trump for misrepresenting his stance on masks. *The New York Times*. https://www.nytimes.com/2020/10/01/world/fauci-pushes-back-against-trump-for-misrepresenting-his-stance-on-masks.html

Rose, R. (1991). What is lesson-drawing? *Journal of Public Policy*, *11*(1), 3–30.

Rose, R. (1993). *Lesson-Drawing in Public Policy: A Guide to Learning across Time and Space* (Vol. 91). Chatham House Publishers.

Sabatier, P. A. (1987). Knowledge, policy-oriented learning, and policy change an advocacy coalition framework. *Science Communication*, *8*(4), 649–692.

Sabatier, P. A. (1988). An advocacy coalition framework of policy change and the role of policy-oriented learning therein. *Policy Sciences*, *21*(2), 129–168.

Santelli, J. S., Kantor, L. M., Grilo, S. A., Speizer, I. S., Lindberg, L. D., Heitel, J., Schalet, A. T., Lyon, M. E., Mason-Jones, A. J., & McGovern, T. (2017). Abstinence-only-until-marriage: An updated review of US policies and programs and their impact. *Journal of Adolescent Health*, *61*(3), 273–280.

Santos, M. (2015, July 12). Washington No.1 for jailing noncriminal kids, spurred by law named for Tacoma runaway. *The Olympian*. http://www.theolympian.com/news/politics-government/article27020662.html

Sawhill, I. V., & Baron, J. (2010, May 1). Federal Programs for Youth: More of the Same Won't Work. *Brookings*. https://www.brookings.edu/opinions/federal-programs-for-youth-more-of-the-same-wont-work

SB 106 open testimony: Hearing before the Senate Criminal Justice Committee, Texas Senate 2015 Legislative Session (2015). http://tlcsenate.granicus.com/MediaPlayer.php?view_id=30&clip_id=9710

SB 6646, 6646 SB (1995). https://app.leg.wa.gov/billsummary?BillNumber=6646&Initiative=false&Year=1995

Schattschneider, E. (1975). *The Semi-Sovereign People: A Realist's View of Democracy in America*. Wadsworth Publishing.

Schattschneider, E. E. (1935). *Politics, Pressures and the Tariff*. Prentice Hall.

Schram, S. F., Fording, R. C., & Soss, J. (2008). Neo-liberal poverty governance: Race, place and the punitive turn in US welfare policy. *Cambridge Journal of Regions, Economy and Society*, *1*(1), 17–36.

Schuck, P. H. (2014). *Why Government Fails So Often.* Princeton University Press.

Scott, J. C. (2008). *Seeing Like a State.* Yale University Press.

Seawright, J., & Gerring, J. (2008). Case selection techniques in case study research: A menu of qualitative and quantitative options. *Political Research Quarterly, 61*(2), 294–308.

Senate Committee on Criminal Justice: Hearing before the Senate Committee on Criminal Justice, Senate 84th legislative session (2015). http://tlcsenate.granicus.com/MediaPlayer.php?clip_id=9522

Senate Committee on Natural Resources & Economic Development, Part I, Public Hearing on SB 600: Hearing before the Senate Committee on Natural Resources & Economic Development, Senate 85th legislature (2017). https://tlcsenate.granicus.com/MediaPlayer.php?view_id=42&clip_id=12205

Senate Committee on Natural Resources & Economic Development, Part II, Public Hearing on SB 600: Hearing before the Senate Committee on Natural Resources & Economic Development, Senate 85th Legislature (2017). https://tlcsenate.granicus.com/MediaPlayer.php?view_id=42&clip_id=12210

Senate Committee on Natural Resources and Economic Development: Interim Report to the 85th Legislature. (2016). [Interm Report]. Texas Senate.

Senate Human Services, Reentry & Rehabilitation Committee Work Session & Public Hearing on SB 5290: Hearing before the Senate Human Services, Reentry & Rehabilitation Committee (2019). https://www.tvw.org/watch/?eventID=2019011203

Senate Journal: 74th Legislature, Eighteenth Day (Pg 3346). (1995). Texas Senate Archive; Texas State Legislative Archives.

Senate Journal: 84th Legislature, Sixty-Third Day. (2015). Texas Senate Archive.

Senate Journal 1995 Regular Session. (1995). Texas State Senate; Texas State Legislative Archives. https://lrl.texas.gov/collections/journals/journalsSenate74.cfm

Sheingate, A. (2014). Institutional dynamics and American political development. *Annual Review of Political Science, 17,* 461–477.

Shipan, C. R., & Volden, C. (2014). When the smoke clears: Expertise, learning and policy diffusion. *Journal of Public Policy, 34*(3), 357–387. https://doi.org/10.1017/S0143814X14000142

Simon, S. (2021, April 8). *Analysis & Updates | Inconsistent Reporting Practices Hampered Our Ability to Analyze COVID-19 Data. Here Are Three Common Problems We Identified.* The COVID Tracking Project. https://covidtracking.com/analysis-updates/three-covid-19-data-problems

Skiba, R. J. (2000). *Zero Tolerance, Zero Evidence: An Analysis of School Disciplinary Practice.Policy Research Report.* Indiana Education Policy Center, Smith Research Center, Suite 100, 2805 East Tenth Street, Indiana University, Bloomington, IN 47408-2698. https://eric.ed.gov/?id=ED469537

Skiba, R. J., Horner, R. H., Chung, C.-G., Rausch, M. K., May, S. L., & Tobin, T. (2011). Race is not neutral: A national investigation of African American and Latino disproportionality in school discipline. *School Psychology Review, 40*(1), 85–107. https://doi.org/10.1080/02796015.2011.12087730

Skidelsky, R. (1986). *John Maynard Keynes: The Economist as Savior, 1920-1937* (1st American ed.). Viking.

Skocpol, T. (1991). Targeting within universalism: Politically viable policies to combat poverty in the United States. *The Urban Underclass, 411*(411), 437–459.

Skocpol, T. (1995). *Protecting Soldiers and Mothers.* Harvard University Press.

Skocpol, T., Evans, P., Rueschemeyer, D., & Skocpol, T. (1985). *Bringing the State Back in.* Cambridge.

Skowronek, S. (1982). *Building a New American State: The Expansion of National Administrative Capacities, 1877–1920.* Cambridge University Press.

Smith, B. L., Mayer, J. D., & Fritschler, A. L. (2010). *Closed Minds?: Politics and Ideology in American Universities.* Brookings Institution Press.

Smith, J. A., & Todd, P. E. (2005). Does matching overcome LaLonde's critique of nonexperimental estimators? *Journal of Econometrics, 125*(1–2), 305–353.

Soss, J. (1999). Lessons of welfare: Policy design, political learning, and political action. *American Political Science Review, 93*(02), 363–380.

Soss, J., Fording, R. C., & Schram, S. (2011). *Disciplining the Poor: Neoliberal Paternalism and the Persistent Power of Race.* University of Chicago Press.

Soss, J., Schram, S. F., Vartanian, T. P., & O'brien, E. (2001). Setting the terms of relief: Explaining state policy choices in the devolution revolution. *American Journal of Political Science*, 378–395.

Soss, J., & Weaver, V. (2017). Police are our government: Politics, political science, and the policing of race–class subjugated communities. *Annual Review of Political Science, 20*(1), 565–591.

States use tax incentives to lure companies. Bipartisan support is growing to stop it. (2021, July 19). *Washington Post.* https://www.washingtonpost.com/opinions/2021/07/19/state-tax-incentives-congress-plan/

Stokes, L. C. (2020). *Short Circuiting Policy: Interest Groups and the Battle over Clean Energy and Climate Policy in the American States.* Oxford University Press.

Stolberg, S. G. (2020a, April 16). Live from her kitchen, Pelosi works to counter Trump's coronavirus show. *The New York Times.* https://www.nytimes.com/2020/04/16/us/politics/pelosi-trump-coronavirus-response.html

Stolberg, S. G. (2020b, July 14). Trump Administration strips C.D.C. of control of coronavirus data. *The New York Times.* https://www.nytimes.com/2020/07/14/us/politics/trump-cdc-coronavirus.html

Stolberg, S. G. (2021, January 21). Biden unveils national strategy that Trump resisted. *The New York Times.* https://www.nytimes.com/2021/01/21/us/politics/biden-coronavirus-response.html

Stone, D. (2020). *Counting: How We Use Numbers to Decide What Matters.* W. W. Norton.

Stone, D. A. (1989). Causal stories and the formation of policy agendas. *Political Science Quarterly, 104*(2), 281–300.

Story, L., Fehr, T., & Watkins, D. (2012). *Explore Government Subsidies.* https://www.nytimes.com/interactive/2012/12/01/us/government-incentives.html

Strickland, A. A., Taber, C. S., & Lodge, M. (2011). Motivated reasoning and public opinion. *Journal of Health Politics, Policy and Law, 36*(6), 935–944.

Tax Break Tracker. (2023). Good Jobs First. https://taxbreaktracker.goodjobsfirst.org/

Tax Incentives for Investment in Research and Development: Sales Tax Exemption & B&O Tax Credit. (2000). Department of Revenue. https://dor.wa.gov/content/high-tech-r-d-tax-incentives-study

Teasley, M. L. (2004). Absenteeism and truancy: Risk, protection, and best practice implications for school social workers. *Children & Schools, 26*(2), 117–128.

Teles, S., & Dagan, D. (2016). *Prison Break: Why Conservatives Turned against Mass Incarceration.* Oxford University Press.

Tesler, M. (2012). The spillover of racialization into health care: How President Obama polarized public opinion by racial attitudes and race. *American Journal of Political Science, 56*(3), 690–704. https://doi.org/10.1111/j.1540-5907.2011.00577.x

Texas Economic Development Act, Pub. L. No. HB No. 1200, 77R 945 JD-D (2001). https://capitol.texas.gov/BillLookup/History.aspx?LegSess=77R&Bill=HB1200

Chasnoff, Brian. "Texas' tax abatement program too broad." (2012, December 6). *San Antonio Express News.* https://www.mysanantonio.com/news/news_columnists/article/Texas-tax-abatement-program-too-broad-4095068.php

Thelen, K. A. (2004). *How Institutions Evolve: The Political Economy of Skills in Germany, Britain, the United States, and Japan.* Cambridge University Press.

Toohey, M. (2015, May 16). *Big dollars, little oversight?* Austin American Statesman.

Truancy Case Processing Practices (pp. 1–35). (2004). Washington State Center for Court Research, Administrative Office of the Courts. https://www.courts.wa.gov/newsinfo/content/pdf/TruancyReport.pdf

Van Cassell, M. (2008, September 20). Charging juveniles as adults poses new questions. *Wyoming Tribune Eagle.* https://www.wyomingnews.com/news/charging-juveniles-as-adults-poses-new-questions/article_acfa3c67-a82a-5d90-9122-e024854d60e5.html

Vetterkind, R., & Schmidt, M. (2020, May 14). Wisconsin Supreme Court strikes down stay-at-home order; Dane County institutes local order. *La Crosse Tribune.* https://lacrossetribune.com/news/state-and-regional/govt-and-politics/wisconsin-supreme-court-strikes-down-stay-at-home-order-dane-county-institutes-local-order/article_49acc610-7294-566b-89a1-0513ffa68632.html#utm_source=lacrossetribune.com&utm_campaign=%2Fnewsletter-templates%2Fbreaking&utm_medium=PostUp&utm_content=634b27b4709cffb4d22087a8815b14d32a348f2c

Volden, C. (2006). States as policy laboratories: Emulating success in the children's health insurance program. *American Journal of Political Science, 50*(2), 294–312.

Volden, C. (2016). Failures: Diffusion, learning, and policy abandonment. *State Politics & Policy Quarterly, 16*(1), 44–77.

Volden, C., Ting, M. M., & Carpenter, D. P. (2008). A formal model of learning and policy diffusion. *American Political Science Review, 102*(03), 319–332.

Walker, J. (1969). The diffusion of innovations among the American states. *American Political Science Review, 63*, 880–899.

Walker, J. L. (1974). Performance gaps, policy research, and political entrepreneurs: Toward a theory of agenda setting. *Policy Studies Journal, 3*(1), 112.

Washington State Center for Court Research. (n.d.). Washington State Courts. Retrieved July 6, 2023, from https://www.courts.wa.gov/index.cfm?fa=home.sub&org=wsccr&page=welcome&layout=2&parent=committee&tab=Welcome

Weaver, V. M., & Lerman, A. E. (2010). Political consequences of the carceral state. *American Political Science Review, 104*(04), 817–833.

Webster, C. (1996). *Truancy: Preliminary Findings on Washington's 1995 Truancy Law* (pp. 1–36). Washington State Institute For Public Policy. http://www.wsipp.wa.gov/ReportFile/1217/Wsipp_TRUANCY-Preliminary-Findings-on-Washingtons-1995-Law_Full-Report.pdf

Weil, D., Fung, A., Graham, M., & Fagotto, E. (2006). The effectiveness of regulatory disclosure policies. *Journal of Policy Analysis and Management, 25*(1), 155–181.

Weimer, D. L., & Vining, A. R. (2007). *Policy Analysis in Representative Democracy: Vol. Promoting the General Welfare: New Perspectives on Government Performance* (A. S. Gerber & E. M. Patashnik, Eds.). Brookings Institution Press.

Weir, M., & Skocpol, T. (1985). State structures and the possibilities for 'Keynesian' responses to the Great Depression in Sweden, Britain, and the United States. *Bringing the State Back In, 107.* https://www.cambridge.org/core/services/aop-cambridge-core/content/view/5BA18E8034F5D81DF757F81D6AB9950E

Weiss, C. (1977). Research for policy's sake: The enlightenment function of social research. *Policy Analysis, 3*(4), 531–545.

Whitehurst, G. J. (Russ). (2018). The institute of education sciences: model for federal research offices. *The ANNALS of the American Academy of Political and Social Science, 678*(1), 124–133. https://doi.org/10.1177/0002716218768243

Wichowsky, A., & Moynihan, D. P. (2008). Measuring how administration shapes citizenship: A policy feedback perspective on performance management. *Public Administration Review, 68*(5), 908–920. https://doi.org/10.1111/j.1540-6210.2008.00931.x

Wilson, J. Q. (1989). *Bureaucracy: What Government Agencies Do and Why They Do It.* Basic Books.

Wilson, J. Q., & Kelling, G. L. (1982). Broken windows. *Atlantic Monthly, 249*(3), 29–38.

Witness List for SB 106. (2015). Texas Senate Criminal Justice Committee. https://capitol.texas.gov/tlodocs/84R/witlistmtg/pdf/C5902015033113301.PDF

Wolfson, J. (2008, June 12). Wyo ranks No. 2 in US for youth in custody. *Star-Tribune.* https://trib.com/news/state-and-regional/wyo-ranks-no-in-us-for-youth-in-custody/article_3e2b39ac-c63c-5c45-9450-c74fc25d711a.html

Woodhall-Melnik, J. R., & Dunn, J. R. (2016). A systematic review of outcomes associated with participation in Housing First programs. *Housing Studies, 31*(3), 287–304.

Wyoming State Advisory Council on Juvenile Justice: Annual Report 2008 (pp. 1–17). (2008). [Document]. State Advisory Council on Juvenile Justice.

Young, K., Ashby, D., Boaz, A., & Grayson, L. (2002). Social science and the evidence-based policy movement. *Social Policy and Society, 1*(3), 215–224.

Young, T. (2018). Generating and using evidence will help to reduce social problems. *The ANNALS of the American Academy of Political and Social Science, 678*(1), 194–198.

Zelizer, A. (2018). How responsive are legislators to policy information? Evidence from a field experiment in a state legislature. *Legislative Studies Quarterly, 43*(4), 595–618.

Index

For the benefit of digital users, indexed terms that span two pages (e.g., 52–53) may, on occasion, appear on only one of those pages.